The
Asian
Century

THE ASIAN CENTURY

The Economic Ascent of the Pacific Rim— and What It Means for the West

Julian Weiss

Facts On File

New York • Oxford

*To the ever-expanding
cadre of philosophers, teachers,
and thinkers whose efforts
build the synergy needed to ease
the transition to the Asian Century.*

The Asian Century
copyright © 1989 by Julian Weiss

Facts On File,® Inc.   Facts On File Limited
460 Park Avenue South   or   Collins Street
New York, New York 10016   Oxford OX4-1XJ
                                                   United Kingdom

Library of Congress Cataloging-in-Publication Data
Weiss, Julian.
        The Asian century / Julian Weiss.
            p.   cm.
        Includes index.
        ISBN 0-8160-1687-9
            1. Asia—Economic conditions—1945. 2. Asia—Commerce.
    I. Title.
    HC412.W4 1989   88-24605
    330.95′042—dc19

British CIP data available on request

Text Design by In-House Graphics
Jacket Design by Berg Design, Inc., Ed Atkeson
Composition by Facts On File, Inc.

Printed in the United States of America
10 9 8 7 6 5 4 3 2 1

This book is printed on acid-free paper.

Contents

Introduction   vi

1. Common Threads: The Fabric of Growth   1

2. Japan: Sunset Over the Rising Sun?   37

3. China: Cracks in the Iron Rice Bowl   76

4. Korea: Post-Olympic Marathon   113

5. Taiwan: Under All Flags   138

6. Hong Kong: The Challenge Before 1997   158

7. Singapore: Father, Son, and Holy Goh   177

8. Malaysia: Quest for Cohesion   204

9. ASEAN: The Next Common Market?   216

Index   225

Introduction

If the "British Century" extended roughly through the ten decades ending with Queen Victoria's death in 1901, and America's epoch—another global odyssey mixed with triumph as well as tragedy—began thereafter, it may be said that the "Asian Century" had evolved by the 1980s.

Asia has witnessed two distinct stages of development. In the first, East Asia achieved rapid growth, harnessing the region's vast resources and dropping a gauntlet before the entrenched commercial powers of the West. In the second stage, she is discovering the problems born of success as she seeks to consolidate her economic gains. This phase is as dramatic as the first.

The Asian Century *has* arrived. It is an unexpected shooting star in the night sky of world events from which great possibilities emerge. The "Asian Century" concept embodies far more than economics. It is the kernel of a new geopolitics, a basic realignment in an information age and postindustrial era. The shape of the next century is being cast in the Pacific.

This text deals primarily with trade, investment, finance, the "stuff" of economics. All are shaped by non-economic elements that are themselves worthy of in-depth analysis.

This treatment of "the Asian Century" omits certain countries by design. We are here concerned only with the major forces propelling growth around the Pacific Rim—those nations most responsible for ushering in the realignment that tilts the balance of commercial power, inextricably and irreversibly.

Most of us realize our relationship with this part of the world will become more important. Beyond generalities, we do not understand why. For example, the perception of Singapore as prosperous and advanced neglects that city-state's precarious transition as oil refining comes to an end. Similarly, our assumptions about Japan overlook serious problems on her economic horizon (see sample chapters attached). We treat Taiwan as a unified entity despite conditions there which might lead to internal disarray. Opportunities in China remain nebulous. Korea's ascent faces stumbling blocks.

Stereotypes abound. Few Americans are aware of the recessions seen across allegedly "booming" Asia during the 1980s. The Four Tigers (Korea, Taiwan, Singapore, Hong Kong) each have diverse economic structures—and are hardly a monolithic bloc (as they are portrayed).

What astounding changes in manufacturing—ranging from textile production to automobiles—will effect competition with not only Japan but her rapidly rising competitors? Which opportunities can Americans tap in Australia, and can the continent-sized nation regain her prosperous legacy? How does Hong Kong fit into the equation? Which countries are winners and losers in the high-tech battles ahead? Which countries can retain their cultural identity while reconciling the import of large doses of Western influence? Will inherent advantages found in the region—such as the celebrated work ethic—remain? Is Japan really as secure as we think—and what nagging problems worry Tokyo? Will China "take off" economically, and if so, when?

A giant is awakening and tearing at its tethers. Three-and-a-half billion people are becoming conscious consumers demanding more than just essentials; they are no longer willing to acquiesce in the strictures of government that deny them fulfillment of their expectations. A new economic and industrial base is forming—consisting of synthetic materials, opto-electronics, and biomolecular developments. The dogmas of yesterday are slowly evaporating, and racial enmities as well as political distinctions of the past are (generally) giving way to the early burst of economic cohesion.

East and West alike are certain to feel the impact of cross-cultural contact unimagined until now.

Will the future bring economic cooperation with America (as well as Canada, and the EEC)—or conflict? This book seeks to bridge an information gap by providing new information and fresh insights, showing Americans just what is taking place in the flagship countries of Asia.

As we go to press, a new cycle in Asia's rise—and especially in East Asia's rise—finds the nations in question not only reassessing their directions but faced with reappraisals of their political destinies. The *average* age of heads of state in China, Taiwan, and Singapore is 72 (in 1988), while Korea and Japan face an end to entrenched political establishments. Hong Kong, of course, will alter its "territory" status in just eight years. Yesterday's underdeveloped economies will rank as tomorrow's masters of commerce—in some cases.

And as the trans-Pacific saga unfolds, the East Asian titan economies face the specter of an EEC intertwined into a single economic bloc.

Midnight on December 31, 1992, heralds the creation of a true Common Market, forging a single colossus out of Western Europe's population of approximately 340 million (a number over 25 percent greater than "America, Inc." and over 2½ times the population of "Japan, Inc.").

And, equally important, the combined EEC GNP is, at $4 trillion, nearly equal to the United States GNP. Compare that to Japan, whose total output is $2.4 billion. The total output for the Four Dragons (Korea, Taiwan, Hong Kong, and Singapore) plus China and the ASEAN is $675 billion.

The North American Free Trade compacts linking Canada and the U.S. in effect launch a barrier-less commercial zone, making the pair a nearly $5 trillion quasi-Common Market. By the EEC's consolidation on New Year's Day 1993 (although these accords are termed "1992"), the planet will face a trio of gargantuan, technology-based, interdependent trade blocs. All three are competing in the same sectors, and only a continuing expanding "pie" would avoid protectionist (under whatever name) maneuvering. For all its strengths, Asia is concerned.

The full impact of these vast transformations has yet to be appreciated. As Tokyo's centrist *Yomiuri Shimbun* noted last year: "The focus of the historic development of the world economy is shifting from the Atlantic to the Pacific. It is still uncertain, however, whether the economic strength in the Asian Pacific region will become a disturbing factor for the global economy, or a powerful stimulant for it."

And, this is only the beginning. Asia's rise on the global scene began, after all, very few years ago.

1

Common Threads: The Fabric of Growth

As the growth economies of East Asia face the 1990s, they are connected by several common threads, most of which pose opportunities as well as pitfalls for the region. This chapter examines these economic factors that propel or imperil all the nations spearheading the Asian Century: technology, trade, currencies, energy and environment, automobiles, textiles, electronics, commodities, and demographics. The dimensions of Asia's unpaid social debt are also outlined here in order to give a coherent view of the region and the often-neglected problems faced by her mostly prospering citizens.

There are a host of issues—such as nationalistic fervor; the status of women; and the impact of imported Western culture—that are not outlined in this chapter, although they too will help to shape the future of this dynamic bloc. Because such issues vary widely from country to country, we will discuss them in that fashion throughout this book.

IMPACT OF TECHNOLOGY: SHIFTING TRADE WINDS

Which factors will influence the outcome of tomorrow's trade wars? Competitiveness is more than a buzzword. In an era when response to customer requests, conformity with evolving styles, quality control, and access to markets are more essential than ever, competing successfully

1

is an essential ingredient of economic vitality. In the years ahead, products that were once on the shelves for a decade (i.e., refrigerators, stereo units, leisure goods), might have a shortened product life cycle that would see them disappear within a few months.

Technology Transfer: East to West, West to East

"The future," says Australian forecaster Phil Ruthvin, "belongs to those nations which are prepared to serve as partisans of the New Technological Society emerging out of the structure of the Industrial Revolution."

Ruthvin makes this bold statement while perched atop downtown Melbourne. He points out the window to buildings and landmarks that depict eras in the city's—as well as the continent's—history. "We were once the richest, but we lost it. We had the highest standard of living [in Asia] for decades, but then something happened. I wonder about it, and I wonder about the relationship between loss of wealth and loss of technological edge."

Ruthvin speaks of a "partisanship" that is a prerequisite for innovation. To succeed, he says, nations must be willing to take risks and to endure unaccustomed self-discipline. This is exactly what the West did centuries ago, when the East held technological sway—and considered Europeans to be barbarians incapable of civilization. The point that many students of history make is this: Who comes up with a breakthrough isn't as important as who takes it to its logical conclusion.

Today, some Asians show a bedazzling ability to beat the West at its own game, applying U.S., Canadian, and European advances in basic research to the assembly line. This is particularly true in an era when, despite the fact that six of the world's seven leading research nations are in the West, East Asia rapidly harvests the fruits of that research. The seven leading research nations are the United States, the U.S.S.R., Britain, Japan, Canada, West Germany, and France (not necessarily in that order). It is estimated that fully three-fourths of the world's manpower in research and development are found in these seven countries and that nearly 90 percent of all R&D is carried out within their borders.

However, technology transfer did not always run west to east. During and after the Dark Ages, civilization was nurtured across Asia. In fact, one can argue that without the bursts of brilliance displayed by Greco-Roman societies, the West (not counting Ancient Egypt) would have a paltry presence in the showrooms of world achievement.

It was left to the Persians, the Indians, and the Chinese to develop a staggering array of technological innovations, from gunpowder to printing. Even literature seemed to be the exclusive province of those who resided east of the Urals. It is not surprising then that these peoples had the natural and financial resources to foster nascent mercantilism. Trade flourished in the East and large cadres of learned men sat in court at the threshold of power.

India was renowned for its intellectual, inquisitive, and advanced culture. Her medicines were eagerly sought in backward Europe, and Indian steel was prized from the Balkans to Britain. Other non-Europeans, including the Moslems—whose territory spanned the Straits of Gibraltar to the Straits of Malacca—were avid scholars, astronomers, physicians, and poets. In fact, Arab ingenuity allowed its standard-bearers to overcome the hardships of climate in a way that few other cultures could.

China was especially well endowed; its neighbor Japan was destined to remain a borrower and imitator. The Chinese could, in the early 16th century, boast an empire of nearly 100 million people, governed by technocrats supported by a vast economic base. In the sciences, Chinese scholarship reigned without parallel. Compasses and water power were but two of the many forms of technology that hummed and churned across the landscape of China.

Europe floundered in many respects in this era, burdened by disease, internal friction, and a pattern of internecine political rivalries. In spite of those impediments, in the early 16th century "Made in Asia" innovations—notably gunpowder, printing on paper, and compasses—were adopted by adventurous Europeans whose horizons were as boundless as their quest for discovery.

The manufacture and distribution of Eastern technology spread quickly in Renaissance Europe. The size of a nation did not inhibit its use of these advances; tiny Holland assimilated breakthroughs just as easily as France, Germany, and Britain. In time, the Europeans themselves became "leading edge" producers of these borrowed inventions; the diverse and frequently hostile nations of Europe simply incorporated the technology into their own societal frameworks.

Thus, the Europeans' golden age of discovery would not have been possible without Asian-born compasses. Similarly, paper and printing were never fully exploited by China, whereas Western Europe fostered whole industries on the premise that commercial, political, and religious institutions would use the hand press to disseminate all manner of information. Thus the stirrings of intellectual development were realized after centuries of repressive ignorance and superstition. After the printed word lifted the lid off the tinderbox of free inquiry, Europeans generally nurtured the flame of learning. Looking to the past as well as to the future, Europe was determined to forge a new destiny built largely on Eastern technologies.

Now, centuries after the Industrial Revolution allowed the West to supplant Asia's early gains in science and technology, the tables appear to be turning. Once again Confucian values appear to provide the conditions that allow high, high technology to thrive. High rates of savings are essential in an era where capital costs for R&D are vast and where short-term guarantees on profitability are virtually impossible. An emphasis on education encourages many Asians to acquire the skills and knowledge essential for success. A cohesive loyalty helps to build relationships that keep both public and private organizations intact during periods of uncertainty or structural change. Finally, Confucian paternalism enables governments in Singapore, Korea, and Taiwan to guide business there, and fosters the sort of monopolistic environment that helped propel Japan to its current position.

Technology transfers to East Asia do not upset long-standing traditions there. Just as the 16th-century Europeans' Christianity did not crumble in the face of imported Eastern technology, today's Asians hold onto what is useful from the past while reaching for what is promising for the future. (The cultural milieu, however, can be overwhelmed at times, as we will see in subsequent chapters.)

"There are cohesive social relations found in these countries," declares Dr. Victor Li, president of the East-West Center in Hawaii. Innovations are readily adapted, and many experts believe that the juggernaut of social progress witnessed during the postwar years has made Asians accept the need for radical transformations within their societies. However, "in the years ahead," notes Dr. Li, "the kind of gentle, nonoppressive, benign authoritarian rule which is supported by Confucianism will still play a role in guiding Asian policies."

Information, Please

The global information technology market has grown for most of this decade at rates of 8 percent or 9 percent annually. This is why worldwide sales for this equipment reached $480 billion for 1988—nearly double sales for 1982. Computer sales alone are growing by over 10 percent a year. A close cousin, telecommunications equipment, constitutes a $300–400 billion market worldwide.

That is only the beginning. Groups such as Nomura Research (in Tokyo) and ITT believe that "information management" systems will approach the $4 trillion mark by 1999—an amount greater than total global output as recently as 1960. Today's 600 million telephones will increase sixfold (while offering radically different capabilities than even the vintage 1989 phone commonly in use), and around the planet, over 200,000 new jobs a year should be spawned. Integrated service data networks, or ISDNs, have the ability to transmit data and voice simultaneously. The rapid rise of facsimile machines, and the early penetration of office markets on both sides of the Pacific by such devices as packet switches and PBXs all attest to a powerful telecommunications contest in the years ahead.

The engine driving these futuristic breakthroughs is, of course, a need for near-limitless quantities of data. With over 60 million square miles of Pacific Ocean, with the Pacific tilt in the world's economy, and with a combined population of over 2 billion people, Asia is rightfully seen as a major competitive battleground for new products entering the workaday world.

Market penetration of these products is astounding. So is the intense, ongoing competition. VCRs have emerged as an $18 trillion industry in under 12 years. They were born of U.S. technology, yet Americans hold under 2 percent of that market. Japan's cost for licensing from reluctant Yankee Traders plus additional R&D needed to commercialize the VCR concept totaled a mere $475 million.

Communications gear is desperately needed throughout East Asia. China's expenditures on such items from 1987 through 1995 should exceed $35 billion, and when Japan entered the contest for sales in earnest five years ago, she captured over 70 percent of the $1.2 billion spent by Beijing in that one year.

Japan's share is impressive. In 1988, according to Intelsat and other official sources, her telecommunications bill was $25 billion. South Korea allotted about $2 billion in 1988.

The trade picture in electronics pits all the global giants against each other in the struggle to capture the same markets. Canada's Northern Telecom, West Germany's Siemens, Japan's Hitachi and NEC, respectively, and a bevy of U.S. corporations are reaching what an analyst at Dataquest terms "unprecedented aggressiveness."

The U.S. information technology industry—computers, office equipment, and telecommunications—recorded a trade surplus in 1988 that may be as high as $400 million. Computer and Business Equipment Manufacturers Association President John Pickitt sees important sales opportunities overseas in the years to come. "We believe that Europe, Canada, the Middle East, Australia, and the Eastern Bloc are continuing to show solid gains for our manufacturers," says Mr. Pickitt.

For telecommunications equipment alone, the U.S. trade deficit in 1988 may have been $2 billion. But exports for that year rose by at least 40 percent over 1987, and all regions except East Asia posted impressive sales by U.S. firms. That is good news for America's domestic industry, whose combined work force of 2.2 million has not grown since 1984. Telecommunications' contributions to U.S. GNP are significant: hourly wages now average $11.51, about a fourth higher than the 1984 level.

While the U.S. held a near monopoly in many sectors of consumer electronics as recently as 1970, its worldwide share has fallen to 5 percent. This fact is inextricably linked to the nature of the contest shaping up during the early part of the next decade.

The ubiquitous chip has found a home in Asia. By 1983, use of semiconductors in Japan had outdistanced usage in North America, and a year later, her use of this substance surpassed total combined use by all foreign industrial rivals. Also in 1983, Japan leaped just slightly ahead of the U.S. in her share of dynamic random access memories. (A discussion of the U.S.-Japan competition in the microelectronics field and related arenas is featured in Chapter 3.)

The real stake in this contest lies in the development of highly sophisticated and customized chips. While their use is miniscule at the moment, it will grow—in large part because of demand within Asia. Hong Kong, Taiwan, and Singapore are all eagerly pursuing independent research to design and produce these customized varieties. Korea has sought to conquer niche markets of memory devices. Malaysia is a key exporter, hoping to see more value added in its own integrated circuits. China has scored a few impressive breakthroughs. All these countries— and Japan, when some of the latest generation chips are considered— depend on America's Silicon Valley for design (and other innovations) as microprocessors and chips take precedence in engineering, and in factory assembly, consumer products, and even in defense industries.

In microprocessors, where the U.S. commands at least 80 percent of a $6.2 billion international market, the reduced instruction set computers are gaining headway. Able to handle 20 million instructions per second, these powerful new entries into the high-tech race are seen as providing America some potent ammunition in its protracted chip wars with Japan.

Just how fast the entire global chip market is growing was revealed by Dataquest probes of sales and exports. 1987 saw a 35 percent increase among the East Asian countries (excluding China). 1988's total market for all varieties of chips and integrated circuits is probably $47 billion, over double the level in 1985. By 1992, it could easily top $60 billion.

Brave New Biotech World

One sign of Asia's commitment to serious technological upgrading comes in the field of biotechnology, and the dynamic economies of East

Asia seek to stake out niche markets in this arena. Singapore, Korea, and Taiwan are embarking on aggressive programs that hope to create industries that are not labor-intensive and yet that yield value added.

The East Asian region may surface as a formidable competitor in global biotech during the 1990s. Following on the footsteps of Japan, Inc., the "Four Tigers"—Singapore, Korea, Taiwan, and Hong Kong—are able to assimilate advanced technologies and, repeating the success stories that developed in electronics and other sectors, adapt Western and U.S. innovations into their own production techniques. Some of those techniques will be increasingly sophisticated thanks to technology transfer from Japanese conglomerates.

Another factor in the biotech equation is demographics. All the countries in this region face the specter of rapidly aging societies, with attendant needs for medical and health care-related products. According to Dr. Robert Yuan, a researcher at the University of Maryland in College Park, the Southeast Asian pharmaceutical market is nearly $3 billion annually.

Although government's role is somewhat different in each of the "Tigers," government-supported science and research centers in all of them provide the general direction of industry, as well as university, action. "This is the pattern that will remain for years to come," asserts Dr. Yuan. A common goal faced by these countries is to increase the number of scientists with managerial skills who can direct others in research projects as effectively as they themselves would conduct experiments. Because hepatitis is a serious problem around the Pacific Rim, companies have directed efforts toward products in that realm. Foreign companies have been leery of collaborating with local firms because of the patent piracy that until recently has been all too common in the region. Attracting qualified top management has also been a problem. We will examine all these issues in more depth in later chapters.

TRADE WARS

The trade winds sweeping the Pacific in the future will be as different from today's as today's are from the era of the Yankee clipper. One cannot fully appreciate the role of trade in certain Asian countries until one sees how the respective economic engines are fueled by trade. Korea's success, for example, is based largely on reprocessing goods from developing countries, goods which are then exported to Japan. Trade—the function that brings prosperity to millions on both sides of the Pacific—has become embroiled in a plethora of issues, such as economic restructuring and competitiveness, that have little to do with actual commerce.

Two decades ago, East Asia constituted a mere 8 percent of the world's output, while the U.S. and Canada accounted for nearly a third of the global total. East Asia is now responsible for 14 percent of the total, while North America holds only 28 percent of the pie. In this period, East Asia's exports have more than doubled, while the once dominant pattern of U.S.-Europe trade has shifted noticeably toward the Pacific. In every year since 1978, more two-way trade was tallied from the U.S. to Asia than from the U.S. to Europe. Even tabulating transnational exports has become difficult, since many products counted as "Made in Taiwan," are in reality built of components from several nations.

Not surprisingly, this change is itself fostering other transformations. New forms of cashless barter and countertrade are emerging as significant factors on the Pacific scene, making up billions of dollars worth of transactions. The ballyhooed dollar-yen realignment is bringing only modest boosts in U.S. exports. America's balance-of-payments crises with fast-rising NICs (newly industrializing countries) such as the Four Tigers (Taiwan, Hong Kong, Korea, Singapore) soared in 1986, reaching $30 billion, compared to $22 billion the previous year. Yet, while Asia gets the attention, consider that Western Europe holds a whopping $36 billion trade surplus with the U.S. Canada boasts another $22 billion, and South America sells $18 billion more to the U.S. than the U.S. sells to them. Clearly, Asia constitutes only about half of the U.S. trade deficit.

The U.S. ranks as number-two trading partner for a roster of leading NICs and commodity-based Asian economies. U.S. consumers and corporations buy about half of Taiwanese exports and 35 percent of Korea's goods sold outside the Land of the Morning Calm. America buys a fifth of all Thai exports, 15 percent of Malaysia's, plus a fifth of both Indonesia's and Singapore's. Two countries—the Philippines and Hong Kong—sell nearly 40 percent of their exports to the United States.

How does the U.S. trade deficit translate in actual goods? Autos make up $40 billion of the $150 billion deficit. Audio equipment is replacing textiles as the second-place item. Each of these categories constitutes about $15 billion in trade red ink. Iron and steel make up about $12 billion of the trade deficit. All of these combined account for 60 percent of the total.

It is difficult to imagine that as recently as 1985, the U.S. held an $11 billion surplus in manufactured products. Today, the deficit in that category is about $110 billion. (Some forecasts insist that a hefty $65–85 billion surplus will emerge in manufactured goods by the late 1990s, assuming that innovative methods of factory automation and ultra-high-tech processes can shave costs while offering foreigners top-quality, moderately priced goods.)

Meanwhile, Japan herself has shifted from her role as an importer of raw materials and exporter of manufactured goods. Her priority is now "high end" goods, with value added originating from producing those components with the highest price. Taiwan's GNP, on the other hand, is made up almost exclusively of imports and exports.

Many in the West fail to realize how dependent Asians have become on the U.S. market. Shouts of joy were heard from Yokohama to the Straits of Malacca in 1983 when an economic recovery in the U.S. opened American ports to more goods from Asia-Pacific. A downturn in the American economy would still spell disaster for Thai textiles, Malaysian rubber, Korean autos, Hong Kong toys, and Japanese VCRs. Nearly all of the Four Tigers' trade surplus is in manufactured goods.

While the U.S. Congress demands more open markets—and few will deny that many Asian domestic markets are de facto closed to outsiders—analysts reason that there isn't that much more America *can* sell, under current conditions, to these countries. As the saying goes, the Japanese must import lawyers, cigarettes, and fast food in order to reduce the trade deficit. However, these are all items that have little real value to their society.

The possibility for trade friction will continue for years to come, and case-by-case resolution may be the only solution.

New Trade Partners, New Partners

"Right now, Asian countries are at a major crossroads," says Dr. Seiji Naya, an expert at Hawaii's East-West Center. "The patterns [of trade] we saw in the 1960s and '70s could change dramatically." Asia is selling to developing countries in a way unimagined a few years ago. In fact, about 42 percent of Asia's trade in 1985 was with Japan and the U.S.—the same percentage as in 1965. Europe's share fell from 19 percent to 14 percent in that period, but it is the developing nations of the world that saw the biggest increases—and which today take in a third of Asia's goods. (The value of those goods has increased, too.)

What has happened has not been noticed widely in the West. Asians have diversified exports to an astonishing degree, moving away from commodities in most cases, and also from textiles. "Manufactured goods were an important part of the export picture as far back as the 1960s," declares Professor Chung Lee at the University of Hawaii. "In fact, by the 1970s, manufactured exports increased in a group of eight East Asian countries by about 30 percent a year." Machinery, electrical products, and upscale consumer goods were all growing in importance, he notes.

"During the 1970s and even in more recent years," says Ronald Danielian, president of the International Economic Policy Association in Washington, D.C., "labor-intensive exports like clothing were less important. Korea took a slightly different path, though, by emphasizing items that were in the heavy industry category, like steel, shipbuilding, and iron." That strategy had paid off well by 1985, when Hyundai expected to sell 5,000 Excels in Canada—their first foray into the overseas market—and actually sold 24,000 of the autos.

The labor-intensive export policy, combined with minimal export substitution (unlike struggling less developed countries in Africa and South Asia) allowed for full employment. Technical skills were transmitted to Asians through export processing zones such as Kao-hsiung, the Taiwanese port city. That duty-free, low-tax zone gave birth to Taiwan's consumer electronics industry. Yet, not all manufactured items have enjoyed success in foreign markets. Some countries, especially commodities-rich Malaysia, oil-rich Indonesia, and the sugar-laden Philippines, were slow to diversify into industry. As late as 1985, 95 percent of Indonesia's total exports, and 57 percent of the Philippines', were in raw materials.

Despite heavy reliance on commodities in those two countries, this has not hurt the region as a whole. According to Dr. Naya, resource-based manufactured products—goods made from wood or timber, leather, or rubber—represented half of Asian exports in 1971 but had fallen to 19 percent of the total by 1981. Textiles also grew in this period from 2 percent of the total to about 15 percent.

The world's longest supply train has surfaced between two unlikely trade partners, Australia and Japan. Resources from Down Under have enabled energy-scarce, resource-poor Japan to diversify her natural resource purchases after the *oil shokku* caused the entire industrialized world to tremble in the mid-1970s.

Few in the West noticed that U.S. trade regulations adopted in the postwar industrial era were probably not capable of sustaining open trading practices during an age of heightened competition. The service sector of the economy burgeoned, and trade negotiators were generally slow to bargain hard for U.S. breakthroughs. Also, few analysts predicted the rapid rise in consumer electronics—a $150 billion global pie by 1985. "There are a number of developments that caught some of us off guard," says Dr. John Alic, a researcher at the Office of Technology Assessment on Capitol Hill. "At the same time, Asians did not fathom some changes."

When the Office surveyed service industries in spring 1987, they concluded that service trade was far larger than had been officially recorded because earlier assessments ignored sales by U.S. affiliates around the world, especially in Asia. "Even excluding banking," says Alic, "service trade reached about $70–90 billion in 1984," which means that the service surplus was several times higher than previously stated. Licensing, construction, data processing, educational services, insurance and management consulting are a few areas posting impressive returns.

If this analysis is correct, it shows there are hidden strengths which, when combined with strong progress in computer-integrated manufacturing and gains in "sunset" industries such as textiles, could alleviate much of the U.S. trade deficit in the medium term. The real problem is getting there.

Looking ahead, some trends are becoming clear. Intra-Asian trade should account for two-thirds of exports by the early 1990s. Already, over 60 percent of Asian exports are sold in Asia, compared with a scant 42 percent in the mid-60s. Exports as a percentage of GNP should increase in every country in East Asia. Dollar devaluation will have a profound impact, too—even for countries like Taiwan, whose currencies are pegged to the greenback. Seiji Naya has reported that Japan's exports to the U.S. nearly doubled from 1979–83, a period characterized by a 260-to-1 yen-dollar ratio. This reveals how the nature of pegged currencies may burden the West, now and in the future.

Future Trade Trends

Let's consider a few trends that will shape what products are made in Asia, and which will be sold, in the early 1990s. External trade is not as important (as a percentage of GNP) in high-income Japan as many believe. However, in the newly industrializing countries— Singapore, Taiwan, Korea, Hong Kong—growth rates will remain linked inextricably to exports. This foursome has middle-range per capita incomes today, and as those incomes increase, more emphasis on internal markets will be seen. In this respect, Japan is again a precursor for economic development in the Four Tigers. But her economic base, and future prospects, differ greatly from those of the Four Tigers.

Asia thrives on complementary trade, with the world's industrialized nations absorbing unprocessed materials from the developing nations. The second half of this decade saw a startling shift, as primary products finally began to become uncoupled from industrial growth in Asia. Malaysia is a good example of this trend; electronics and semiconductors—which are a $4 billion export market—are gradually, steadily taking the place of overseas sales in oil, tin, rubber, and edible oils.

George Sternlieb, an expert on economic development at Rutgers University, believes that, since Asia's labor pool will grow by 240 million in the next 11 years (or 40 times the European increase in working population), trade flows will rise rapidly before the next century.

The new players are gaining some trump cards. Korea accounted for 8 percent of all world trade in 1988. China's role as an exporter is seen by a 28 percent increase in value of her exports in 1987—a year where exports made up a fifth of all output.

Today, and in the foreseeable future, value added is replacing the stress on primary products, which means that the developing nations can upgrade their exports, price them higher, and export them to regions outside Asia—just as the industrial world is leaving behind "sunset" industries.

Within all East Asian countries, public and private agencies are trying to adjust to these shifts. There is an inevitable lag between understanding the data and acting on it. Delays in decisions about which markets to target, which products to manufacture, etc., create job losses and stagnation in all economies, whether centrally planned, market-oriented, or a combination of both.

Complicating the process is the fact that we have entered an era of surpluses of nearly all goods—an era that will continue through the early part of the next decade. "It's a situation which resembles the 1920s, pre-Depression years," according to forecaster A. Gary Shilling. Shilling and other savants argue that many products— including such traditional engines of trade as autos, commodities, and even electronics—are in excess supply. "There's too much around," he insists, creating a buyer's market.

This is good news for some nations and bad news for others. Just as the oil shocks created winners (Singapore, for its refining, and Malaysia, through its increased petroleum exports, as well as China, through incentives to explore vast offshore reserves), and losers (Taiwan, Japan, the U.S., the European Economic Community, and all other customers), those whose incomes depend on goods in the oversupply category will face rude disappointments. However, these can be offset by price drops their citizens will enjoy on other products. There is no clear trade-off, and no way of gauging whether an equilibrium exists—or can be found—to balance losses, since nearly all of East Asia's citizens will be purchasing and selling those products and commodities.

In the 1990s, automation will sweep factory floor and office alike. The relationship between production itself and employment levels will continue to decline. This alters all previous assumptions about economic development, of which trade is a central component.

The Asian NICs and Japan are opening up, albeit slowly, to pressures from the West to admit more imports. Most Occidentals fail to appreciate the great surge in exports to Asia. American sales to Japan, for example, rose from under $10 billion in 1975 to $26 billion in 1986. During the same period, Hong Kong purchased nearly four times as much as previously ($800,000,000 compared to $3 billion). Other countries follow the same pattern, and China imported ten times as much in that ten-year period, buying over $9 billion in 1987. Chinese trade was all on the plus side of this balance-of-payments ledger for the United States.

From 1980–87, U.S. trade with Asia more than doubled and surpassed the $200 billion mark. Experts are cautious about the volume of exports and imports in the 1990s, but a level of $500 billion is not unthinkable. A moderate level of GNP growth in the United States—the country that absorbs between 40–60 percent of all of Asia's products—would, throughout the next few years, assure rising flows of exports and imports. If you assume real growth to be about 3 percent or 4 percent a year, then a healthy volume of trade can be sustained well into the next century. Volume is a critical component in the equation, because it responds to currency shifts.

In the foreseeable future, how will continued trade deficits with East Asia affect the Western bloc? Exports to Asia benefit service, managerial, and white-collar jobs, while imports from the Pacific Rim continue to cripple blue-collar "sunset" industries. A $10 billion increase in foreign sales, coupled with a $10 billion jump in imports, creates 150,000–185,000 jobs, according to Chase Econometrics and to studies produced by other experts. It is assumed that those exports would be in sectors safe from foreign competition, i.e., agriculture, services, or high technology. At the same time, a constant level of imports—which affect heavy industry— can claim an equal number, or even more, American jobs. This equation will remain true for some time.

In international trade, the statistics are often tallied after trends are cast. Response to that data may likely be inadequate.

Capital Flow

Beyond exports and imports, the 1990s are ushering in an era when capital flows across transnational boundaries are gradually becoming far more significant that pure trade in stimulating growth. "This is a complete 180-degree turn from the last few years," says Dr. Michael Borrus, chairman of the Berkeley Roundtable on the World Economy. "In fact, it's vastly different than anything else we've seen at any time since investment flows, and specifically direct foreign investment [meaning investments in plants, factories, and such rather than in stocks, bonds, and in paper assets] were recorded."

Consider one cornerstone of Asian postwar growth: the great multinational "offshore" investment game. Although the basic formula is still in place: companies set up branch plants and factories in order to control costs in LDCs (less-developed countries) or NICs, in the alphabet-soup world of direct foreign investment (DFI), LDCs still hope to attract those multinational corporations (MNCs) or transnational corporations (TNCs) by dangling attractive incentives—low or no taxes, land, free industrial space, a guaranteed infrastructure—and then set conditions for those TNCs. However, today, the introduction of new skills and other forms of technology transfer are just as important to the host countries as are the numbers of jobs created when the MNC opens its offshore factory gates.

Asia has prospered from overseas investments by West European and U.S. TNCs. Consumer electronics industries have thrived in places like Hong Kong and in Taiwan's Kao-hsiung export processing (low-tax) zone. Semiconductors have spawned 40,000 jobs in Malaysia's Penang State. Textiles industries established by TNCs are an important foreign exchange earner throughout Asia, from Sri Lanka to Singapore.

Since the mid-1980s, a number of significant changes have affected "offshore" investment. For one thing, it is slowing dramatically. This would normally cause severe economic downturns in many countries, especially since development assistance from organizations like the Asian Development Bank are also on the wane. However, Asia will continue to fare well, because while the Europeans and Americans are retrenching, Japan's current alignment—as well as rapidly rising labor costs—forces her to shop for new plant sites. Also, LDCs outside Asia are not attractive to foreign investors: South America is debt-ridden; Africa is facing uncertain political (as well as economic) times; and the Middle East's former petrol glamour has faded.

The overseas arena had been dominated by the United States, which commanded about 70 percent of offshore investment in the mid-1960s. Today, that figure is about 45 percent, and in fact North America and Western Europe became a target of Asia's direct investment on a vast scale.

Data is often difficult to gather—and can obscure the true story of the DFI saga. "Many of the statistics," says Britain's Dr. John Dunning, for years one of the leading experts in the field, "disguise the globalization of production and marketing. That is what offshore investments have actually produced in Asia." Yet, according to economist A. Gary Shilling in New York City, "every indication now is that [DFI] has been slack in most sectors for the past few years." Others agree with his perception that "Asia is the only ... region still part of the picture in this scenario—

one essential to growth among *all* developing countries. And, Asians are using the identical 'offshore' strategy: Singapore farms out labor-intensive ingredients of production to Jahor (Malaysia), where factory wages are 40 percent Singaporean averages ($3,200)."

Countertrade

Barter began in earnest during the late 1980s, with countertrade becoming a convenient means of exchanging surplus goods in lieu of formal cash contracts. In 1987, Singapore concluded over $50 million worth of swap deals with its Asian neighbors, according to the Economic Development Board in that city-state. Malaysia estimates the volume of countertrade for that year at over $100 million, five times the amount in 1986. China and other countries short of hard currency favor this method; South Korea eagerly swaps abundant petrochemicals and fertilizers for scarce foodstuffs.

It is in industrial products that countertrade is growing most rapidly. The East-West Center's Dr. Seiji Naya estimates that Taiwanese exports of industrial products to the United States rose over 100-fold during the two decades ending in 1985, a year when those export items reached the $8 billion mark. Korea also achieved a more than 100-fold increase (to over $6 billion), while Hong Kong's exports rose from $310 million to $6 billion in that time. Singapore, however, saw the most dramatic rise of all: A scant $8 million in manufactured and industrial products exported to the U.S. in 1965 became $2.5 billion 20 years later—a 300-fold increase.

American sales of the same types of items (but more sophisticated units) rose rapidly, showing that providing the East Asian economies with tools for development has indeed borne fruit. Even Japan—which bought $715 million worth of those types of products in 1965—purchased over $12 billion worth two decades later, an increase of 15 times. While $300 million was sold to the Four Tigers in 1965, that amount neared the $12 billion level by 1986, representing a 40-fold increase.

Countertrade increases seem to prove the theory of oversupply. As the NICs continue to move upstream, competing in arenas where supplies are plentiful (and can be readily produced in large quantity), they will still require the feedstocks for their industrializing economies: petrol, raw materials, minerals, and machinery.

The question is whether the "pie" is big enough for all, and whether it follows that nations in this dynamic region can move up the value-added ladder successfully with a minimum of destabilization and structural chaos. Of more than 80 experts, business leaders, futurists, diplomats, academics, and statisticians of whom this author asked that question since the early part of this decade, the responses were inconclusive. This is the Great Riddle of the era immediately preceding the Asian Century itself.

Other Trade Factors

Concerning competitiveness, other quandries confront all the leading- edge countries in the region. The debt load was amassed by the East Asian NICs, and by other nations both during years of growth and in the brief periods of spiraling petrol prices. Will it overwhelm countries in the region? The Philippines is usually cited as a serious case; her collapse in the midst of debt would trigger collapses across the region—and almost as suddenly, throughout much of Western Europe as well as North America. No other nation in the region is as imperiled.

Economists of the World Bank and other institutions studying this issue believe that, when measured as a percentage of exports (a good barometer for export-led economies), Taiwan's $11 billion debt is not an obstacle; that figure is a mere 29 percent of annual sales abroad. The Philippines' $29 billion is far more serious, since it constitutes about 330 percent of yearly exports. South Korea's debt burden is far greater, at $46 billion, but first, this is a relatively modest 14 months' worth of sales overseas; secondly, the products sold outside her borders are those least likely to be affected by gyrations in the volatile commodities markets; third, the debt is declining—and will be a surplus in a few years. The opposite is true of the Philippines. In a world of potential oversupply in the early 1990s, Korea would not be as secure, because her $2-4 billion worth of automative sales would plummet by as much as 15 percent.

Diversification can count for plenty; Korean leaders assume that textiles and an array of other goods can keep sales volumes healthy even if prices fall markedly on steel, electronics, or in other sectors. Diversification of the customer base is more difficult, since Latin America will remain debt-ridden and burdened by other woes through the remaining years this century, while Africa continues to confront serious problems. The U.S. and Japan, respectively, will remain half the trade in both imports and exports for much of East Asia, including China and the NICs.

In response to barriers, protectionism, quotas, and the difficulties in direct sales, joint ventures are increasing and are themselves taking new directions. These bilateral, or even multilateral, projects allow for shared risk, pooling of expertise, and for the West, access to industries, resources, and other advantages that Asians are hesitant to provide unless Western capital and technologies are shared. For those seeking entry into the heralded Chinese market, for example, joint ventures are the only way of achieving that penetration.

Carnegie-Mellon's Dr. David Mowery notes that the parameters for joint ventures—a relatively recent tool—are growing very quickly. Since the mid-1980s, we have seen an explosion in joint ventures, and from modest bases, every conceivable field, including semiconductors, aviation, and telecommunications is involved. Structuring these deals is still more art than science.

Issues connected to trade and competitiveness include both worker and equipment productivity. Some experts, such as C. Fred Bergsten, former Treasury assistant secretary for international affairs and now president of the Institute on International Economics, believe that Americans measure the wrong indices—and emerge with an overly negative view of export penetration. Bergsten notes that since 1980, fixed investment, looked at as a share of GNP, has risen in the U.S. faster than even in Japan and the successful NICs.

Bergsten told a meeting of the Washington Roundtable for the Asian Press in November 1987 that current account deficits, measured by trade outflows and inflows, show we are in pretty much the same position as Japan was during the mid-1960s. Capital then was entering Japan for much the same reasons it is now coming into the U.S.—because this country is attractive to outside investors. Whether in real estate, technology, or even in some sectors of manufacturing, currency fluctuation is a far better indicator of economic malaise.

None of this means that there are no problems affecting Western trade vis-a-vis Asia's export juggernaut. But, as we shall see below, investments made in the NICs are temporary, and the relatively tiny domestic markets in those countries cannot sustain the level of growth possible in North America.

While U.S. productivity increases have often paled since the 1970s compared to those of East Asia, the American base was so much higher that there was little basis for comparison. In 1987, the U.S. Department of Labor noted that the United States was the only country to reduce costs of labor per unit in manufacturing, and in that year productivity gains in manufacturing—which we have been led to believe were all but dead—rose by 3.5 percent. Japan, in contrast, reached 2.6 percent, behind the U.K. (2.8 percent), while France and West GErmany had increases of under 2 percent each. Those figures represent actual output. Moreover, as we go to press, the U.S. is scoring a substantial resurgence of its manufactured exports.

Vulnerability

The debate over Western trade policy has been shaped by economic considerations, and, for understandable reasons, most of the debate ignores geopolitical considerations. The question of political stability around that region has not surfaced, yet it is a critical consideration in geopolitical strategies for both the near and long term. At stake is not only stability around the Pacific Rim, but across the globe.

Curbs on sales of traditional exports from countries in the Asia-Pacific region may trigger unwanted results. Even a relatively small cutoff of one major export can dry up hard currency, stalling further development and increasing unemployment after years of rising expectations. This grim scenario includes severe economic dislocations that produce "solutions" from committed extremists of both right and left.

In Malaysia, Islamic fundamentalism has growing appeal—and would disrupt not only that nation but goals of the Western alliance. This largely Moslem republic is a nerve center in worldwide shipping lanes and figures in the larger Pacific geopolitical equation. A delicate balance between ethnic interests may unravel if a severe downturn occurs.

Stability in the export-dependent city-state of Hong Kong is also of prime concern to the Western World. With negotiations over its future after 1997 concluded, autonomy and economic vitality remain paramount considerations. Former U.S. special ambassador (to Asia) Richard Fairbanks describes Hong Kong's position as "unquestionably strategic"; he is one of many experts insisting that Western protectionism will dismantle the economy.

Korea is another country that is far more vulnerable than imagined. Data from the U.S. Department of Commerce reveals that this country had been, as recently as 1985, the second biggest purchaser of U.S. cotton, third in military aircraft, sixth in U.S. wheat, plus second in iron ore. This northeast Asian ally was the United States's third biggest customer in lumber, fifth in corn and soybeans, and purchases large stores of scrap iron each year. To pay for six McDonnell-Douglass twin-jet MD-82s Korea must sell the U.S. the equivalent of 15 million Nike tennis shoes or 25 million dress shirts.

One problem in Singapore is what *The Economist* terms a tendency to be "too dependent on the American economy," in large part because sales to America fell in some sectors. This "shakeout" caused this affluent country to experience its first major economic downturn in 1986.

The Brookings Institution's Robert Lawrence cautions that chances of Asian retaliation are "extremely great." Leaders of the Association of South-East Asian Nations, or ASEAN (Singapore, Malaysia, Thailand, Brunei, Indonesia, and the Philippines), would "be very harsh on the United States" and act "in unison as much as possible," according to Anand Panyarachun, chairman of the (Association's) Task Force on Co-operation.

CURRENCIES

In summer of 1985, after considerable bargaining and acrimony, the U.S. and Japan agreed to address the legacy of enormous American account deficits—deficits that seemed to parallel surpluses on the part of nations like Japan and the Four Tigers. Taiwan, for example, accumulated $64 billion by summer 1987, or an average of nearly $4,000 for each of its 18 million citizens. This is not a treatise on currency alignments, nor is it a succinct analysis of the arcane components of devaluations. Devaluating a currency is a step taken as a final resort; it in effect cancels out debts, and by unilateral fiat it erases wealth in the way that deliberate inflation eradicates true values.

After the Bretton Woods, New Hampshire, pact in 1944, the world agreed to exchanges determined by the dollar, and in turn the dollar was orbiting around a fixed price for gold. The arrangement provided stability and was credited with boosting trade flows and yielding other benefits. By 1971, disorganization in an inflationary era resulted in floating rates, and there were a few calls for establishing targets on exchange rates.

Now, according to John Williamson, a colleague of C. Fred Bergsten, targets would prevent a forthcoming crisis around East Asia wherein deliberately undervalued currencies have allowed for great surges in foreign exports. This is true, says Williamson, but the countries in East Asia (and he means the Four Tigers) have no incentive to upgrade their product lines. "They have become complacent because cheaper products keep them making even more cheap products," while the industrialized countries outside Asia-Pacific are given a chance to emphasize value-added goods. "In the long run, the expert strategy won't keep running by itself. It has to run out of steam."

And he believes that is what will occur unless currency shifts are forthcoming—ones that raise the value of respective currencies. But they must happen in some orderly fashion, with targets. "This is what is the most difficult to convince ... governments," he says.

The ways of governments and central bankers are mysterious indeed. Results of behind-the-scenes manipulation and arm-twisting by the primary industrial powers led to an end to overvaluation of the green-back, which traded for some 260 yen in 1985. The dollar has lost over 40 percent of its value since then.

As Japanese decision makers realized what was happening, they scurried about, building factories offshore and implementing severe cost-cutting measures in order to survive. IBM and other corporations insisted in winter 1987 that their plants could, with a yen-dollar ration of 160:1, compete successfully. Japanese plants in the U.S. now manufacture with the intention to export, and through the magic of currency exchange are able to do so effectively and profitably.

Currency upswings are confounding, but even counting the numbers on exports and imports is difficult in the new era of the globally interdependent economy.

Currency shifts have made the rich poorer and the middle-income countries wealthier. It was the heralded yen-dollar shift that boosted actual values (pegged against the dollar) of the yen in such a way that Japan's per capita savings rate nearly doubled from 1986–87, to an astounding $27,300, according to the Geneva-based International Savings Bank Institute. The thrifty Swiss actually fell into second place (at $23,800).

However, unless analyses of currency rates factor in inflation rates, real relationships are hard to conjecture. While the yen has appreciated 42 percent against the American dollar, Singapore's dollar rose by 7 percent, the Korean won rose slightly by 4 percent, and Taiwan's currency increased 22 percent. The growing economies of the Pacific Rim are in a similar bind but face a somewhat more difficult hurdle than do the Japanese. Koreans are being squeezed, especially in the export-dependent industrial goods sectors; they and their won are trapped between the stronger yen and the weaker greenback. Taiwanese companies shrug as pressures at home and abroad mandate appreciation of the new Taiwan dollar. Hong Kong has had its dollar linked to the greenback for nearly a decade, and while trade with America is not adversely affected, its commerce with other nations can suffer because of swings in the U.S. dollar.

Extremes on either end—highly valued currencies or intentionally undervalued ones—can serve to "hollow out" national economies in the short term and in the medium term. The dependency that Williamson and others caution about prevents NICs and would-be NICs from jogging far ahead of less-developed nations, which are now thoroughly capable of handling a large share of identical low-end export items.

THE ENVIRONMENT, ENERGY, AND MINERALS

The Environment

Across Asia-Pacific, a tremendous ecological price has been paid for industrialization and for overcrowding. Both are unavoidable, and the pell-mell race to improve standards of living cannot simply be dismissed as reckless ravaging of a pristine environment.

Environmental issues are of concern to a small band of leaders within all the Pacific Rim countries. Slowly, the present rulers are becoming aware of the issue's importance to future development. Dr. Mohan Munasinghe, assistant energy director at the World Bank, notes that the issue of hazardous waste will change the outlook of anyone reluctant to commit resources toward environmental cleanup. At least 70,000 chemicals, many of them extremely hazardous, have been used, and are still widely used, in industry (a number of these, perhaps as many as 1,000, are banned in Europe, Japan, and North America). According to Dr. Kirk Smith at the East-West Center in Honolulu, about 800–1,000 new chemicals come into use each year. However, Smith, director of a multilateral consortium on the environment, thinks management of hazardous waste is not impossible. He believes the cost savings would be in the range of 20 times or even 50 times expenditure if preventive steps are taken.

Smith and others assert that the full commitment toward solutions to environmental problems—solutions that are in keeping with the style of indigenous institutions and that can be incorporated into policy-making operations in existence today—comes at an enormous cost. "There is no doubt that all of these countries … will have to be involved," he says.

Another problem that will determine policies in the 1990s is the way in which major cities worldwide are sinking, as groundwater, gas, and oil beneath them disappear. Problems with land subsidence occur in regions where river floodplains and unconsolidated sediments accumulate. Tokyo, Shanghai, and even Bangkok are imperiled. It is an issue the countries must confront within the next few years before options become limited. Rising seas levels are another issue that must be faced soon, as they jeopardize the future of the same cities as well as cities on the Pacific Coast of the U.S. and Canada.

The movement off the land continues across Asia. According to the World Bank, urbanization will transform rural sectors in Malaysia, Korea, Taiwan, and congested Japan.

Energy

Energy futures are clouded by lack of a consensus on petroleum prices during the years ahead. After a peak of $35 a barrel in 1981, price drops slowed development of alternate energy sources. The International Energy Agency believes that, with oil consumption growing by only 2.4 percent a year across East Asia, the previous conservationist trend has diminished. Should the price of a barrel of oil approach $50, as projected, it would slow development and cause a few Asian economies to contract.

Is Asian energy secure? It seems so during the decade ahead. Markets around the region are undergoing a fundamental change. Strides in offshore drilling technologies, conservation in factories, homes and other buildings, plus changes in demand—based on increased production levels of certain types of petrol used for different applications—are interacting to produce a generally optimistic scenario.

Diversification of use has meant energy substitution in Asia. In power generation, a shift away from oil is occurring, freeing more petroleum for cars and trucks. Smaller power plants are emerging in East Asia, and their generating capacity is expected to rise markedly during the next several years. Conservation has helped the region. Oil use was 15 percent higher in 1980 that in 1973, the year of the OPEC embargo, yet output in Asia grew by nearly three times as much. Oil consumption in 1987 was only 6 percent above the amount used by industrial as well as industrializing nations in 1980, and output continues to increase at higher rates. When measured as units of GNP, oil consumption in 1973 was 100, but Japan yields the same output with only 65 percent of the 1973 units of oil. In the U.S., the proportion is 75 percent, and in the slightly less conservation- minded EEC, it is 85 percent.

China's emergence as an oil player, with 18.4 billion barrels of reserves as of January 1987, is another change. Saudi Arabia is still the kingpin, with 196 billion barrels in reserves, but the U.S. has 27; Indonesia is the only major supplier (with 8.3 billion). Although China's coal needs cleaning before use, Dr. Xin Dingou of the China State Economic Commission reports that production reached 900 million tons in 1986—a 10-fold jump over levels seen in 1980. This figure should rise to 920 million by 1990, he believes, and 1.4 billion tons nine years later. Reserves of coal are estimated to be 325 years' worth.

Minerals

Many analysts ignore the role to be played by minerals. Japan uses more minerals and oil than all the other nations in Asia combined, and use of both oils and minerals in heavy industry will grow substantially in Southeast Asia, as well as in China. Fuel minerals—the types of coal employed in industry—are one area where Asia is well endowed; yet Asia possesses only 4 percent of world oil reserves.

Natural gas is relatively abundant in Asia, and exports of this substance and of liquified natural gas (LNG) are considerable. In fact, countries such as Malaysia are factoring LNG into their long-term strategies; the infrastructure needed to handle this highly volatile substance is coming into place.

The nuclear power drive has slowed, although plants up and running allow Taiwan to gain half its energy from this source, while Japan, as of 1986, secured 27 percent of her energy by atomic power; Korea, at 22 percent, was not far behind. Those percentages will grow slightly in all three of these countries, with Taiwan's total reaching 60 percent by 1994. In Japan, reservations after Chernobyl have curbed construction on many facilities, but political decisions in the post-Nakasone era have yet to be reached.

Yet another issue bears upon natural resource development. A once-overlooked aspect of seabed mining is suddenly receiving considerable attention around the Pacific, with far-reaching implications for that part of the world. Problems confronting exploration and mining of those manganese nodules—with their store of increasingly scarce natural resources as well as metals—force multinational corporations and island mini-states alike to consider another untapped resource, cobalt crusts.

Dr. Charles Johnson is a raw materials expert who has worked with governments in Tanzania, Botswana, and Asia. "Even the limited area where we conducted tests shows tremendous potential. The crusts are technologically easier to recover than nodules, and they fall within the 200-mile limit." Their location would, say experts, eliminate problems surrounding the not-yet ratified Law of the Sea conventions. Many rich deposits are in relatively shallow waters, about a fourth as deep as waters containing the nodules.

Cobalt crusts are found in a wide swath across the Pacific. A small portion of the region surrounding Hawaii and nearby islands would yield between 25 and 300 million tons of manganese, 10 million tons of cobalt, and substantial amounts of nickel and copper. Researchers believe that if a mere 4 percent of the crust area can sustain mining operations, centuries' worth of cobalt as well as manganese is available. With cobalt prices climbing, the dollar value of these crusts might easily reach the trillions.

Cobalt is a strategic material. Jet planes, cutting tools, electrical components, and other essential products rely on it—yet nearly all imports to the industrialized countries come from insecure suppliers such as South Africa.

Deposits are found in undersea mountains, and the hurdles that prevented exploitation of manganese nodules do not pose as many problems for those seeking to develop the crusts. Ray Jenkins, a mining consultant based in Hawaii, has had wide international experience. "The costs of developing each cobalt site would be high, but major difficulties are being worked out. Recently, we found out that much of the saltwater taken up with ore can be eliminated with freshwater washes or conveyors."

Private industry committed vast sums to seabed mining, much of it during the 1960s. Many are concerned that a proliferation of bureaucracy—especially on a global scale—will curb utilization of these resources. Yet, Amoco, International Nickel, U.S. Steel, Kennecott, and others remain interested in the prospects. Another possible player is the State of Hawaii, where officials hope it will assist in the islands' economic transition.

Dr. Sam Pintz at the East-West Center in Honolulu is optimistic. "Planning cannot proceed unless resources are known," he says, "and we have the task of getting geologic models disseminated." Dr. Johnson supports more research to ascertain other parts of the Pacific where crusts yield mineral treasure. "The crusts represent a long-term development option for Pacific Island countries," he says.

The possibility of seabed mining was suggested in the 1870s, but technical hurdles (and stratospheric costs) inhibited serious efforts. Most feel large-scale mining cannot begin until the 1990s. Cobalt crusts might exist in economically extractable amounts off the shores of Indonesia, China, and in other regions. The extent will be known in the near future.

THE BULLS AND BEARS THINK ASIA

There were tremors reverberating throughout most of the Asian stock exchanges before the last week in October 1987. While money-earners such as the G.T. Fund, Merrill Lynch Pacific, T. Rowe Price, and Putnam International continued to perform well, the stage was set for a rude awakening. Capitalization more than about doubled in Japan during the previous 14 months, reaching $2.8 billion (and outdistancing the venerable New York Stock Exchange by $700 million). Hong Kong more than doubled in the same period, and others gained paper assets that were far, far in excess of actual worth. Just as on Wall Street, gains on paper covered up the fact that in many cases there was no foundation for real wealth. In Japan's case, the Tokyo markets recorded price/earnings ratios of 60:1 and 80:1.

In local currencies, Singapore, Hong Kong, and Tokyo lost 18 percent–20 percent. (Wall Street declined by a scant 4 percent by comparison.) Results were truly mixed. For example, Taipei suffered a severe 40-

percent drop in October, but was still above 1986 levels even after the mini-crash.

Asia's partially interdependent bourses include markets that rank as true financial titans. Australia's capitalization of $800 million is seen as becoming slowly meshed with those of neighboring Pacific Rim nations. Hong Kong's totals $46 billion, and Singapore's is over $30 billion. Malaysia, Taiwan, and Korea hold another $18 billion. While America's share of capitalization was 60 percent just seven years ago, it is now half that amount.

The impact of "Black Monday" ranges from Asian national plans for privatization to prospects for global economic cooperation, to company expansions, and of course, to investment plans. The post-October jitters affect everything from auto sales in the U.S. (on which the Four Tigers depend) to consumer purchases on both sides of the Pacific. Also, some developments in the background are shaping future transactions on the bourses. Currency realignments foretold of major shifts in trade, GNP growth, and other indices.

"Currencies have not affected the thriving Asian bond tradings. Since the era of floating exchange rates in the 1970s, 18 percent of the gain in Asian bonds came from changes in the dollar's value," said Jim Mulally, director of the San Francisco-based American Funds Group. "The remaining 82 percent came from price appreciation and yield."

Has competitiveness been affected by October 1987?

"If it affects American consumer demand, it may ultimately send forecasts for growth in these countries," said Kirk Sweeney, vice president for international research at Drexel Burnham Lambert. "For instance, what one of the 'Four Tigers' believed would be a year with 4 percent GNP growth, could be 2.5 percent."

Economic analyst A. Gary Shilling echoes those concerns.

"Stockholders account for about 70 percent of all new car and home purchases," and their post-October "collapse of confidence" would force them to abandon "discretionary purchases," said Shilling.

Any consumer retrenchment compounds recessionary pressures if plant and equipment spending, less hiring, and inventory drawdowns take place.

Therefore, the 1980s stampede toward high-yield Far East stocks is only one facet of a global economic matrix whose linchpin rests upon a fulcrum more truly balanced between the East and West. U.S. purchases of Asian stocks rose nearly sixfold from 1980–88 (when they surpassed the $110 billion level).

RISING—AND FRUSTRATED—
EXPECTATIONS

Some characteristics of the four newly industrializing countries (NICs) of Asia—Taiwan, South Korea, Singapore, and Hong Kong—evoke metaphors. The countries are credited with ferocity ("The Four Tigers"), and are alleged to breathe economic fire ("The Four Dragons"). Inspired by the Japanese economic miracle, forged out of cheap labor and sustained by the world's appetite for high-technology consumer products, East Asian countries are creating stiff competition for the industrial giants of North America and Europe. Meanwhile, both China and Malaysia are creeping up behind the Tigers and Dragons.

But try another metaphor: The newly industrializing countries are a rising ride crashing against the shores of the global economy. A familiar maxim asserts that a rising tide lifts all ships. Yet a visitor to East Asia will see not only an economic boom but poverty, urban squalor, illiteracy, and disease.

Can the foursome meet the terms of this metaphor? Besides wage levels, the standard measure of how well the fruits of economic growth are distributed among the populace is the degree of social development. Adequate housing, plentiful and affordable food, water and sewer facilities, medical care, and education form a quality-of-life index that ultimately nurtures economic growth. In the East Asian context, however, entrenched values and cultural mores—often revolving around Confucianism and the mixed-economy models found in the region—have played a major role in shaping social policies. The ideal of a common good, intertwined with national priorities, allowed these NICs to put critical social needs on the back burner as they strived to attain their economic goals. Now, however, just as many Pacific nations are beginning to see signs of an economic slowdown, demands and expectations for social advancement are increasing.

Despite the economic boom, more than two-thirds of the population in the entire region have incomes below the poverty level, according to Dr. Richard Estes, a specialist at the University of Pennsylvania. The East Asian NICs must seek to balance the inequities that exist and to balance rural versus urban development. They also have to restructure their school systems to equip citizens for the next leap in industrialization. "The task of providing this type of infrastructure," notes a specialist with the Asian Development Bank in Manila, "is more difficult than before" in all but a few of the countries. "For the first time, a large number of policy-makers are listening to academics and others in leadership, and the message they're getting is that strong commitment in housing, schools, and the rest is essential."

Environmental policies are starting to take effect, but the side effects of industrialization still extract a heavy cost on health and on life span. The use of cooking stoves has created a "second energy crisis." According to Dr. Kirk Smith of the East-West Center, pollutants absorbed by tens of millions of people every day are equivalent to the effects of inhaling two or even three packs of cigarettes.

Adding to these gathering social storm clouds for the NICs is the demographic dilemma of an aging population. In the 1960s, those in the over-60 age bracket were but 4 to 6 percent of the total population. That figure is rising. In Singapore, the figure is 7 percent, and in Hong Kong, more than 11 percent. In just two decades, more than one-fifth of Japan's population will be over 60. China will catch up just 15 years later, when one in nine people in Taiwan will fall into that age group. Sustaining quality of life for these nations is more difficult as once-productive workers are pushed into the category of social service recipients. (Malaysia, however, officially favors tripling the current numbers of its citizens as rapidly as possible.)

Not surprisingly, urbanization is growing, and in 35 years, Shanghai's population will near 30 million.

At the same time, the shift to smaller family size by the Chinese, wherever that ethnic group resides, compounds the demographic problem; there will be fewer young wage earners to support the retirees. Throughout the East Asian NICs, the new emphasis is on providing services for the handicapped and on educating the mentally retarded. "Whether what is offered can match the needs," says a source at the Asian Development Bank, "is the big question for the 1990s."

National snapshots given below are discussed in more detail in subsequent chapters.

In Japan, "rabbit hutch" housing is another fact of life that the Japanese will have to try to alter; the stress of long hours at blue- or white-collar work is compounded by cramped housing conditions— like others, the Japanese yearn for sheer physical space. The price tag for recently proposed home construction is estimated in the billions of dollars. Long commutes in the major industrial and commercial centers are taking a toll, too. So far, the consensus on growth has placed all these issues low down on the list of priorities. A craving for leisure time, an end to prearranged marriages, the changing role of women, and other assorted life-style changes all point to a Japanese society in flux. So far, the country has given almost no attention to mental health; once this ideal is accepted, it is certain to highlight other long-ignored social needs.

Despite successes in Taiwan, social problems still remain in that country. A major issue facing this island NIC is improving the quality of life in Taipei, where one-fourth of the population is clustered. A subway system will relieve traffic congestion, but concomitant pollution should receive some attention. Also, wage policies and labor standards could be improved, declares Dr. Parris Chang, an expert on both Chinas. All these changes will require the shifting of resources. Another battle ahead lies in the struggle to preserve the island's cultural identity. Ironically, the enemy in this battle consists of the way of life that accompanies some of the products that Taiwan itself produces—blue jeans, radios, and televisions. Increased trade contact with the West has spawned Western ideas that may prove disruptive because they defy traditional values and modes of decision-making. Here, as elsewhere in the region, the challenge is to reconcile an increasingly rapid influx of contact from the West—vital if development can be sustained—while retaining indigenous socio-cultural characteristics.

The major social issue confronting Singapore is providing quality care and amenities for an increasingly elderly population. A recent medical insurance scheme, Medi-Save, is supported by 6 percent of employee wages.

The Republic of Korea is a Dragon with an extensive social agenda awaiting it in the 1990s if wealth is to be shared equitably. While great strides in housing and some other measures of living standards have been made in the past two decades, much remains to be done. For example, infant mortality is relatively high, sewage and water treatment are inadequate in much of the country, and health care is costly and often limited. Rural sections simply did not cope with a loss in population as the capital city grew, says Swarthmore College's Dr. Lawrence Westphal. Today, metropolitan Seoul is home for one-third of the population. Moreover, the government did not begin to address many of these issues until the mid-1970s. Education expenditures climbed to 22 percent of the national budget in 1985, and 8 percent of the outlays went for social welfare and health. Family planning, also instituted in the past decade, has lowered birth rates to 1.7 percent, which will improve the quality of life in future years. Urbanization occurred rapidly, and more than three-fifths of the population lives in cities. Some attention was given to urban conditions as the country prepared for the 1988 Olympics.

Hong Kong, with a GNP of U.S. $34.2 billion, has resources to allocate for its 5.4 million inhabitants. The costs are staggering, however, and more attention to housing and amenities in this polluted, overcrowded city-state imposes additional burdens. In 1985, 47 percent of the citizenry lived in public housing. Refugees pour in, straining a U.S.-funded $300 million social welfare budget as well as the U.S.-supplied $90 million in aid to the unemployed and disabled. However, achievements here are impressive. The New Towns settlements, for example, continue to relocate hundreds of thousands of people north of the city core. Ultra-high-rise conditions trouble some observers—and desperate use of mass-produced, institutional buildings as residences is criticized around the world, as these buildings force large families to split up. The limited space and daily cacophony cause frustration for many residents. To some extent, incomes are negated by the pressures found here and in other NICs, declares Westphal. Expenditures on public amenities and parklands are rising. A commitment to the elderly and retired was slow in coming but has brought tangible results since the 1970s. Net reproduction rates should tumble to below half the 1970–83 levels by 2010, when more than 7 million people are expected to live in Hong Kong.

Malaysia's controversial economic policies were designed in the 1970s to raise living standards for "sons of the soil," or *bumiputras*. The policies had broad implications as ways of equalizing income—and thus many social services—between native Malays and the ethnic Chinese minority who form much of the commercial elite. The needs of the rural sector must also be balanced in a country where some 40 percent of the work force is in agriculture—double the number in manufacturing and mining. Natural rubber is a mainstay of the economy, and rubber-industry workers have seen their lot improve greatly in recent years, with sanitation and housing now provided as a matter of course.

SHIPPING: CARGOES GOING EAST WITH EASE

Without question, shipbuilding is vital to economic prospects across the entire Pacific Rim; subsequent chapters will reveal the enormous stake in jobs and GNP directly linked to both shipbuilding and shipping, which moves hundreds of billions of dollars in merchandise by sea each year. As we go to press, cargoes are overbooked—a welcome change from the half-empty loads of 1987.

Shipbuilding has become a major industry in Japan, Taiwan, and Korea. A fourth of the world's cargo tonnage in 1985 was built in Korean shipyards. Also, the Taiwan-based company Evergreen now ranks as the world's leading shipping firm.

It is not difficult to understand the impact of Asian shipping on all international trade. Vital trans-Pacific shipping routes have already led to a boom on U.S. West Coast ports, from which cargo now moves eastward aboard high-speed, all-container trains.

Asia continues to have a growing share of all flag and registered tonnage. These nations, falling in the top 16 of the world's fleets, made up nearly 100 million deadweight tons (dwt), or a fourth of the 1986 worldwide total. Today, they hold a greater share. Japanese vessels carried 39 million dwt in 1987, followed by China with 16 million dwt and Hong Kong with 8.2 million dwt.

The economic calamities that befell shipbuilders and shippers after the boom of the 1970s are now improving. Titan shipbuilders have learned to cope with the legacy of financial calamities such as that which befell Sanko, the Japanese group whose losses neared $1 billion.

During the downturn, the grim scenario forecast in Paul Erdman's bestselling novel *The Crash of '79* based on the premise of a collapse of investments in oversized, globe-trotting tankers, seemed quite possible. Few could foresee the vast changes, so over-capacity mounted and tonnage volume fell. Magnates like Hong Kong's Y. K. Pao saw their empires crumble after the 1970s boom was followed by a deep, prolonged slump.

Asia's shippers thrived when commodities sales were rising, capital costs were low, and rate structures made their services competitive. But in the 1980s automated production changed the whole basis of this earlier strategy. Shippers found it necessary to meet demands for high-speed transit and intermodal links to other forms of ground and air transportation.

Established groups in Japan saw neighboring competitors, Korea and Taiwan, pick up greater shares of this "sunset" industry, as Japanese rates were too high for many North American and European shippers, while customers elsewhere complained about service. Meanwhile, some countries entering the fray for the first time discovered that their timing was off, and their governments were saddled with heavy costs for a fledgling industry.

Sharp increases in shipbuilding contracts for Asian companies came after 1970, but they are by no means ancient history. When 1985 gross tonnage was tallied, the 1,900 Korean and Japanese-built ships comprised 60 percent of the figure, according to the Korea Shipbuilders' Association. Last year, the combined Korea-Japan gross tonnage orders were over 70 percent of the world's total.

Japan has been phasing out its shipbuilding industry for several years. But several of the giant Japanese trading companies were slow to get the message. Mitsubishi, Sumitomo, Mitsui and others will handle much of the 4 million tons of world output by 1988. There were 60,000 workers in this industry in Japan in 1984, but the number has been reduced to less than 20,000 today.

It is impossible to escape the fallout from years of mounting losses, but around the region there is some sense that at least the worst is over. "We understand that major shippers can avoid being caught without dependable carriers," said Reginald Kent, director of Hong Kong's port authority. "It's fair to say there's some optimism around the whole shipping community." "Freight rates have stabilized (in 1988), and business is returning to profitability," said an executive from Singapore-based Neptune Orient Lines.

Trends indicate that a rebound of the world shipbuilding industry, combined with very efficient facilities at these East Asian ports, will give a potent economic edge to the region—and to its U.S. partners.

Asia's leading shippers are adjusting. They are changing their lines of business, reducing dependency on commodities, quietly investing in fuel-efficient craft, and attempting to satisfy the needs of high-tech manufacturing.

Long-standing shortcomings in domestic transportation systems within some Asian countries are being addressed by both the public and private sector, which is crucial to speeding up deliveries. It is also an issue about which many experts feel the U.S. is far ahead of Japan, as well as other shipping giants.

The widespread use of computers in American ports can give Asia-minded traders significant "lead time" where information is vital, explained a Japanese shipping executive. The contents of the sprawling container lots and shipyards can be on personal computer files, along with detailed data on status, shipments, and destinations. Commerce is beyond the initial phases in standardization of codes as we go to press. Strides in electronic mail formats and in paperless communications will facilitate the movement of all goods by shaving several days off Pacific transit routes. Knowing precisely where goods are at each stage of transportation, and the status of inventories, greatly assists commerce (and saves substantial costs). In addition, new intermodal concepts—linking rail directly with trucks—should enable further savings of time and expenditure. Improvements have allowed Neptune Orient to decrease to 19 days the transit time from Taiwan's west coast port of Kao-hsiung to Long Beach, California. This is a solid decrease from 25 days in years past.

Other factors likely to improve the shipping outlook include a rise of between 10 percent and 15 percent annually in air freight rates. Declining petroleum costs this year will also help give shippers more breathing space. Massive infrastructure projects in Japan and Singapore meanwhile are expanding port capacity. As demand for trans-Pacific cargo runs is growing, so are rates rising from the depressed levels of 1984–86. American President Lines reports that 40-foot containers coming into U.S. harbors from Asia averaged just over $4,000 apiece in 1986, but that figure had increased by at least 5 percent in 1987.

Even containers with goods going the opposite direction are seeing some price jumps, pleasing shippers. American President—the U.S. heavyweight—estimates that the average price in 1986 for containers of comparable size was under $2,200. In 1987 that figure increased by more than 10 percent.

Several future strategies are being proposed. Korea has offered deficit-laden companies an extensive bailout plan. Others emphasize speed by which containers are unloaded. Hong Kong and Singapore are attempting to beat each other in that respect.

"If we are to become a regional business center for Southeast Asia, then we must establish ourselves as a leader in container turnover time," said Phillip Yeo, chairman of the Economic Development Board, with regard to the effects of Singapore's port modernization plan on shippers in this city-state. "Turnaround is improving every year, and I think we can hold our own in that respect," he says, pointing to construction under way on a new $500 to $600 million container terminal. With more automation, unloading and other procedures can be made more attractive to multinational corporations scouting for shipping sites.

An innovation by the Japanese shipbuilding industry is being watched carefully as a new tool for economic development in many parts of the world. The concept of "throw-away" factories has been around for some time, but few promoted the idea—and even fewer paid attention. An official with Mitsubishi in Tokyo thinks that the market for large numbers of temporary structures is there. "The floating factory, or whatever you wish to call it, can last for a period of approximately four to seven years without undergoing major repairs. The number of people employed on it is small," says the spokesman, "and we never see that number going beyond 100 or so workers."

At the same time that the shipbuilding industry was seen in peril, a second major event was taking place: Orders for factories to be built in the Third World were booming, a sharp reversal of the earlier pattern of Western- and Japanese-dominated production. Spinning the globe around, businessmen at Mitsubishi, Sumitomo, and Nippon Kokan thought that newly-developing countries would be the place where most plants in nonferrous metals, chemicals, and related fields would be built.

Since the factories are well beyond the drawing board stage and can be transported safely, Japanese concerns declare remote coastal areas and other areas previously off-limits at last to be opened up.

Platforms can be constructed quickly under the much-heralded quality-control techniques used in Japan. One specialist at Stanford Research International notes that "many environments require extensive site preparation, and construction equipment and skill aren't always available through conventional means."

A few setbacks have been experienced, however. An extension of the idea was floating airports, and for $4 billion, a 10,000-foot runway plus tarmacs and auxilliary strips were offered by the Shipbuilders Association. But they weighed an astounding 5 million tons and would be many times heavier than the world's largest supertankers.

MATURING INDUSTRIES

Steel

Just as in shipbuilding, Asian countries face a problem similar to one encountered by the West. Steel is undergoing a restructuring across the Pacific Rim—as well as on the other side of the Pacific. In the late 1960s, it was rightly deemed an underpinning of economic growth. Japan saw the handwriting on the wall, although her transition through stormy seas of NIC competition is not without discomfort.

With Korea scaring even Japan, Inc. (mostly through wages of under $2 an hour but also through efficient output), only a transition that considers new markets as well as the impact of new materials can withstand foreign competition. Flexible production methods plus white-collar restructuring are essential.

Steel around the world greatly expanded capacity in the 1970s, while consumption tumbled. The metal isn't being used as much as before, with major infrastructure programs such as railways completed, and replacement by synthetic materials. Were usage to match GNP increases, declares Dr. Stephen Barnett at the World Bank, U.S. consumption alone should have doubled from 1979–87. Production in the U.S. sank during that period from 100 million tons to under 70 million—and was under 60 million in 1982. Although imports are high (about 21 million tons today), they rose only during the 1984 recovery, and have fallen every year since.

Over 400 steel plants closed around the U.S. during the past decade, and over 250,000 jobs were lost, according to Lionel "Skip" Jones, director of a competitiveness study at the congressional Office of Technology Assessment.

Today, Taiwan and Korea are clearly picking up the slack, attempting to best competition from the most recent entry into the field of aspiring NICs, Brazil. Just as the U.S. witnessed employment in steel production shrink from 400,000 in 1972 to a third of that figure 15 years later, so Korea appears concerned that her fortunes in this classic Rustbelt industry are not secure without diversification, capturing specialty, low-volume market opportunities, nor devising orderly blueprints for worker retraining.

New transnational joint ventures are a tactic that both Korea and Japan embrace. Korea has taken the mantle held by Japan from about 1981–88: that of the low-cost, state-of-the-art steel champion. Taiwan has not, according to many observers, plotted out its gradual phasing out and/or diversification. On the horizon: Chinese potential, using modernized cold-rolling techniques, a merger of new synthetic materials to production processes, and energy-efficient methods.

Steel is not actually mature, in the usual sense. It has a future, but lower volumes and the advent of Brazil are certain to impact on what has been a piston in Asia's economic engine for over three decades.

Autos

The automobile industry has a cloudy future. With so much of many countries' economies based on motorcars, the prospect of a glut in the market is troublesome.

Newcomers to the ranks of would-be auto exporters include Taiwan (which has attempted since 1986 to secure access to the U.S.), and Malaysia—whose government had anticipated sales of 80,000 Proton Sagas to American consumers in 1989. Those plans were modified, and far fewer are seen as entering the loading docks by year's end. Other countries such as Thailand are beginning to open auto plants, fueled by partnerships with, and investments from, Japanese as well as U.S. automakers. (It was this type of partnership, led by Mitsubishi, that launched Malaysia's Proton line.)

Proton executives proclaim the car to be a cornerstone of industrialization for that nation. Leaders in other countries share identical hopes. Yet there is danger in linking economic development plans with the fortunes of auto sales.

Are those plans realistic? Clearly, autos do not have the same capacity to propel growth as they once did. (The Ministry of International Trade and Investment is aware of this, and only strong pressures by labor and government in both the U.S. as well as Canada are forcing the Japanese to continue high levels of output.) Overcapacity in autos by 1992 worldwide may be as high as the 5 million car range. Only 75 percent of capacity sold in the U.S. last year.

The situation is already worrying some in Asia, according to Dr. Seiji Naya, former vice president of The Asian Development Bank and now a director at the East-West Center. East Asia still thinks the U.S. will consume autos at current rates. "The data," he said in a recent interview with me, "shows a desire to focus on exports," which really drains resources from other projects. "It could be a mistake."

Some experts believe a severe glut in the early 1990s will produce a buyer's market. America is the intended customer for these vehicles. While Korea's Hyundai has succeeded, it is probably the last to stake out a claim to the once-lucrative market in North America.

Most producing countries are emphasizing sales of upper-range, high-cost models. With very modest growth rates forecast worldwide, and cars lasting two or three times longer than in times past, grandiose plans for formulation in the early 1980s are no longer relevant. Consumer spending habits show "reluctance about big-ticket discretionary items," says National Association of Manufacturers' chief international economist, Dr. Stephen Cooney. A severe slump in 1989–90 would force debt-laden consumers to cancel many plans.

"Autos were the classic engine of growth" since the 1960s, declares economic analyst A. Gary Shilling. "Here, as in other basic industries such as steel and shipbuilding, we are approaching an oversupply situation."

If that assessment is correct, the shock waves will reverberate: As Asia hopes to produce more, America (as well as Canada and Western Europe) is preparing to host more Asian plants. Dependency on car sales overseas is so great that, according to the World Bank, some 14 million direct jobs in East Asia are linked to automotives.

Textiles

The "rag trade," as textiles is often termed, makes up a tenth of all manufactured trade from developing countries. It is significant because it was the first evidence to the West of Asia's potential economic prowess—and her threat. It has been the linchpin of acrimony in Western Europe as in the U.S., as thorny export-import pacts were crafted in the last few years. Textiles offers hope for beleaguered non-Asian industrial countries; the advent of data networks to facilitate up-to-the-second, "just in time" production, inventory, and transport has saved the U.S.

producers a half-year on all phases from design, production, and finally, sales. That came to $28–34 billion saved in 1986 alone. And, although textiles cannot respond to not-so-nimble robotic "hands," use of lasers to cut patterns is ushering an ultra-customized, instantaneous manufacture era.

The pattern is similar to what is happening in other industries, and several cities such as Hong Kong and Tokyo as regarded as possibly supplanting Paris as fashion capitals in the 1990s. "Asia has moved upscale, from contra manufacturing to centers of design and marketing," declares Peter Harding, an expert at Kurt Salmon in New York City. Just how upscale Hong Kong is moving, for example, is evident when visitors have to search for T-shirts priced under $10.

The day when the NICs' Asian neighbors dine at the "rag trade" table is not far off. The trade wars in this maturing sector, though, show how economics and politics are embroiled in rationalization, and thwart that process in both East and West. From 1980–85, over 142,000 American jobs were lost in the $110 billion textile-apparel industries before a modest recovery.

"Textiles is a mainstay for our country," insists Kang Ki-Chae, director of Korea's Federation of Textile Industries. "We plan modest increases in our sales through the 1990s. But, the jobs that came in the 1970s were important, because they really allowed us to take on other new types of industries. Even when we were selling a lot, we prepared to drop our reputation for clothes in favor of other export products."

His country sold $4.7 billion in textiles to the U.S. in 1985, and two years later, the dollar values still increased (to $5.8 billion). "But, we know how sensitive all of this is to your Congress. I would say, the days of textiles here are really over, except for older workers who still may have a future in these occupations."

Having reviewed these general trends, we are now in a position to examine nation-by-nation the milieu that will shape the Asian Century.

2

Japan: Sunset Over the Rising Sun

Evidence from many sources reveals a behemoth beginning to show signs of stress after its mercurial rise over the past three decades. This northeast Asian titan has come a long, long way, but it is not quite the juggernaut Americans were led to believe. Shacks in Hokkaido, the sea of "homeless" in Osaka, lines forming outside Tokyo's bankruptcy courts, and displaced blue collars across the Kansai industrial region are all in contrast to the mythical monolithic economic glitter palaces characterized in the Western popular press.

Our lack of understanding about this amazing country follows a pattern. We were caught off guard when war clouds gathered over the Pacific eight decades ago, when ascendent Japanese prowess devastated the czarist armies. Surprise struck American shores just 35 years later. Most of us were caught off guard again when the nation laid a foundation for recovery in the 1960s, while we were still mesmerized by images of geishas and Commodore Perry memorabilia. This reactive stance has remained one constant on the ever-changed latticework of East Asia. Today, our continued lack of understanding about the real problems facing Japan once again warps our perception.

While our Asian ally has an impressive track record—and deserves the highest respect for its economic muscle—the great Japanese challenge, while not about to disappear, is taking a new direction. Parity is likely in many fields such as microelectronics, biotechnology, and superconductivity, while some of Japan's future triumphs will be felt as much in the cultural sphere as in finance and manufacturing.

As the yen has risen, Japanese companies have had to compensate by either automating, pinning their hopes on labor-saving devices and computer-integrated manufacturing methods, or on moving facilities offshore in search of cheaper labor and materials.

Seldom has a country's future been so directly dependent on not only continuous growth—and that growth is slowing down rapidly—but on sales beyond her borders. In fact, performance as measured by GNP increase has been modest throughout the 1980s and is not expected to rise to above 4–5 percent at any point in this century. Okhita Masayoshi, a specialist at the Asian Development Bank, recalls: "My estimates are down now, and in six months maybe it will drop again ... We have made these readjustments before. Look at petrochemicals, look at electronics, shipbuilding, even furniture industry and processing."

Japan makes mistakes; some of its recent sales campaigns overseas were flops. In the Middle East, for instance, tractor fleets were offered for sale. the tractors carried a telltale Japanese sun, and they were compact models. Potential Arab customers had enough of the blazing sun, and found the logo a scorching reminder of the climate. In addition, the oil-rich buyers, like their Texas counterparts, favored full-size models. This relatively minor anecdote is one of several one unearths from non-American sources. This writer was told by an Asian head of state that "lemon" autos *are* coming off Japan's assembly lines, but only reach countries "where product liability laws" are not in effect.

Even machine tools, one of the company's "stellar performers," according the the *Asian Wall Street Journal*, is in trouble, with "critical problems" affecting this industrial cornerstone. The *Journal* reported in June 1987 that "machine-tool makers are booking orders at a loss just to keep factories operating. The number of companies posting losses is growing." Prospects for the early 1990s are no more promising in many sectors. Also, as Kyoto University's economics professor Katsundo Hitomi indicates, debt/equity ratios—some 19 percent, compared to 49 percent in the U.S.—indicate a weak financial base despite outward appearances.

Even the heralded Ministry of International Trade and Investment (MITI)—which has become an invincible wonder in the eyes of Westerners—makes some blunders. Years ago, they failed to bankroll autos, thinking that the industry would not fare well. (MITI told Toyota not to try for U.S. sales, and the *soga shosha* trade company cartels agreed. Now Toyota holds half the total foreign auto import market in most sections of America.) MITI also clung to losers such as aluminum, while turning thumbs down on support for Sony, now a top performer in consumer goods.

Just as in the U.S., signs concerning economic performance are mixed in Japan. No less a source then the prestiguous *Far Eastern Economic Review* noted in April 1987 that the "economy is fast slipping towards recession." It has, of course, conducted a turnaround, but like the economies of its neighbors in the Pacific Rim, Japan's remains vulnerable to the impact of any decline in the volume of exports.

In 1988, $40 billion in new private capital spending helped propel a 4 percent GNP growth, an amount about equal to growth in the previous year. Output was impressive; Japan continued to make great strides in both industry as well as science. Yet, weaknesses in some sectors revealed that the picture is more mixed than most imagine.

Spending by Japanese industry has been flat recently, increasing by less than 1 percent in 1987. "This means," according to Justin Bloom, former U.S. scientific attaché in Tokyo and now a consultant to prestigious groups such as the Japanese External Trade Organization (JETRO), "that many manufacturers are actually not spending to keep their exports, their plant, and equipment running full steam ahead." According to Mr. Bloom and others, some of the sectors cutting back on their expenditures include auto companies (by between 7.5 and 95 percent in most cases), electrical machinery companies (3.5 percent), and an assortment of manufacturing companies (whose general level of reduced spending in 1986 was projected at over 5 percent). According to the Keinendren, a confederation of all industries, from March 1987–88, new spending on plant and equipment rose 11 percent.

Steel continues to be a sunset industry that the giant trading companies held onto for far too long. The handful of steel giants have over $80 billion in assets and a labor pool of 175,000. It was the dollar-yen realignment that dealt a knockout blow to once-mighty Japanese steel, and losses of the leading producers—Nippon Steel, Sumitomo, Kobe Steel, and Kawasaki—were almost $2 billion in 1986 alone. Sources at the Ministry of Finance and in MITI itself believed that, in order to compensate for the rush of lower-cost Korean and Taiwanese steel, a massive public spending program is required.

Problems facing this vital sector go beyond low-cost imports. Not all Japanese steel facilities are fully modernized, while glowing (and accurate) reports of the state-of-the-art steel plants have captured most media accounts outside Japan itself. In addition, the sinking prospects of Asian shipbuilding have affected Japan's steel colossus more quickly than had been anticipated in the mid-1980s. What lies ahead for the steel producers is unclear, but diversification is proceeding. Kawasaki is planning to move into electronics in a big way and has recast its corporate structure—with over $13 billion worth of assets in 1986—so that electronics will constitute over 40 percent of its business in 1999. Projections call for new economic activity, some of it in chemicals and petrochemicals, on the part of Kawasaki's domestic "Big Four" competitors.

Another demonstration of Japan's weakness came with a downturn in the engineering/construction sector. In part, the decline stems from the collapse of Middle East projects in the early 1980s—and the inability of a stagnant world economy to make up the gap between those orders and hoped-for demand on other continents. The entry of serious contenders into this sector—especially from the European Economic Community and from Canada—threatens Japan's frontal assault on Asian contracting. Japanese authorities are concerned. This is a $4 billion industry, with some 500,000 companies—and a work force of over 5 million (as of 1985), according to the *Engineering News-Record*. Not surprisingly, it is dominated by an entrenched lobby, one that sees its mission as protecting jobs, even at the cost of imposing nonproductive featherbedding on the nation as a whole.

The rise in bankruptcies that afflicted much of Japan in the protracted recession of 1982–84 has surfaced once more. Because it is already a society of small business, with unique distribution systems and subcontracting arrangements, Japan is especially vulnerable to downturns sweeping through the retail sector. The number of small businesses, on the whole, has fallen by some 20 percent since 1984, according to official census data. There are 1,150,000 today, and most of those function in 1,000 square feet of space. Sales revenues will continue to tumble, with a heavy social toll. This collapse of the "mom-and-pop" operations may be accelerated as the change from an export-oriented economy to one stressing domestic spending creates shakeouts, each with their own ripple effects.

Japan, Inc., while still resilient, dynamic, and destined to remain the number-two economic superpower, is partially dis-"inc."- orporating. This notion is enforced by seldom-discussed statistics. Only one-third of Japanese homes are connected to sewerage systems; even in Tokyo, 200,000 houses depend on sanitary trucks. A Tokyoite enjoys only 2 square meters of park space, while a Washington, D.C., resident has 45 square meters and a Londoner, 30. Machinery is outmoded in 35 percent of industry—excluding glamour sectors like steel, autos, and electronics. Even those sectors are largely becoming "sunset" industries, and eroding in the face of competition from Asian neighbors.

Only half of Japanese roads are paved. The per capita value of its dwellings, roads, and other public facilities stands at $4,600, less than half that of the United States ($9,700), West Germany ($10,900), and Britain ($12,700).

Spiraling budget deficits place a strain on the financial system despite phenomenal personal savings levels. This portrait sounds like a mirror of the U.S. (complete with lagging academic test scores and a rising crime rate), but other similarities are more striking. For example, the population is aging rapidly, placing additional stress on resources.

This sounds like a different Japan than the one that captured our imagination in recent years. We look in awe at the success stories (and, of course, there are plenty of those) without examining what lies just beneath that layer of good news. Toshiko Wada is a widely respected economist in his native land. Like many of his fellow Japanese, Wada refuses to accept the myth of Japanese invincibility. The rave reviews of "Japan, Inc.," reaching America portray an infallible nation poised for world economic conquest. "Everything in these books is just too splendid," he said as far back as 1984. "These overgeneralities may lead to an incorrect understanding of Japan."

Myths distort our view of this mighty, but *not* all-powerful, country. Some little-known facts:

- Japanese success depends largely on U.S. economic health.
- Labor rates are reaching parity with those in the West, ending one key advantage.
- The heralded lifetime employment system covers less than a third of the entire work force.
- Not all businesses are scoring huge profits, and bankruptcies are much higher in proportion to the population than the U.S. level.
- Statistics show an unemployment rate one-third that of the United States, yet one need work one hour per week in Japan to be officially "employed"; also, featherbedding is widespread.
- Production has been flat in many industrial sectors for most of the past several years and Japan barely escaped recession.
- Chronic inefficiency plagues key industries, such as machinery, steel, and oil.
- Most output comes from mom-and-pop operations, not giant multinational combines.
- There are, as experts point out, no more "free rides" in high tech, patents, or licensing originating in the West.
- Resentment toward Japan is strong throughout much of Asia.
- Japan lacks food supplies, energy, and raw materials.
- Key elements needed to spark innovation are missing (thanks largely to a school system committed to rote learning).

No single book chapter, not even an entire book, can completely unravel these issues and do justice to the concepts that befuddle scholars, statesmen, and businesspersons on both sides of the Pacific. However, let's take a look at some of these issues and expose some myths that will have major consequences in the future.

What are Japan's strengths? Her economic priorities? How do leaders there assess timetables for capturing markets and retaining them? Japanese policymakers in business and government understand the hurdles ahead; what are their game plans to cope with those obstacles to growth?

To get a glimpse of the future, we will continue to examine lesser-known aspects of the present situation. Then, by reviewing aspects of competition in selected high technology fields, we can explore the nature of this protracted, yet dynamic battle.

WORK FORCE PRODUCTIVITY

One feature of the trans-Pacific struggle is productivity. Those in the United States have lagged, but America is still far ahead of Japan. Incredible? According to the Productivity Center in Tokyo, labor productivity there falls far behind that in the U.S. in all sectors except steel and autos. America was about 60 percent ahead in 1984, leading the world (Japan rates fifth, edging out the U.K.). Americans held a 54 percent lead in services and commerce. Overall, production per worker in Japan was just about 70 percent of the U.S. level of $16,000.

Japanese companies are thought by many to be managed better than those dominated by the "quarterly report syndrome." In *The Art of Japanese Management* author Richard Pascale presents a favorable picture of the much-heralded techniques that are supposed to rescue floundering U.S. firms. However, the situation was more gray than black-and-white—in half the cases, he concluded, the Japanese firms were less productive, with higher levels of absenteeism and tardiness. This was in 1984; in fact, the situation is worsening.

The reason for low turnover is not loyalty, but, says Yoshio Higuchi of Keio University (in Tokyo), the form of company-specific (not task-oriented) training which prevails. There are changes in the 1990s labor situation in Japan that will alter a few existing features of worker-management relations. One is the bonus system. Ronald Dore, in his 1986 book *Flexible Rigidities* (Athlone Press), was among the first to take note of how bonuses—which make up a large part of the total incentive package provided by quasipaternalistic employers—are also declining. Since the yen collapse, hourly wages in manufacturing are equal between the U.S. and Japan at, according to the U.S. Department of Labor, $9.20. By 1995, the U.S. is projected to overtake Japan slightly in this wage-rate contest, when the gap is forecast to be $1.80 ($12.95 to $11.15).

In autumn of 1988, a survey of over 300,000 Japanese metalworkers showed that their general perception was that working conditions were not as good as those in the West. And, when the recently formed, 5-million member Trade Union Confederation announced its agenda, workplace improvements—ranging from hours on the job to forms of democratization—were high on the list of its goals.

Unionization is on the decline. The Economic Planning Agency in March 1987 reported that union membership for industrial workers—who work some 45.9 hours a week as opposed to Korea's 54 hours a week, the world's longest workweek—fell to 27 percent from 30 percent in 1983. By 1995, according to the Tokyo-based agency, union membership will fall to under 20 percent, and as the next century dawns, it will drop again to 14 percent. "What happens there mirrors the situation here," says Bill Vatt, a specialist at the U.S. Department of Labor. "Even the causes of union membership falling off in this period are probably the same as here—namely, the lack of leadership in some craft unions, and their failure to capture the imagination of workers moving into service and technology-intensive occupations." Other trends in the 1990s are causing unions to become less popular, including stores' longer hours, which have caused a mini-boom in the part-time work force.

Women are now one-third of the Japanese labor force, a factor that is creating tensions. Furthermore, more Americans are happy on the job than are their counterparts in this Asian nation. In 1983, an Indiana University survey found that 83 percent of U.S. workers reported being content, compared with 53 percent in Japan. American workers had more favorable responses to their supervisors and enjoyed their tasks more than did their counterparts. Similar studies in 1986 showed the gap widening—with a 45 percent "satisfaction" index in Japan.

DECLINE OF THE *SOGA SHOSHA*

Ask any U.S. export-import executive, and he or she will tell you that Japan's legendary trading companies are considered a threat to American successes. After all, the *soga shosha* post upwards of 45,000 staffers across the globe. Several unique characteristics made these titan traders a formidable obstacle to their non-Japanese counterparts. They coordinate sales of thousands of products ("from noodles to missiles" as a popular adage goes). They prefer products with little after-sales servicing. All stages of production are directed from the company's interdisciplinary division. They locate the raw materials and price all aspects of the products' components (and potential markets). The *soga shosha* handle about 40–45 percent of all imports and exports; in 1988, this figure was $470 billion. They have been the cornerstones of the Japanese economy, with connections to Japanese financial institutions and conglomerates. If the *soga shosha* stumble, shock waves will reverberate across the country.

Can the trading companies continue as a viable institution? John Choy, a researcher at the Japan Economic Institute in Washington, D.C., believes the companies face some hurdles but is confident they can overcome them. "It's true that some are too involved with what we've come to think of as 'sunset' industries...It's also true that the giant trading companies make mistakes and do miscalculate their own objectives." Their traditional high-volume, low-commission, low-profit strategy may be scrapped. Their reliance on commodities has often proved disastrous and may also be shelved.

Several *shosha* have faced stunning reverses; all must recast decades of traditional modes of operation. The trading companies have grasped a "high-tech" strategy as a way of coping with short-term difficulties. It is a race against time.

ALL ABOARD

One celebrated Japanese institution, while boasting many laudable achievements, is surprisingly vulnerable: It is the Japanese National Railway. Here, the single fleeting image of the famed high-speed "Bullet Train" forms our complete impression of an entire transport system indicative of Japanese prowess. In reality, the JNR is staggering under a debt burden of $77 billion. The railroad is the single biggest enterprise in Japan, and an unusual mix of public and private track forms the network. It is boxed in between unions, politicians, and many demands that overwhelm Japanese ideals of consensus.

JNR started service in 1872. Indeed, the Meiji masters of this epoch were fascinated by trains. They rode in small-scale replicas of the "iron horses" that crossed the American prairie. Most of the existing system was completed by 1910. It is today comprised of 15,000 miles of track, but in recent years, rail transport has declined as a share of the total transit pie (as measured in passenger-miles). Nearly 80 percent of all passengers took JNR in 1960, but by the mid-1980s the figure fell to about 35 percent. While the system handled 38 percent of all freight (measured in ton-kilometers) a quarter-century ago, it carries a paltry 8 percent today.

A commuter run from Tokyo to Osaka earns high marks for rapid, safe, and efficient transit. Shinkansen lines, although no longer a novelty, boast strong ridership. But most other parts of the system are performing less spectacularly. With the opening of new ports, rail freight lines started to suffer in the mid-1960s. They were never abandoned because of enormous political pressure, including that from constituencies in agricultural regions who insist on keeping reasonable service levels.

The Kokuro (National Railway Workers Union), keeps membership high by supporting featherbedding. While union membership fell by a fifth over the past five years, most experts think that the 340,000 workers still bearing Kokuro cards represent a bloated, wasteful exercise. Even rail yards are said to be the results of boondoggling. Construction campaigns built impressive tunnels yet suffered from cost overruns.

Today, with strains on the national budget—and with soaring deficits threatening to dismantle the delicate coalition behind the Nakasone government—criticism of the railroad is not muted. Diversification is being considered by JNR officials. Multipurpose station buildings could succeed in raising revenues, and a pilot program to this end was unveiled in Osaka in 1983.

One little-known opportunity awaits foreign firms. Some 180,000 acres are in JNR holdings today, with a value exceeding $150 billion. Officials in Tokyo will look for a way to develop some of this land, or rent it out to corporations. Five thousand acres have already been sold; raising over $1 billion for JNR. Americans in particular will be allowed to participate in these ventures because trade friction should force concessions from JNR.

A related investment opportunity comes as NTT (Nippon Telegraph and Telephone) is being privatized by the Japanese government. Some analysts believe that a telecommunications system will be developed along the right of way, following the model in Canada, where CNR (Canadian National Railways) competes with Trans-Canada Telephone. It seems that a move toward further privatization of JNR would be generally supported in the Diet; most members will continue to accept the role of private enterprise in sustaining the "miracle" of economic ascendancy. The chance for foreign groups to participate should appear soon.

SCARCITY

With nearly 100 percent of her oil imported, Japan's race to find alternative energy sources is considered a life-and-death quest. No country that dependent on stormy foreign seas for fuel can feel secure—and nuclear fusion as an energy source is at least 15 years away. About 90 percent of Japan's natural resources are imported, and nearly all the scarce minerals needed by low- and medium-tech industry alike come from a single source, Australia. Small wonder that experts such as Dr. Marvin Cetron, president of Forecasting International, conclude that the island chain is far less secure than most outsiders imagine.

Half the entire world's imports and exports in lumber involve Japan. An import market passing the $8 billion mark provides a fourth of all sales to American suppliers—and this figure should reach $10 billion before declining in 1992.

Japan's plywood industry is one of the world's largest, and more sawmills are found there than in the U.S. The country earns substantial export revenues from sales of finished wood products, and U.S. traders contend that a lowering of tariffs—which range up to 15 percent—would benefit Japanese consumers. The costs of a house would drop $700–$800, they say, if American two-by-fours—a standard industry size in North America—are used. Such standardization is slowly catching on in Asia.

In Japan, each prefecture has its own custom-sized market, and the U.S. manufacturers claim they are already adjusting specifications to satisfy potential buyers abroad. Housing starts in Japan nearly equal those of the U.S., in a good year, and demand for wood is enormous. The market opportunities are as great as chances for severe trade conflict.

Food is sometimes termed the "oil of the 1990s," since the specter of scarcity appears as a possibility, at least in some portions of the globe. Most of the 5 million Japanese farmers are part-time workers and are over 50 years old. An oversubsidized, inefficient farm sector (most plots are 3 acres or less) produces half the nation's food and contributes to food costs that are double the U.S. rate of 16 percent of family budget. The Japanese pay over four times as much as Americans for wheat; over twice as much for rice (!); and twice as much for equivalent amounts of pork and rice. High as these figures are, they represent a steep decline over prices of a few years ago.

SPENDING SPREE ENDS

Recently, as in North America and the European Community, the Japanese government has come to rely on public works and other projects to stimulate the economy. Government spending has grown nearly fourfold in the past 15 years to $300 billion, and the budget contains the world's highest deficit in proportion to expenditures: 21 percent or $61 billion. The U.S. deficit, by comparison, is 14 percent in the current fiscal year. A third of the Japanese budget is pure subsidy. The outstanding debt is approaching over $700 billion, or over 50 percent of 1987's $1.3 trillion GNP. (The U.S. proportion of net debt in 1986, a year laden with red ink, stood at 36 percent of GNP.) Interest payments alone tap 5 percent of output. Even the high personal savings rate (which in the past allowed for large debt levels) will be put under strain. In the 1990s, deficits will reach 70 percent—and possibly a higher share of the GNP—according to the Economic Planning Agency.

Ironically, despite this tight budget, 1986 witnessed a net flow of Japanese capital into America of $76 billion. (Even the U.S. Federal National Mortgage Association which supports home building in America, not Japan, borrowed $71.2 million of it last year.) "If this trend were to persist," says a United Nations Conference on Trade and Development (UNCTAD) report, "Japan would become the largest creditor country in history by the turn of the decade, with an unprecedented $400 billion of net external assets and a substantial net investment income."

Taxes, land price policy, deregulation of the financial industry, and public investments—and deregulation of government itself—are all issues of mounting urgency in a society and a political system where time-consuming consensus-building and centralized bureaucratic regulation have been traditional.

JAPAN LOOKS INWARD

The great transition in Japan's general economic direction is a bold gamble destined to reconcile some of the nation's problems with the preconditions for continued growth. In the coming years, Japan's economy will look inward for the first time, concentrating on domestic infrastructure as well as on consumer spending. Shifting gears to a domestic (not export) demand-based economy is the cornerstone of this proposal. In 1985 then Prime Minister Yasuhiro Nakasone requested a comprehensive report on how the nation could shift away from export-led growth that had propelled the economy during the past few decades. It came after some American pressures convinced them that the old formula couldn't continue to work, explains the East-West Center's Charles Morrison, long-term director of that institution's Japan study project.

Drafted by the Advisory Group on Economic Structural Adjustment for International Harmony, a private panel of specialists commissioned by Prime Minister Nakasone, the report has come to be named after the group's leader, Bank of Japan Governor Maekawa Haruo. After receiving the report on April 7, 1986, Nakasone publicly pledged to follow through on its recommendations, first on the occasion of his visit to the United States later that month and again at the Tokyo summit of industrial democracies in May.

The Maekawa report has been controversial from the outset. Most early commentators agreed with the general thesis that a change of course was needed, but some criticized Nakasone for promising other countries that Japan would implement a set of policies drawn up by a group of private advisers before it had been deliberated in the national legislature. Others ridiculed the report's recommendations, calling them impractical and overly abstract.

However, that report—and the adoption of its findings—will shape the Asian Century in a variety of ways. The Maekawa proposals suggested that Japan reorient toward a domestic economy and that she internationalize in a manner consistent with her new role as leading global creditor. This new openness must be conveyed to the world in an un-Japanese style, requiring radical changes in the Japanese perception of what is proper. Justin Bloom believes that the new, more Western role makes people there uncomfortable. "Yet," he says, "they sense there is a cultural bridge they must cross as they build the 'Pacific Community' they've talked about for the past 15 years or so."

We can assume that, throughout the mid-1990s, elements of Japanese management and corporate philosophy will remain intact. These include the heralded participatory quality-circle techniques, the core of guaranteed employment in most (but not all) top industrial firms, and the predominant role of engineers in key decisions.

Yet the economy is likely to change in several ways. Taxes, government policy on land and its use, construction of new cities, and deregulatory steps are part of the new plan to address the next century. It is a gamble that comes as financial resources are strained and opposition to spending is stronger than ever. But there is no real choice on the direction of the country, according to Mark van Fleet, director of Asia-Pacific affairs at the U.S. Chamber of Commerce. "Without this type of concerted action, they could face a degree of stagnation," he says.

Financially, the traditional notion of requiring excessive cash down payments for consumer items will evaporate. That policy made it possible for vast hordes of personal savings—ranging in different years from 18 percent to 30 percent of personal income—and currently 23 percent—to be forcibly "saved" (and hence invested). This change will occur as credit cards become more commonplace. Today, Japanese carry huge bundles of yen around for such purchases, but according to Charles Morrisson and other experts, that habit is going to change markedly, and perhaps a third of the populace will prefer "plastic" by the mid-1990s.

Home purchases have also been generally hindered by the requirement for large down payments, but the implications of this single change go far beyond housing. They come in conjunction with plans to ease restrictions on capital—thus freeing up even more funds to pursue opportunities outside the country. James L. Mooney, vice president at Landauer and Company, the New York-based investment firm, suggests that "the flood of real estate money coming out of Japan hasn't been felt," despite the fact that an estimated $5.2 billion has come into the U.S. alone. "The new regulations about to take effect," declares Mooney, "mean that pension funds will get involved for the first time [in real estate investments overseas]."

Debt has caused public expenditures to remain effectively frozen during the past five years. Why, ask many observers, cannot the mountain of cash invested abroad be put to work in Japan itself? It cannot right now. "The real estate system is very cumbersome, in a way," says a Japanese consultant working with one of America's major realty firms. "You have a situation where land is held so tightly that it doesn't change hands ... for generations," and therefore there is little option but to invest in property—or industry and services—in the West. Other factors at home make the U.S. extremely attractive. Land prices are astronomical in Tokyo, where monthly downtown office rents can average $650 per square foot. A 1,000-square-foot home can cost between $900,000 and $1.2 million.

Despite the high rents, vacancy rates for offices in Tokyo haven't been greater than about 1 percent for some time. Pressures to build will continue, with estimates that the equivalent of more than 200 60-story office buildings will be built by 1990. Real estate holds a big piece of the Japanese overseas investment pie. About $6 billion was invested in such properties in 1986, which was double the amount of the preceding 12 months. In the current phase of investment, the Japanese are diversifying, with medium-sized investors joining their larger transnational brethren.

Manufacturing absorbed one-fifth of the total direct foreign investment in '86, amounting to $2.27 billion. This new breed of foreign investors prefers certain regions of the U.S., especially the two coastal regions and central or midwest locations (for distribution purposes).

Japan is simply not structured now to accommodate the type of investment needed in the great domestic-based transformation. As the world's largest creditor she has the financial resources. Some $181 billion in net foreign assets—after liabilities are subtracted from $727 billion in total foreign assets—were tallied during 1986. (This represents a 40 percent increase over $129 billion for the preceding year.) Japan's previous deficit has turned into an overwhelming surplus—one that outdistanced OPEC's at its peak—over the course of three stormy years in which America became the world's leading debtor nation.

So, cash-rich Japan will be able to absorb more of that largesse—if the Maekawa report is adopted in toto. She must end regulations on how money is spent, and turn her sights inward in a way that has yet to occur. The new emphasis on domestic markets is critical, and as much as 20 percent of Japan's GNP from 1984–88 was based on U.S. imports alone. Economist A. Gary Shilling notes that a "devastating" effect is possible if the decline in those exports is not compensated for by sales elsewhere, or strong domestic demand. A 2 percent drop in American consumption, says Dr. Stephen Cooney, international affairs vice president at the National Association of Manufacturers', would "probably lead to zero growth" in the northeast Asian archipelago.

Is there a "miracle" cure for the financially strapped government? One little-discussed solution comes through the $1 trillion found in her postal savings network. This 19th-century device, common throughout parts of Europe as well as Asia, might be tapped in a way that has not been possible because of shortsightedness and political squabbles. Like the Japanese National Railway, the postal system is guided by political concerns and subtle lobbies that make it difficult for the government, or for quasi-government agencies, to utilize postal savings to issue bonds. The amount in postal savings compares with over $3 trillion personal savings deposits in banks, and the postal system constitutes a potent source for funding internal development.

Discount rates in Japan have been as low as 3.5 percent in this decade, but real interest rates (when inflation is discounted) remain above 5.9 percent. In 1920 Japan had 2,036 banks. By the end of World War II financial panics, mergers, and the growth of government financial institutions—especially the postal savings system—had reduced that number to 69. Today the banking community has recovered its health, but dark clouds have reappeared on the horizon. If the postal savings system is permitted to continue growing, the future of the private-sector institutions will be in jeopardy.

The privileges already enjoyed by the system are tremendous. It is able to use the whole Japanese market as a tax haven, while benefiting from cross-subsidization on a large scale. Unlike banks, the system need not set aside any fixed portion of its deposits as reserves, nor must it pay deposit insurance premiums. Furthermore, interest paid on postal savings deposits is tax free.

THE GROWTH OF THE LEISURE CLASS

Some portion of the new wealth is being spent by an emerging class of Yuppies, or *shinjinrui* ("the trendy ones"). As consumers everywhere across the globe discover that they do not have enough disposable income to acquire what they wish to, they choose less-expensive alternatives. In Japan, a home of one's own is the obvious item that is deemed too far out of reach for nearly everyone. Enter the growth of a leisure orientation. *Business Week* reported in a July 1987 issue that leisure spending is slated to grow at 6 percent a year, nearly double the 3.1 percent growth expected for overall personal consumption. Data from the Hawaii Tourist Board indicated that, in 1985, the typical Japanese tourist spent some $285 a day, or between two and one-half and three times what the typical Canadian or American spent per day while on a Hawaiian vacation. The potential for leisure spending in golf-crazed Japan—with its host of other pent-up "holiday" and recreational demands—is enormous. And the system there will determine a suitable way of plowing back much of this money into activities that afford some future-minded return on investment.

In September of last year the magazine noted that "quality of life" for the typical Japanese lags far behind that of American and Western European counterparts. "Improvement looks elusive," added *Business Week*.

Meet Akira Chizuka, a member of Japan's middle class. A government planner, he spends almost three hours a day commuting to and from his job—like millions of employees living around Tokyo. At 34, Chizuka makes $33,000 a year but budgets nearly half his $1,615 monthly take-home pay for rent and utilities for the three-room, 484-square-foot apartment he shares with his wife, Keiko. To save on electricity, he unplugs the television set when they're not watching it. Despite Tokyo's stifling summers, the Chizukas do without an air conditioner, which would easily drive their utility bill up by 30 percent.

As the northern sections of Hokkaido open up, and as youth in the great megalopolis from Tokyo to Osaka are given more personal freedom, there is little doubt that leisure spending can accomplish several objectives. First, it can be channeled into the types of investment and domestic consumption plans proposed by the Nakasone group.

Second, it can serve to ease the emotional pressures on a quasi-workaholic nation. Third, it can be diverted to a tourism industry that will contain its own value-added components (high-tech amusements will have an educational component and, as one official in MITI declares, any railways or bus lines to Sapporo (one section already opening up to tourism) will be built so as to lure the tourist yen so that these lines can pay for themselves. Job creation is another benefit of leisure spending.

Whether a leisure mentality creeps into boardrooms and seeps into the work ethic is not an issue—in the short term. Leisure attitudes *are* rising. When the Organization for Economic Cooperation and Development studied per capita income among its member countries in 1988, it found that Japan's GNP per person was $13,000, compared to over $18,000 for the U.S. Yet, the popular perception in Japan itself is that the nation is overwhelmingly middle class, though most feel denied perks such as spacious housing. By the 1990s, experts see escapism and mild adventurism finally surfacing in a culture yearning for some expressions of individualism. The old Japanese adage "the nail that sticks out will get hammered down" is probably not destined to be taken as gospel by the majority of students by the late 1990s. Japanese leadership will do everything to channel occasional outbursts of individualism that are identified with Western-styled "degeneracy."

Cultural barriers are being broken as Japan adapts a worldwide standard—a form of "Californization" of products, ideals, tastes, and mores. That Japan must do this while reconciling her own cultural milieu is a given. The glittering specialty shops along Tokyo's Ginza and Harajuku's avenues will not be mirrors of Western-based Yuppiedom. "When I went there [Spring 1987]," declares a State Department official with years of previous service in the country, "I was surprised at the types of stores springing up. Record shops were more plentiful than before, and boutiques, restaurants, that sort of thing."

DEMOGRAPHICS

Demographics gets a very watchful eye at the nerve centers of Japanese economic planning. The islands face a problem very similar to that in the West. The demographic landscape is being transformed, with those age 65 and older climbing steadily in the next few years. That is the first problem. This group, 7 percent of the population in 1970, now represents 10.3 percent and will soar threefold in less than 25 years. The nonproductive under 14 age group will remain almost a quarter of the population in that period, creating additional strains on the working majority. Those in the 15–64 age bracket, now 70 percent of the 116 million Japanese, will fall to 60 percent by 2010. Translation: Fewer working people supporting many more retired than ever.

Longevity is rising, with men reaching an average of 73 years and their spouses 78. Increasing the retirement age from 55 to 60 was one strategy advanced to cope with stress on the pension system, yet some believe that this method—even when combined with employment for senior citizens—cannot neutralize an oncoming crunch as retirees' ranks swell. One fifth of the work force will retire by the early 1990s at 80 percent of their pay rate.

The 26 million Japanese aged 65 and over, a fifth of the population by the year 2010, demand that solutions and new attitudes emerge. Even this society, steeped in respect for the aged, is capable of developing a backlash if the financial and social stresses become overbearing. (According to government data and census reports, those over 75 will make up one in eight of the total population in that year. Many will require special medical care and more social services than have been historically available.)

A so-called Silver Plan has been suggested as one means of coping with the large numbers of "non-productive" senior citizens who grasp at pieces of a seemingly dwindling economic pie. It calls for sending qualified seniors overseas, when the yen is valued high, to mingle with inhabitants of other countries, and bestow the blessings of advanced civilization on those societies through direct, prolonged personal contact. Not all Japanese feel comfortable with the idea— especially those from older generations, who are more xenophobic than are their offspring.

Hitoshi Kato, a well-known author who has written about the seniors' plight in forthcoming years, takes the view that encouragement of volunteerism, community involvement, and providing the currently missing ingredients for a thriving social life in Japan—amenities such as more park space and less crowded conditions—can go a long way toward improving senior citizens' lives. He believes that the difficulties faced by the elderly will probably increase should the Silver Plan take root.

An underlying issue facing Japanese society is whether filial piety, the centuries-old trait found throughout much of East Asia, can withstand the pressures of the new global economy. It ranks as another one of Japan's unique problems—problems ironically borne out of swift and undeniable success.

Social problems have yet to be confronted. They constitute a major challenge for the decade ahead, every bit as significant as the economic blitzkrieg of the '60s and '70s. Housing, recreational facilities, and other projects are all on the back burner, with little hope of receiving attention until pent-up demand reaches unimaginable levels. Seiji Toshida, until recently economic counselor at the Japanese embassy in Washington, D.C., speaks of the situation as a "crisis." The price tag for housing improvements is inestimable. Free medical services for the elderly are jeopardized, and health care for all age groups has its shortcomings.

The overcrowded megalopolis stretching outside Tokyo is taking a toll on many Japanese as the idea of community weakens. Seventy-seven percent of Japan's people now live in cities, and a staggering one-third of the total population lives in Tokyo and its seven surrounding prefectures.

Pressures on land—as on population—are enormous. According to the Center for Econometric Data Development, the present total of 26 million people living within the fifty-kilometer region of downtown Tokyo will grow to 32 million (a quarter of the total population).

By the year 2000, nearly 45 percent of all Japanese will live within fifty kilometers of Japan's three great cities, Tokyo, Osaka, and Nagoya. Thirty-one smaller cities within the metropolitan region will experience population increases of more than 50 percent in less than 15 years.

Some observers think that the stress of long hours at work and the intense demands placed on students and businessmen are beginning to affect large numbers of people. It is a recognized phenomenon that societies undergoing rapid cultural change and "modernization" experience increases in mental-health problems. Japan—a nation many felt could avoid such disturbing trends—appears to be less immune to psychological dislocation than suspected.

Religious thought in this traditional society had for centuries identified mental illness as a spiritual malaise. Those who did not seek enlightenment, says Buddhist doctrine, are incapable of achieving the state of consciousness needed to avoid disorders of the mind. This "therapy" was unchallenged until the postwar era. As the world learned during Emperor Hirohito's passing, subjects such as death (and even cancer) are taboo in this homogeneous society.

The transformation in Japan after the war saw drastic changes in housing and employment. Women entered the job market, a fact that altered relationships between the sexes. It has left problems unresolved. "If women are second class citizens in most industrial countries," notes *The Economist*, "they are third class in Japan." The extended family—a support group that handled individual psychological problems—is being replaced by nuclear groupings.

HIGH-TECH WARS: THE COMMANDING HEIGHTS

We will now examine several key industries that will help shape Japan's future and the Asian Century. The first is computers.

Japan knows that IBM has an automatic lead over high-tech firms like Hitachi, since the entire world is "IBM-compatible," (and must be) not "NEC-" or "Hitachi-compatible." The big push is for a new generation of computer, and for artificial intelligence (AI), respectively. The best minds from Tokyo to Tsukoba (a new science city and site of the 1982 World's Fair) are working on these breakthroughs. Without having to spend time and yen on defense, they've been able to link computers with industrial processes—which, like computer-aided design and computer-aided manufacturing, were a product of American ingenuity—and capture consumer goods markets.

In 1987, over $30 billion worth of computers and peripherals were produced (of which a third were exported abroad).

The Japanese have been training large cadres of engineers and scientists. But the school system there, despite its other strengths, is mostly geared to *rote* learning. "The Japanese education methods are by no means adequate," cautions Toyoaki Yoshida, an expert on his country's industry and economy who spent 16 years at MITI's top planning councils. The futuristic fields that both nations are counting on require innovative thinking. This is one reason why mechanisms to raise startup and venture capital are in a fledgling stage in Japan—and will remain so for the next few years, according to observers.

Too few Japanese corporations are keen on taking steps to design new products. According to a popular story, Portuguese seafarers landed on Japan in the 1500s and left behind a single pistol. Two years later, when they returned, their Japanese hosts greeted them and pointed proudly to over 10,000 guns, each exactly identical to the original. The manufacturing effort was indeed impressive, but no changes in any feature were introduced. Technological copying is one tradition still revered.

In the quarter century beginning in 1985, Japan entered into 40,000 agreements—licensing, patents, marketing, and other contracts— gaining invaluable technology transfer for a cost of only about $9 billion over a period of 28 years. They skimmed the richest cream from the U.S., a bargain for Japan since America spends $50 billion *a year* on R&D. However, the era of virtually free rides is over.

High-tech competition will be shaped in, and by, several key sectors. We will examine these to gauge the future that is rapidly closing in. A few developments in the archipelago will affect the twists and turns of the overall high-tech effort.

Industrial research will be the cornerstone of the overall high technology effort that is Japan's master game plan for the 1990s. Most of the vertically integrated electronics companies have kept R&D outlays consistent with levels seen in the early 1980s, but what the experts recognize as deficiencies in basic research will continue to plague the country. "It is being overcome in some specific areas of electronics," says Dr. Omri Serlin, one of the world's leading authorities on parallel processing and fifth-generation computers. "You cannot now quantify with exact detail where research lags and where basic research applications are advancing." Some of the past obstacles—the ones that forced Japan to adapt so much European and U.S. technology, are finally being overcome. With little need to emphasize military applications, there was always the opportunity to plunge directly into commercialization in a way that other countries find impossible. But, he and others believe that the advantage of Japan's well-established expertise in product launches is neutralized by a lack of continued access to the best secrets that once came to Japan at bargain basement prices.

The debate over the impact of Japan's rote educational system, and her historical lack of basic research, continues. Gary Saxonhouse at the University of Michigan at Ann Arbor asserts that Japanese industry witnessed the smallest levels of increases for research and development during 1987, a fact that "will count for something in the years ahead, in both their knowledge-based industries and in other industries as well." His assumption is based on analyses of spending by 2,000 universities and 1,500 research institutes. When 12,000 companies and integrated trading companies are added to the pool, it was discovered that some $70 billion were allotted to R&D that year. This represented an increase of under 4 percent above level in the previous 12 months.

According to the Japan Economic Institute, the percentage of R&D funds as a share of the GNP amounted to 2.7 percent, which was slightly lower than in previous years. It is the corporate share of this outlay that continues to remain far ahead of either campuses or special institutes targeting areas of research.

Gains made by any side in the three-way (Western Europe-America-Japan) battles ahead are a result of many different conditions, opportunities, and initiatives used to support science-industry links. Among the more significant issues is a shift in the way funding of research occurs in Japan that has been evident since the late 1980s. There will be more *kouza* money, which is geared for specific professors at certain campuses. Dr. Martha Harris, director of Japan Affairs at the (U.S.) National Research Council, speaks for many observers. "I would not expect really dramatic changes soon in the structure of research, and in the way companies allow individuals to break away from teams. The applied research area, however, will remain impressive, and should provide Japanese science with continued inroads in development of consumer goods."

There is no single nerve center in Japan to coordinate information pools, R&D dissemination, and the host of other activities required to undertake a full-scale, global assault on high tech. Mr. Uneohara, NEC vice president for research, explains that several key entities "relay information" across the board, with a little-known group, ERATO (Exploratory Research and Advanced Technology) calling many of the shots. Justin Bloom, who served in the early 1980s as science counselor in the U.S. embassy in Tokyo, reflects on long-term trends. "You will always have a lot of power in places like Musahino Labs [sometimes termed Japan's "Bell Labs" or the "Jodrell Bank" of high tech in Asia]. What is happening right now is that we are starting to see more vertically integrated companies, and even competing sectors, share enough bits and pieces of information. The automakers, for example, are working much more closely with the ceramics and synthetics materials engineers, to develop breakthroughs in automotives and ultra-strong, lightweight vehicles."

Joint ventures planned on U.S. and Western European research and science parks will surpass all current expectations, because in the next few years, an insatiable need for fundamental research will force Japan to give up parts of the laboratory and "clean room" work they formerly kept on their own soil. Some estimates are that the current pattern whereby the Japanese stay in partnerships only long enough to pick the best process from their *gaijin*, or foreign partners, will at last come to an end in a few industries. "Of course," says one leading expert on global trends in microelectronics, "the reluctance to share information *must* come to a close in the near future … the Europeans are less tolerant, they've taken all they can in that respect." And, he adds, the Americans are "boiling over" because they've been stung too often by close-lipped Japanese who "still carry about with their notepads and cameras" around the corridors of our own laboratories and research parks.

Internationalization of industrial techniques in the next several years will mean that Japan will be faced with the need to restructure many of its practices in the industrial lab—practices Westerners view as secretive. "This is going to be another very big change for them … very unsettling in many respects, too," according to the RAND Corporation's Dr. Charles Wolf, director of international studies.

The computer/communications "pie" totalled $140 billion in 1984, and revenues for deserving companies in the U.S., the EEC, and East Asia should hover in the $940 billion range by 1994. It will reach $1.5 trillion by 1999, according to Dataquest.

Information technologies are generally projected to be 40 percent of the world's value-added industrial wealth in a mere 13 years. Computers, services, and telecommunications are rightfully considered *the* battleground that pits America against (largely imitating) rivals. More than that, this still-infant sector will transform the globe in ways we can't even imagine.

It is a rich harvest, with low energy inputs and very high value added, the very ingredients Japan seeks for its economic blitzkrieg. NEC, Hitachi, Fujitsu and other cartels see the net export earnings, high unit value, potential for standardization, low margins, price-sensitive products, and businesses where they can use a mass distribution approach. Another critical element is high manufacturing content, essential in terms of selection of target segments. What does this mean for the future? Consider the mathematics. A product that sells for $100, but costs $80 to manufacture, is a low-margin product. The Japanese could manufacture it for $60 because of pre-1988 foreign exchange rates. Japan sells it for $70, and the probability of success is great. Japanese competitiveness was based on that feature, plus low labor rates (70–80 percent of the U.S. level). In the early 1990s, these will change.

Furthermore, Japan was never in the computer business per se, but was in the component and peripheral business. The Japanese adopted, as a guiding principle, a strategy that relies on sales of components to future rivals, eating away the integrity of their hardware. The corollary of this technique was to develop peripheral presences around the mini-computer and mainframe businesses, and in microcomputers. In the early 1990s, this plan calls for direct selling, direct service, plus a direct brand systems approach to those markets (and to PBX markets in telecommunications). This specific system strategy is very much in force today, and the overall thrust still propels the Japanese to a commanding lead in many consumer product categories. That is the secret of the "commanding heights" strategy of the decade ahead. The ability to produce excellent quality peripherals for office systems is going to give Japanese companies a competitive edge extending well into the mid-1990s.

Future battlegrounds will be in such areas as parallel processing and artificial intelligence (AI). AI would demonstrate that the island nation is no longer simply a technology copycat. The prestige accorded Japan for being first to unveil this marvel would add luster to all her products and stand as a powerful promotion tool. It would also hand the Japanese new capabilities.

Use of kanji characters, cumbersome written representations, have curtailed Japan's hoped-for gains in high tech. English remains the language of high tech, of science, of music, and of business. However, by 1987 great strides were made in the effort to include the Japanese tongue and its complex character system in the world of high tech. (It is often said that even the best typists in Tokyo can only master 2,000 characters, and even today, the vast majority of business correspondence is handwritten.) Until recently, it was thought that a truly Japanese keyboard would have to contain some 7,000 characters in order to satisfy *wahpuro*, or "word processing," capabilities. Recent breakthroughs, after years of concentrated research, have enabled Sharp and Brother word processing units to identify Japanese characters and convert them into English words, using a simplified code that condenses the number of possible characters. Of course, the reliance on Western operating systems such as DOS has made it cumbersome for many Japanese to pursue a number of sensitive—and strategic—computer projects. Western alphabets seem facile, mobile, and futile when compared with the thousands of characters in Japanese.

Ken Sakamura, one of the leading computer scientists in Japan, began in 1985 to enlist support from dozens of companies as he devised one way to end run the dependency on the Western tongues that cripples Japanese strides in information processing: the TRON system, a new standard operating system to rival DOS, which is currently holding sway in Asia. Matsushita recently produced the first TRON personal computer.

What will TRON do for Japan? A joint project of Mitsubishi, Fujitsu, and Hitachi includes Japan's first truly indigenous microprocessors. TRON represents a success (after repeated failures) in developing a national operating system—the foundation of a serious drive to devise common formats for all electronic equipment, ranging from sophisticated office gear to relatively mundane facsimile machines. "Because the 'guts' of computer architecture worldwide is dominated by U.S. standards and protocols," declares forecaster Dr. Marvin Cetron, "it has given IBM and other leading manufacturers a real advantage." With what *The Economist* describes as support from a group of eight major Tokyo- and Osaka-based multinationals, the TRON quest for a common tongue gives Japan an opportunity to shatter the U.S. monopoly in one critical arena of high tech.

Week to week and month to month, the battlefronts and commanding heights of this protracted—and epic—struggle changes as new banners of conquest are unfurled and, at other strategic points, white flags raised in surrender (and in America's case, often by default). We are looking at the wrong set of criteria, and interpreting a temporary stage of world history, with all its gray areas as a black-or-white fierce, winner-take-all competition. The concluding sagas of this classic East vs. West combat are probably years ahead; the ultimate prizes, if they exist at all, lie along those further shores of both destiny and history. Today's events in licensing, innovation, commercialization, product design, and the rest, cannot adequately be interpreted by mere recitation of date or by the short-lived triumphs or tragedies accompanying each skirmish between the Pacific-based contestants.

In the end, or not the end, but in succeeding chapters of the postindustrial drive for national self-upgrading by a handful of nation-states, the legacy may find new definitions for competitiveness, and a fundamentally different paradigm for economic growth. Today's observers, the dynamic Four Tigers, currently relegated to the status of observers in this titanic ring match, might emerge themselves as participants when future bells are sounded, signalling resumption of the fray.

Japan's scorecard is mixed as she pursues high tech. At present, she lags in development of new technologies but has been adept at improving upon existing ones and in commercializing them rapidly. However, many quandaries over ties between business and government are surfacing and will impede the future collaboration of groups that have relied on a host of special relationships and partnerships unfettered by concepts of antitrust. Also, the lack of U.S. licensing and patent bargains will hinder some of Japan's high-tech development. "Europe is not going to give anything away, either," says Justin Bloom.

Chip Wars

The Japan of the 1970s planned its electronic campaign well. The island nation, then clearing away the last charred debris of war, could boast 6,700 computers—large, mini, and micro—valued at $2.7 billion. A dozen years later, a census of computers tallied 106,000, with a value reaching $21 billion. By that point, six giants—OKI, NEC, Mitsubishi, Hitachi, Fujitsu, and Toshiba—ruled the roost over electronics, components, computers, and communication equipment. Her share of the global semiconductor market reached 37 percent in 1983 while, according to Dataquest, 90 percent of all 256K RAMS bore the "Made in Japan" label in 1987.

Several trends affect Japan. The structure of the semiconductor industry is changing, with many diversified companies in Europe as well as the U.S. recognizing the need to seek internal chip capabilities. This will impact on many Japanese firms. Also, the Japanese advantage in the area of capital costs will end; they have only a temporary labor market advantage. Public support and consensus is no longer assured as the nation looks inward at its social agenda.

Future markets will evolve beyond the current semiconductor contest. It is often said the Fujitsu and the Tokyo-based conglomerates control a major share of the "chip" market, but a deeper probe shows that America's and the EEC's concerns have often been misplaced. Consider the American microchip market, which in 1986 stood at $9 billion, or one-third of the world total. While experts point to a doubling of Japan's share of that market since 1982 (to 45 percent), few include so-called captive production. This is, production by major manufacturers that caters exclusively to their internal needs. Titans such as IBM and AT&T prefer to manufacture the higher-grade microchips themselves, allowing rivals and smaller competitors to focus on the less powerful chips. It is the more widely used microprocessors and chips that have suffered the most dramatic price drops in recent years, and giants like IBM do not want to endure chip shakeouts alongside other manufacturers. If the captive markets are included in the totals, Japan's share drops to below 36 percent.

The Japanese, who have three of the five leading chip makers today, have flourished because of the way in which their respective design centers are sited on U.S. territory. These plants usually carry a steep price tag, as much as $150 million, but the location here allows Asian manufacturers to capitalize on the availability of large cadres of trained research scientists, especially those geared toward individual research.

It is in the linking of high-tech chips with commercial and industrial applications that Japanese companies are likely to stay ahead of their Western rivals. Refinements in those techniques can be applied to manufacturing of semiconductors as well as other cornerstones of the postindustrial epoch. At the beginning of this decade, the 16-kilobit DRAM (dynamic random access memory) was in volume production, replaced only three years later by the 64K DRAM and by 256K DRAMs. As memory size increases, production of chips becomes more demanding. A 1-megabit DRAM has more than a million transistors on a piece of silicon; the separation between devices on the chip is one micron, the limits of current manufacturing technology. By the time 16M DRAMs are manufactured that separation will have to be .5 micron. Few companies can afford to develop such complex equipment.

It is too late for U.S. manufacturers to enter the 1M DRAM market, and they lag in that for 4M DRAMs. Costs of developing memories and miscellaneous production processes required for their manufacture are increasing rapidly. Many are expected to appear before the end of the decade, so development of a 64-megabit RAM would be an attempt to "leapfrog" over both the 4M and the 16M stages. The semiconductor industry may have coalesced a suitable manufacturing sematech to make this possible.

The European economic community is not sitting still. Philips and Siemens have had a joint project to develop 1- and 4-megabit DRAMs since 1984. Partly financed by the Dutch and West German official agencies, the $2 billion project is beginning to show results. Siemens has begun sample production of 1M DRAMs and expects to produce 4M devices by 1989. Philips is expected to begin sample production shortly. These companies, plus French firms, are all serious contenders.

Recent discussions with experts from different companies, as well as research labs, and other pertinent institutions on three continents points to some clear trends in the early 1990s. Their conclusions mirrored those of a special task force set up by the U.S. government in 1986, which conducted a comprehensive examination of some 25 fields in which semiconductor competition between the U.S. and Japan would be critical during the next few years. In only one field, linear devices, did the United States appear to hold a clear lead that could withstand the Japanese assault into the early 1990s. Logic memory chips, computer-assisted manufacturing/computer-assisted design, plus assembling micro-processing equipment were areas where American firms held on to leads—but where maintaining those leads was in doubt.

However, looking at the short term, the weaknesses of some export-minded Japanese multinationals are hurting their chances to leapfrog ahead of the U.S. Toshiba's net profits were sagging—down 43 percent in 1987 compared to the 1986 fiscal year ending March 31. The titan corporation still posted $23 billion in sales. "If Toshiba starts to slip," remarks one American electronics authority, "it automatically gives the competition here, and for that matter in Europe, breathing space."

Toshiba has been in the forefront of efforts to develop yet another artillery piece in Japan's high-tech assault. It is the ASIC— applications-specific, customized chips that can replace hundreds, or even thousands, of standard microchips. They perform better, work faster, and have other advantages as silicon chips are brought more directly into the world of manufacturing itself, guiding "intelligent" factories (see below), programmable devices, and literally shaping the products coming off those conveyor belts.

ASICs will grow in both quantity and value eventually doubling from the 1987 $2 billion level to $4.7 by 1989, then reaching the $15–17 billion level by 1995. *The Economist* reported in April 1988 that they are 12 percent of the world market now, but will rise to 20 percent of that market within four years. Nervous companies are concerned about Japan's tendency to monopolize markets, undercut prices, score long-range "deep pocket" deals, and carry out other established practices that ultimately deny market share to her opponents. Therefore, European Silicon Structures in the EEC, and the newly created Semantech consortium in the U.S. (a creature of Intel and IBM) hope to reach breakthroughs on their own.

One change affecting this type of competition is the occupational structure of high technology and its increasing tendency to divide functions into select geographic regions. "There are very sharp distinctions emerging," says Brian Jeffrey, now president of Technology International in Palo Alto, "that mean these [high tech] companies are going to break up production and keep certain types of personnel in certain locations, instead of bundling them together. As globalization increases, and Asian firms are required to sit closer to the large American market, they will have a need to locate professional, managerial, and technical staff in certain regions of the United States, and to a degree, Western Europe." It is possible, according to Mr. Jeffrey, that we will find electronics' location strategy having a much more significant impact on their joint ventures, and on the character of those ventures, than we once thought.

The EEC has recently launched its own anti-dumping investigations. Semiconductor imports in 1986 rose beyond the $3 billion mark (compared to $2.7 billion in the previous year). This figure is nearly three times the amount of Western European semiconductor exports—and this disparity troubles people. (About half of those imports came from the U.S. and about $580 million were from Japan.) As recently as 1985, Japan captured 80 percent of the EPROM (erasable programmable record only memory) market, which while tallying $175 million in sales represents one of the dynamic, strategic sectors within the overall nifromarityon industry. It is linked to 1990s business information processing, the field called an ultimate battleground by experts in the West. According to *Europe* magazine, some manufacturers are criticizing EEC authorities for not taking a more vigorous stand. The magazine reports that last year Europeans were forced to slash prices by as much as 30 percent in order to prevent Japanese hegemony.

The perspectives of the global chip trade war are perplexing. In a Nikkei Research Institute poll released in June 1987, 1,000 Japanese executives were asked which of the two great economic superpowers was responsible for trade friction in chips. According to that survey, 63 percent blamed MITI itself, and half of the respondents indicated that

MITI was not doing enough to reduce disagreements over semiconductor trade. Fewer than 25 percent of respondents felt that MITI was taking a strong enough stance to avoid future trade friction over these vital components, the "brains" of the new information era.

Will Europe be left out of the short-term competition because of the U.S.-Japan semiconductor, or chip pact of 1986? The 1986 trade agreement between the United States and Japan on semiconductor quotas is not working as intended and could threaten the stability of the European computer industry, according to an official of Britain's largest computer company. John Dickson, director of manufacturing operations for International Computers Ltd., made his remarks to 200 delegates representing leading suppliers of semiconductors, subassemblies and peripheral equipment in July 1987.

"ICL procures semiconductors and other components from the United States, Europe, and Japan in roughly equal proportions," Dickson said. "Since the U.S. government protectionist action, component prices in Europe have risen and will rise even further if the anti-dumping complaint before the European Economic Community by European semiconductor producers is successful." Dickson urged suppliers to resist the temptation to raise prices during the current trade friction. "Such moves will seriously destabilize the market," he said. "We therefore believe an immediate return to free trade conditions is essential for the medium- and long-term success of the indigenous computer industry." Dickson said that ICL's purchasing expenditure for 1987 will be about 10 percent more than the 1986 figure of $670 million.

Supercomputers

There is another high-tech battleground of extreme importance. It is the supercomputers, ultra-fast—able to calculate a billion arithmetic equations per second—and ultra-expensive, costing $20 million apiece in most cases, that can speed up design and production, solving the most thorny quandaries imaginable today. Spaceflight trajectory, aerospace design, and other activities probed only through the most intensive calculations rest on strides in this arena. To perfect synthetic materials, for example, many millions of calculations are needed in the quest for new structures made from composites of existing elements.

Considered a major prize in the whole protracted high-tech war, supercomputers would carry out many of the same functions, such as analyzing image data from satellites and handling tasks helpful to industry, including analysis of highly complex nonlinear problems, structural analysis, searches for natural resources, engineering, and aeroengineering—all very important to the economic survival plans of the industrial world. AI, whose goal is to duplicate or mimic human reasoning, would enhance strides seen in the fifth-generation effort. The University of Hawaii's Dr. A.J. Marshall Unger has theorized that AI's quasi-secret purpose is to allow the Japanese to bypass complexities of kanji. Those features of their language confound the ability to tabulate, communicate, or express concepts. AI would provide a means of circumventing such cumbersome restrictions, he insists.

In current Japanese AI projects, functions of a human neocortex's estimated 10 billion neurons would be carried out through intricate techniques of "memory" and association of concepts, words, and "images." All this is inextricably linked to a drive to recreate the human brain with high-powered biochips, the product of work in biotechnolgy.

New targets for high-tech industries were unveiled by MITI in 1988. Space limitations prevent discussion of all of these. One critical field, however, interfaces with electronics, telecommunications, and with the all-important quest for value-added products that are the cornerstone of future growth and national stability.

Two U.S. projects began in artificial intelligence and supercomputers, respectively, in the mid-1980s. For the latter, a $225 million drive called Superspeed aims for a rival to Cray and Control Data by 1989. The $500 million-plus AI venture spearheaded by those giants is a 10-year plan, while the Defense Advanced Research Project Agency at the Pentagon is holding fort against MITI with its own AI effort.

In 1985, the Pentagon announced a $10 million special operation to gain new, key technology in the semiconductor business because of increasing reliance on Japanese sources.

As of June 1987, only 2 percent of the world's supercomputers were "Made in Japan." Of about four times as many operating in the United States, all were "Made in the USA." That ratio, at press time, remains unchanged.

High-Definition TV

High-definition TV (HDTV) is termed the next electronics for good reason. Since the mid-1980s, research laboratories in both the U.S. as well as in Japan, and to an increasing degree in Western Europe, are turning their attention to this field. "The affect on communications is not readily understood," according to Dr. Marvin Cetron, author of *Encounters with the Future*, "but it promises to be significant." Breakthroughs and innovations, he asserts, "would be more revolutionary than the advent of TV itself."

Communications would simultaneously be "transformed in major ways," declares Dr. John Gibbons, since 1981 director of the congressional Office of Technology Assessment.

Dr. Larry T. Darby, who for years has organized Pacific telecommunications conferences, terms advanced TV "a blend of new technologies" in analog and digital—among others. It will enable us to realize "real sci fi" interactive communications for the first time.

HDTV is far more than the ultra-sharp, near-lifelike images possible on the ubiquitous boob tube. It is seen by the experts as what John Pickitt, president of the Computer and Business Equipment Manufacturers Association terms "a battleground." Reasons are clear: The Semiconductor Industry Association supports contentions of seasoned observers that some $400–500 billion worth of consumer products (an amount over double the present global telecommunications market) will result within a dozen years.

Spinoff products (including new chips) will provide other far-reaching multiplier effects. Furthermore, it is estimated that half of today's consumer electronics products originated within the past nine years. Therefore, HDTV potential to spawn new industries is hardly unrealistic.

Calculations of TV units requiring replacement over the next 20 years indicate that a vast sales potential will be realized by more aggressive organizations or multinational groups pursuing an HDTV strategy.

California Rep. Mel Levine (Dem.), one of a handful of telecommunications point men in Congress, asserts HDTV will "dwarf" the economic impact "of today's consumer electronics industry."

New TV sets—as well as converters needed for current, "ghost"-laden fuzzy-screen models—are a vast market. Advanced TVs, with double the current 532 definition lines (which was unchanged for three decades), would constitute a $40 billion market worldwide in just eight years. A wide range of products—electromedical devices, graphics screens, VCRs, and such—are allied to breakthroughs in the field. (Over $2 billion in graphics terminals were sold in the U.S. during 1986 alone.)

Industrial uses abound, and an assortment of new multiplier effects should be felt in entertainment. Defense-related uses are realistically envisioned. Market penetration in consumer products is profound, especially when one recalls growth in one sector: Fewer than 500 personal computers were sold in the U.S. as recently as 1978. It is anticipated that, in 13 years, household penetration of advanced television sets could easily reach (or surpass) 20 percent.

We know what happened when Japan, Inc. and the U.S. were rivals in autos and in semiconductors. Protracted war is raging in biotech and superconductivity, but HDTV is clearly a "sunrise" industry with significant possibilities.

While the U.S. contributed most basic R&D, it appears to be letting product development slip away. The EEC seems destined to play a role as a joint venture partner, with participation by Thomson CF, and possibly Philips. In Japan, Inc. corporations there are—through a cartel-like style witnessed in other arenas—attempts to gallop ahead of the U.S. Toshiba, Sony, NHK, and others are in the forefront of this field, busily overcoming long-standing obstacles. Before 1990, NHK in Tokyo will unveil advanced HDTV receivers.

At press time, there are questions of technical standards that must be resolved by the Federal Communications Commission. (Bandwidth and capacity of many broadcast stations is incapable of accommodating HDTV.) In addition, views are mixed concerning which transmission mode is deemed to be acceptable to the Commission. In television broadcasting of the 1990s—and beyond—that mode is yet another critical matter to be resolved.

Brave New Biotech World

The field of biotechnology—enzymes, new plant strains, plant cell culture, DNA techniques, gene manipulation is an industry of the future … a future already upon us. Despite its still-infant stage, biotechnology is regarded as one of the most promising scientific activities of this, as well as the next, century. It is an area with future opportunities for tremendous economic growth and commercial expansion, in food production and industrial uses, among many other areas. The two key players are Japan and the United States. Few doubt that this "sunrise" industry has the potential to become another electronics. Biotechnology will produce better crops, cure age-old diseases, slice genes, synthesize new substances, and even bring innovations to the factory floor. Biochips—complete with biologically-devised switches—tantalize researchers. By the 1990s, great strides will be made in these arenas.

Japanese strengths in biotech are renowned, and farsighted companies there recognize the seeds of another industrial/postindustrial revolution. Skill in handling complex microbes is proven by many advances, and MITI estimates that a $27 billion industry will exist in this one sector within just two decades.

Furthermore, biotech is the cornerstone of Japan's $9 billion program to link science with overseas assistance—while spawning more indigenous research to smooth a postindustrial transition. Proof of Japanese determination comes through the efforts of Sharp, Hitachi, and Fujitsu, as they race against American firms striving for "biochips"—a technique of utilizing nature's chemical structures to transmit information far more efficiently than silicon chips currently used in computers. In only one area, fermentation, does Japan appear to hold a clear lead over the U.S. (due to centuries of expertise in rice wine production). In 1987, $90 million was spent by the Japanese for basic research, probably an eighth of what the U.S. allots. And, basic R&D coming out of the U.S. can, and is, being utilized by Japan's industry. Recently, attention to the basic research quest has been emphasized in Tokyo and Osaka, and applied R&D still receives support of nearly $500 million. Also, long-discussed coordination of Japan's biotech efforts is happening at last. A new consortium in Tokyo will bring together major companies, grafting input from computer giants Fujitsu and Hitachi onto a more coherent national effort. Not surprisingly, MITI actively monitors these developments. Yet, one problem inherent throughout much of Japan's high-tech quest plagues her strides in biotechnology. "Basic research remains a stumbling block," declares Lehigh University's Dr. Arthur Humphrey.

Several companies without any presence in biotechnology are planning to enter the fray. When Toshiba announced plans to allot 20 percent of its total R&D budget by 1992, its moves were in keeping with those of many other major Japanese companies yearning for a chance to seize sunrise opportunities. Toshiba has emphasized biotech in its intensified drive, one that depends on stimulating non-Japanese basic research. "They have to take the risks of investing in research that has uncertain results," declared M. Maruyama, a Hitachi executive, in an interview with *The Asian Wall Street Journal* in June 1987. Noting that "researchers chose their own themes," the *Journal* reported that biotech research in 1986 alone increased by 16 percent over the previous year, to $2.68 billion. "Manufacturers are starting to woo more theorists," notes the publication. Experts like Justin Bloom think that increases in basic R&D expenditures of 10 percent a year through 1999 are not likely in many large corporations. Much of this outlay will go to build plants and equipment. "The question is whether they can overcome institutional barriers quickly enough to make the most of these very large expenditures," notes Dr. Bloom.

Can the trade friction we have seen in electronics and computers be avoided during the next phase of high technology? Biotechnology remains one of a handful of key high-tech battlegrounds between the U.S. and Japan, although Japanese firms are catching up to American competitors. A surprising degree of bilateral cooperation has been taking place, just as biotechnology's tortoise-like (and disappointing) pace is accelerating. "Both sides understand there is no immediate pay off," according to Richard Godown, president of the Industrial Biotechnology Association. "The regulatory hurdles here in America, and concern for product safety are only part of the reason for what was until recently somewhat slow progress."

"Mapping and sequencing DNA and chromosomes are one area where both countries are starting to work together," says Rachel Levenson at the National Institutes of Health (NIH). Once this is done, science can have the control over the genes that critics warn is a curse—and others see as a blessing unlocking biotech's true potential. And, this year, teams in both the U.S. and Japan are moving in that direction. The NIH is considered a nerve center for U.S. biotechnology research, and it has funded nearly 300 Japanese researchers on-site since 1984. "Japan is now telling us what they are doing," she insists, "and we can provide some assistance. Their scientists feel that, after all, they're getting information from [the] U.S. ... they're not as reluctant as they once were to share information."

This is a new trend. American companies working in Japan have complained about one-way communication in the pharmaceutical, biomedical and other industries. Until recently, even conferences and exchanges of research papers between the two countries were rare.

However, the new give-and-take approach is carried out cautiously. Dr. Ed Chaitt, vice-president at DuPont, finds Japan's catch-up phase in biotech "remarkable during the past ten years." Their knowledge of our language provided the Japanese a lot of access to our own research." It's that catching up that scares some Americans who are mindful of the bitter experiences in other arenas. A California biotech executive compares this new attitude with earlier efforts to secure information from non-cooperative Japanese companies. "My colleagues and I think it's like day and night, and we're happy. Unquestionably, both countries will benefit."

Industry strengths in both countries are being reassessed by the biotech community to see how the most fruitful types of joint ventures can be arranged. In Japan, "effort, equipment, and the knowledge base" are about equal to the U.S., according to Dr. Arthur Humphrey, director of Lehigh University's Biotechnology Center.

Indeed, joint ventures are starting to shape the course of U.S.-Japan work in biotechnology. Kirin's 1987 alliance with U.S.-based Amgen is looked upon as an example of future biotech collaboration. The California firm provided $8.3 million in technology and equipment to aid its quest for new hormones and pharmaceuticals, while the beer maker matched this with over $10 million in cash. Takeda, the titan pharmaceutical, is teaming up with Harvard University on a project to design protein cells to eradicate cancer. Licensing deals will become more sophisticated in these types of arrangements, and can allow both countries to score respectable market shares. It's a market that will rise to over $70 billion in Asia alone by 1997. Part of the reason is the vast need for pharmaceuticals and medical products in the Asia-Pacific region.

While cooperation characterizes some aspects of the biotech field, heated competition characterizes others, including the automation of biotechnology. Since new and commercially valuable products— peptides, immune regulators, neuropeptides—are useless unless sufficient quantities can be harvested, automation is an essential step in producing commercially viable product. Automation has been elusive for many firms. Adequate purification and separation of substances is a problem, since these high-value-added pharmaceuticals and chemicals are prone to contamination. When companies seek high-quality products, they are often forced to trade off quantities, and conventional cell-harvesting methods lose as much as 25 percent of the product.

Thus, the country forging ahead in automation has a significant advantage. Companies like Ajinomoto and Kyowa Hakko gain recognition for use of computers in the process, giving Japan a lead in two segments of automation: amino acids and enzyme production. But American firms scored important breakthroughs since the mid-1980s. Experts are divided on who is in the lead (and on how to precisely define criteria for that lead).

The Space Race

The principal research objectives of the "Star Wars" program (Strategic Defense Initiative-SDI) include laser weapons intended to stop enemy missiles in the first moments of flight, before they release warheads and thousands of decoys.

Three such space-age weapons are under development in the United States. The first is a ground-based free-electron laser that would bounce intense, high-energy light beams off orbiting space mirrors to destroy enemy missiles. The second is an X-ray laser used to harness the energy of a nuclear explosion in space. The third is a space-based particle beam that could theoretically destroy a target by combining the burning heat of a laser with the destructive effects of jolts of particles supercharged with high energy. Guidance and battle satellites needed to launch these weapons would, in turn, be protected by space equivalents of tank corps and carrier battle groups to ward off enemy hunter satellites and orbiting space mines.

These technologies are still too theoretical to be of interest to most Japanese companies, and Japan herself will not benefit from research contemplated by the SDI project, even when civilian applications are considered. However, Japanese firms are interested in some of the essential SDI technologies. Superfast computer chips, composite materials for microelectronic device applications, optoelectronic device technologies, fiber optics, artificial intelligence, and ultra-state-of-the-art software are all slated for continued research.

Off quiet Tanegashima, on the southeast coast, rockets are launched into space. The crimson flares offer a sobering perspective on the future—as America struggles to overcome the disastrous setback in its shuttle program. The launch on February 19, 1987, of Peach— formally known as Marine Observation Satellite (MOS-1)—was a milestone in Japan's space program. MOS-1 was the last to be carried on what was essentially an American Delta rocket assembled through a license agreement. Launches from now on will rely more on indigenous technology. Japan has already put up over 25 small (130–550kg) satellites, mostly without a hitch, since 1975, and by 1992, a 50-meter H-II rocket will lift some 2,000kg into space. A manned Japanese shuttle in the 1990s and a Japanese space station in the early 21st century are both on the drawing boards.

The goals are to put a two-ton payload into geostationary orbit cheaply enough to make it commercially worthwhile. When a payload intercepted Halley's Comet in 1987, the NASDA established credibility for itself. It was speculated that a plan was afoot to develop new industrial materials in space—thus launching (literally) a true sunrise industry, with tremendous economic spinoffs.

Developing a new engine for the H-II with ten times the thrust of earlier models will require a major stride in this technology. America's NASA already uses it for its latest double-combustion rocket engines, but it is reluctant to give it to Japan. Western Europe is similarly slow to provide too many secrets about Arianne. Dr. Iomonao Hayashi, a top scientist at the NASDA, concedes that these gaps in aerospace technology could derail some ambitious plans. "Our rocket guidance systems are … in need of catching up [to the West and the U.S.S.R.]." He confirms reports that over $35 billions will be spent by 1996 by his countrymen in the space race.

Japanese satellite launches are expensive by international standards. One reason is that NASDA can launch only during two 45-day periods a year. Tanegashima is populated by not only fish but by strong fishermen lobbies. A second launch site is sought, possibly in Hokkaido (in the north).

The space budget was over $70 million in 1985 or a tenth of the U.S. level, in 1986. A year later, it rose to $800 million. The European Space Agency is now spending about $1 billion.

Superconductivity

The Houston breakthrough in superconductivity scored by Dr. Paul Chu and his colleagues in February 1987 changed history and allowed science to realize a generations-old dream of conducting resistance-free electric current—an event that only occurs under difficult conditions and at extreme temperatures.

Potential applications in both first-generation and second-generation modes of superconductivity are astounding. Small wonder the *Christian Science Monitor* of July 13, 1987, noted, "It's a race with enormous stakes. If the new materials prove practical, and especially if the temperatures at which superconductors work can be pushed higher, intuitively you know that the market will be larger than you can imagine," says Richard Cyert, president of Carnegie-Mellon University in Pittsburgh. New transmission lines and power generation, ultra-efficient electronic products, superfast microchips, and magnetic levitation railway trains are only a few breakthroughs realistically forecast before the next century.

There are two leading competitors for advances in this particular technology: Japan and the United States. Western Europe is, however, carving out its own niche.

The Technological University of Nagaoka is taking Japan's lead, and it has developed a task force that collaborates with the country's atomic energy agency in a $20 million program. The total spent by others on superconductivity is at least $15 million, and Japan's outlays for this field are projected to rise to over $55 millions by 1990. In 1987, American expenditures came to nearly $50 million, nearly 95 percent of which is estimated to come from federal coffers. Yet, by April 1988, nearly 2,000 patents were tallied in the archipelago, while a paltry 40 superconductivity-related patents had been filed in the U.S.

The *Monitor* notes that within a month of the historic Houston breakthrough, over 100 Japanese companies formed a consortium slated to coordinate R&D. While the Defense Advanced Research Projects Agency (DARPA), a branch of the Pentagon, may hold most of the cards—directing policies, determining where R&D is carried out, hiring staff, dividing funding, etc.—Japan's drive is entirely in nonmilitary hands.

MITI has persuaded giants of Japanese industry to join forces in creating a massive new research center. The center will serve two purposes: joint research efforts and information clearinghouse. According to Professor Shoji Tanaka of Tokyo University, a member of the advisory committee to the as-yet unnamed organization, over 80 companies are interested in joining the information clearinghouse at an annual subscription rate of $10,000 per year, which would result in an annual operating budget in excess of $1 million. However, the really large commitments are reserved for the research consortium. According to Tanaka, over 35 companies have expressed interest in joining that effort, each making an initial investment of $700,000, and an annual contribution of $140,000.

The center may also receive some of the largess requested by MITI and the Science and Technology Agency in their 1988 budget proposal: $42 million. The new center will seek tax-exempt status, and will be located in Tokyo.

THE TECHNOPOLIS QUEST

Japan is going to change in other ways during the 1990s. Tokyo seems destined to be replaced as the nation's commercial center.

Through the efforts of its engineers and technicians—and as a result of an ambitious high-tech development plan luring U.S. biotechnology firms to the metropolis—Osaka may again take the mantle as *ichiban*, or number one.

It's not the first time that Osaka has been on the economic development warpath. One fifth-century emperor actually prescribed tax abatements for merchants when he suspected that a declining commercial base was sapping Osaka ("The Big Slope") of her preeminence in trade. After Japan opened its gates to the world in 1868, trade there flourished, and the town became headquarters for many of those legendary Japanese trading companies, the *soga shosha*. Thus began a classic "Rustbelt" saga, because this port city—which for centuries held sway over Tokyo in commerce, manufacturing, and finance—is today strapped with many sunset heavy industries. Chemicals, textiles, steel, and pharmaceuticals have been mainstays of Osaka and the Kansai industrial belt, of which it is a part. However, future prospects for those sectors are not good. Tokyo, by contrast, some 300 miles eastward, saw its rise in the postwar era, when it hosted a growing share of factories, banks, and occupying Americans—whose billions in aid spurred the resurrection that followed.

Osaka grew to a population of 2,820,000. Industrial decline set in during the 1960s, and town fathers were bedeviled by conflicts with environmental groups. Osaka became the butt of many jokes around the country. Effects of the oil shock and trading slumps took their toll on the port. New business was moving to Kyushu Island, or to Hokkaido in the poor, rural north. The "Slope" lost its edge over Tokyo in every way.

Farsighted plans advanced by long-term Mayor Yoshiso Oshima, now nearly two decades at the job, are seeking to restore Osaka to economic vitality. The infrastructure is there, although officials concede they've had to finance hundreds of millions of dollars' worth of new roads, port improvements, and public transportation. Results are noticeable, and some innovations—extensive land reclamation, futuristic pneumatic refuse disposal—all attest to recent strides.

The phase of growth that should propel Osaka to the status of number one is tied to its plans for incubators and research parks. Although Japan has scored remarkable success with its Kyushu Island (the equivalent of Silicon Valley), there are concerns about the track record in university-business-local government experiments to date. Osaka's development plan far outdistances anything else happening in Japan. Its emphasis on biotech—stemming from an existing pharmaceuticals base—is significant, because this sunrise sector is viewed as a cornerstone of national economic advances during the 1990s. A "Technopolis" plan across the Kansai region uses the city as its hub. Nearly two dozen research institutes and other facilities could, in theory, be tapped.

The second prong of Osaka's plan comes through the 3,200-acre Kansai International Airport. Construction on this $8 billion-plus project is in its early stages. City officials boldly proclaim that air travelers from the West will be able to bypass Tokyo after the 1992 opening. A pair of 4,000-meter runways and one 3,400-meter runway are part of the present configuration.

Such heavyweights as the Ministry for International Trade and Investment and a network of public and private agencies are actively promoting the city. Prefecture Governor Sakae Kishi says that an incentives campaign will begin within three years—and U.S. firms are being targeted. "It is an unsurpassed location for technologically advanced industries and for industrial labs," he says.

Conceived in the early 1970s, Technopolis is Japan's planned leap into the next century. Technopolis is a $24 billion venture that will build over 20 strategically-located "science cities," or "smart cities," across the Northeast Asian nation. While the goal of planned communities is not new, relieving congestion in the Tokyo-Osaka corridor is viewed as critical. The Japanese concept calls for cities that use fewer scarce (and imported) resources. Another chief reason for the ambitious plan is that university-company links have not evolved as quickly as they have in the U.S., and planned towns might foster that form of communication—one vital to demands of high-tech industry in the 1990s.

Other goals are part of the Technopolis plan. Since many rural areas have been left out of the Japanese economic miracle, there is a historic opportunity to generate growth in those regions. They are currently characterized by the universal "brain drain" syndrome.

Activity to date stemming from the overall program shows mixed results. A handful of cities are importing workers, retraining others, and constructing factories according to a master plan revised earlier this year. Strides in robotics and in chip design occurred, yet technology transfers from titan corporations to medium-sized suppliers lag. European and U.S. firms are not responding to incentives that would help them set up shop in places like Kyushu Island. A Texas Instruments manager cites "confusion" over development plans there.

Technopolis, complete with teleports, near-universal videotext, and features of futuristic daily living, represents technology-based economic development on a nationwide scale. Outlays are measured in the hundreds of billions before completion in 1999–2002.

3

China: Cracks in the Iron Rice Bowl

China's economic landscape is dotted with contrasts. From one end of the mainland to the other, there is a realization of the promise that this vast nation holds for its own people during the 21st century. Despite China's stunning successes under the new "Open Door Policy," the sparkle of a "billion-person market" has evaporated. For the remainder of this century, the bloom is partially off the rose: investments soured, would-be opportunities never materialized, and there is a realization that China's own goals are very much different from those of the foreigners.

AN ECONOMIC REVOLUTION

How great can growth be? When the U.S. National Security Council probed economic trends among leading nations, it appeared that China would spiral itself into second place in terms of growth (after the U.S.) by 2010. This 1988 study—considered part of a long-range strategy review issued for the White House—placed Japan in third place, with projected annual GNP increases of 3 percent after 1990 and for much of that decade. (The U.S.S.R. came in fourth place.) China's output, increasing at rates 4.6 percent and higher over two decades, is what enables the People's Republic to achieve stupendous growth. (The countries forming the six-member ASEAN group, discussed in a later chapter, doubled output in only a decade by maintaining consistent 6–7 percent yearly rates.)

The Chinese economy's growth in the past decade has been nothing short of phenomenal in many respects. "They accomplished it principally through the unleashing of their human potential," notes Dr. Harry Harding at the Brookings Institution. Representative Stephen Solarz (Dem.-NY), chairman of the House of Representatives Subcommittee on Asia-Pacific Affairs, is no less enthusiastic. "The short burst of freedom we've seen," he told the Washington Roundtable for the Asian Press in autumn 1987, "allowed a true consumer revolution to take place. It would have been completely impossible without the introduction of the steps taken by Chairman Deng."

Per capita consumption is only one indication of this gentle yet profound revolution sweeping the mainland. According to the Statistical Bureau in Beijing, the per capita expenditure for consumer goods reached $237 in 1987, more than double the 1981 level.

When controls over farm prices and farm output were lifted, the revised "responsibility system" yielded a harvest of profits and agricultural surpluses. Yet inefficiency is difficult to eradicate. "While we saw a lot of land used for grain going to waste," says Jeffrey Bader, head of the State Department's China desk, "we also should appreciate something else. The new land reformist policies hope to end the situation where you have underused agricultural lands, by giving farmers the freedom to sublet parts of their allotted plots, or by working through the village councils to devote part of their land to specialty crops. It's a very big step, even if it's partially experimentation."

That is as important as any transformation in consumer demand or any change on the factory floor. What happens in farming ultimately affects 750,000,000 to 800,000,000 people—the estimated 80 percent of the Chinese population that is rural. Grain harvests in 1987 reached 400 million tons, a small boost above previous totals but still below the record level of 410 million tons seen in 1984, while overall farm output increased by 3 percent in that year.

Agricultural productivity remains low, which, according to Dr. Alan Crane, at the congressional Office of Technology Assessment, a researcher familiar with the economy of this would-be developing land, is why output is not nearly as high as it is in other parts of the region. "Industrial output is consistently higher because massive investments over a long time have changed a few of the primary factories," he says. With the reforms has come more attention toward balancing the economy.

China's move toward a centrally planned economy probably did not become formalized until after the Cultural Revolution. This is ironic, since shortly after lines of authority were finally established, Deng

Xiaoping was ready to announce his bold initiatives toward decentralization. "Therefore, tensions built up," says Crane, who directed a benchmark study of technology transfer to the People's Republic that was completed in 1987. "You have to understand how many chains of command existed throughout the 1970s and 1980s to appreciate how reforms have often been slow" to permeate the whole economy. This—and the impact of local decision makers—is why gains appear skewed, with certain provinces along the southeastern tier seeming to show the most impressive growth compared to regions such as Gansu (in the center). There, the poverty line is about U.S. $50 a year (and many experts insist that as many as 125,000,000 people fall below that poverty line). Per capita income for the nation as a whole still falls in the $350 range. (It is only slightly higher in cities, at $390, according to the official Xinhua News Agency.)

Even in the poverty-stricken western and central regions, the tally of progress is noteworthy. Reports have surfaced about families pooling literally their entire combined wealth in order to take a stab at the promise of advancement offered through new incentive-oriented liberalizations. One of the most popular tales today is about the families who cater to a common need in China. Since housewives must spend hours daily gathering vegetables for meals (and refrigeration is nonexistent in many provinces), why not have the children collect them for a modest fee and market this service around the villages? A seemingly simple business such as this can raise cash (or bartered goods) year-round.

"Guidance plans" have replaced stringent guidelines for quotas for all forms of output. Managers may initiate their own changes without entering a maze of regulations mandated by Beijing. The establishment of banks to finance factory operations is another major stride. These helped stimulate growth in the early 1980s, a factor that was essential for Communist leaders to continue their support of the changes, according to Pennsylvania State University's Dr. Parris Chang, for years an internationally renowned authority on both Chinas (and one of a handful of experts with access to all political factions in Asia).

Changes on the outside face of the Chinese Dragon were no less substantial during the decade of post-Maoist reconstitution. The PRC joined the global trading system in a formal way when it became part of GATT, the tariff-governing mechanism. She replaced Taiwan as the "real" China at the Asian Development Bank. The mainland now takes part in the World Bank—which allows it to tap billions' worth of low-interest "soft" (long-term) loans, plus technical expertise. Other ideologically inspired barriers also crumbled.

LIMITS ON CHANGE

In the People's Republic, those who are in the business of trade understand what few outsiders, constantly exposed to enthusiastic reports, yet fathom: The commanding heights are still very much state-run. As China's commercial counselor at his country's Washington, D.C. embassy, Ye Jian, reveals, "Most reporting here [in the U.S.] has not really explained what we can do and what we can actually do."

It is unrealistic to anticipate a wholesale privatization of the economy, and Brookings' Harry Harding estimates that only about 2–4 percent of the urban populace are taking part in the private sector. Other experts point out that labor rates are controlled for the most part, and that even the agricultural experimentation is confined to limited acreage.

The changes are a commencement—not the end in themselves suggested by some of the glowing accounts in the press. None of the modifications come without dislocations. Rampant inflation, the advent of commercialism with its sometimes excessive elements, plus a sudden influx of people to the cities has led to a number of complications that now confront China.

Certainly the suddenness with which policies can shift in China is a factor. Those factions closely allied with purist forms of Marxism might well conclude that the Open Door swings too widely; its new freedoms on the press, its Democracy Wall project (that allows for sloganeering on public graffiti spaces), and other features of the Dengist period may create new stresses and strains for traditionalists. Other Asian countries have been known for unannounced policy reversals when leaders concluded that liberties were ill-advised and menacing to the social good.

A two-tier economy has slowly started to emerge. The first tier consists of formally planned sectors—transportation, energy, natural resources, power, aviation, shipping, and such. Heavy industry remains a responsibility of central planners. So is trade. Prices at the provincial level and for the country as a whole are still set by central authorities.

The sectors outside this central network consist primarily of rural industry, the special economic zones (SEZs, discussed below), and most of agriculture. Dr. Michael Oksenberg, a veteran "China hand" at the University of Michigan, estimates that rural industry output is growing by 30–50 percent a year.

In the planned spheres, reforms are harder to implement. Communist Party leaders struggle to keep the main financing tools (chiefly represented through national budgets) in their own hands. Local authorities enjoy privileges such as the right to invest in favored economic activities.

Interaction with the rest of the world has been another hallmark of the modernization program. Yet, although the percentage of China's exports in the total worldwide export pie has doubled in the decade 1978–1988, it is still only .25 percent of the total of all countries.

Formidable hurdles confront the current leadership. The stated aim is tripling of output by the year 2000, a goal that could bring the GNP to $900 billion (equal to that of Japan in 1978).

In 1987, the GNP grew by 9 percent, and investment in new machinery rose to new heights, indicating an earnest desire to replace the prewar equipment that predominates in 75–80 percent of all industrial plants. GNP in 1988 surpassed the expectations of some, which may enable the country to achieve the lift-off that might forever end a centuries-old legacy of poverty and deprivation. John Frisbie, director of the China-U.S. Business Council, concedes there are sharp turns in policy at the macroeconomic level. "They're still ... in a period of experimentation," he asserts.

China is divided into several unequal economic parts. A Dickensian version of Industrial Revolution capitalism flourishes throughout the land, under the watchful eyes of both Adam Smith and Karl Marx. In the future, a reconciliation of these seemingly contradictory viewpoints will prevail, making for creation of a first-of-its-kind, truly mixed economy—as well as for tantalizing calculations about long-term macro prospects of this Asian superstate. In addition to these features, geographic regions offer their own blends of development philosophy, with the southeast coast (long populated by entrepreneurial-minded groups) outpacing other sections.

In much of the country, little has changed for centuries. There is truth to reports that villages in Jiangsu and Hunan are unaware of Mao's ascent in 1949, or of subsequent changes. More inhabitants endure a life-style comparable to that of the 17th or 18th century in the West: machinery on a limited scale, fragile, labor-intensive farming systems, and a thoroughly provincial perspective. The tens of millions of jobless in the countryside, the millions of homeless in the cities (over 100,000 are on the official list in Shanghai alone), and the nonexistent infrastructure in most of the nation remain obstacles to growth. Oil is still the leading export, and it will not be until the early 1990s that reports gain the momentum and revenue that the Chinese hoped for when the globe shuddered under the specter of the oil shocks of the 1970s.

Yet, successes and surprises abound: Dairen's thriving management cottages train eager, industrious, capable managers of tomorrow. The *Christian Science Monitor* noted in 1987 that China was "unexcelled" in "competitive spirit" at the International Exhibition of Inventions in

Geneva, where native sons won awards for such innovations as breeding mitten crabs, a new microthermometer, and a cyanide-free gold brush-plating technique. (Rival Taiwan had a similar star-studded impact on the previous year's gathering.) The People's Republic can rightfully claim a mantle in the superconductivity race, and its space program is impressive.

Industries spawned during the late 1970s are bearing fruit. Manufacturing exports are valued at $12 billion, or three times the 1978 (pre-Deng "liberalization") amount. Where barren streets awaited visitors to the heralded special economic zones just three years ago, a patchwork of skyscrapers dot the horizon now. And, China is intrepid: While Asia's (and the world's) shipbuilding flounders, China has manufactured over 4 million deadweight tons, nearly half of it for export.

We can project a number of general trends in China. As this most populous of all nations nears the midway point in its seventh five-year plan, it is believed that population growth will continue to rise at a level of 1.2 percent a year. Not until the period 2025–2040 will the number of citizens decline.

The $300 per capita output might climb to triple that level by the year 2000. This ambitious goal is linked with projections of a 7 percent GNP rise per year—a rate comparable to what was seen from 1980–84. At that rate, the GNP could (at rates not as spectacular as the statistics suggest, since the base upon which increases are made is so modest) reach $1.3 trillion in just 11 years, and triple to nearly $4 trillion by 2030.

The PRC's GNP was a modest $240 billion in 1980. Six years later, it reached $270 billion. By 1988, "lift-off" was evident in some sectors, and the stop-and-go Four Modernizations plan produced GNP growth that topped $320 billion (according to best estimates). Despite official expectations, it is more realistic to expect that a few years of more moderate growth, ranging from 4.5–5.5 percent, will occur during the next decade. This is for several reasons. Some instability is likely; the overwhelming forces of change sweeping this land invite more of the stop-and-start policies that surface periodically in the Deng era. At some point early in the next decade, inevitable battles over succession—supposedly worked out at the last Party Congress but still in doubt—would take place following the premier's removal from the scene (he is a robust octogenarian now). This may trigger the sort of ideological donneybrook that characterized earlier years, especially the chaotic and economically traumatic Cultural Revolution of the late 1960s.

It can be assumed that some resistance to Chinese goods will be evidenced in vibrant trade markets of the early 1990s, including the EEC and North America. China is already the 16th biggest trading partner for the United States, and after slumps in the 1980s, exports and imports reached $8 billion for 1986—a 25 percent boost over 1985. In 1987, China's lust for foreign exchange, and her cumulative $18 billion trade deficit, causes her leadership to remain wary of overextending both credit and the welcome mat to foreign investors. Such moves have eroded some of the base of Western support, as well as the fascination of Western business leaders, who for years lusted after the elusive "China market."

As the People's Republic gains greater industrial stature, she will no longer be perceived as an investment opportunity but as a legitimate competitive threat in certain sectors. The billion-person consumer market is not likely to be realized before 2025, but low-cost labor—at 35 cents per hour—multiplied by an enormous labor pool with increasingly sophisticated hardware at their disposal—casts a specter across not only industrialized nations of the West but across Japan and its newly industrializing neighbors as well.

Allotment of capital is probably one of the least understood of all problems confronting the Chinese economy in the years ahead. Capital is not being channeled in the most constructive ways, and has not been for the past few five-year plans. "Far more money has been put in to obtain the increases in worker productivity than in other countries," says Harry Harding of the Brookings Institution. Chinese savings are a staggering 28–30 percent, far higher than even the Japanese (22 percent), but unless these resources are better allocated in the next decade, growth in output will never exceed commitment of capital. This affects recent improvements in productivity, which are nonetheless evident to observers. According to the World Bank and other sources, productivity increased by about 70 percent in the quarter century ending in 1983. Yet, in 1985–86, output rose by about 30 percent, according to best estimates. This indicates a misalignment between capital and productivity.

With a labor force of over 500 million, this largely rural nation still has 20 cities with over a million persons. Most of the work force—probably 80 percent—still labor in agriculture, and (a point most Westerners ignore) industrial production is geared toward the farm sector. In the value of output, industry and agriculture equal about 40–45 percent each of the total GNP. Construction and transport each account for about 4 percent. Commerce, according to the World Bank, makes up some 6 or 7 percent of GNP. These percentages are not likely to change before the year 2000.

China is no stranger to commerce, and the Chinese have succeeded in all aspects of trade and finance in the most unlikely parts of the globe. This is one difference between China's straying from Marxism and

Russia's attempts at *glasnost* (as well as inherent economic incentives in the policies). Buddhism itself thrived along the famous Silk Route during the Tang Dynasty era. It's worth noting also that the Chinese have been remarkable innovators, giving the world the magnetic compass, gunpowder, and even paper and printing, among other technological breakthroughs.

Significant developments affecting the future of the economy of the People's Republic include the following:

1. A sharp downturn in purchases of foreign goods
2. Clarifications and modifications of investment guidelines
3. A better understanding of the true climate in China on the part of foreign firms, which provide the technology and modernization essential to China's growth
4. Diversification of investment by American business
5. Opening of the great expanse of China's southeast

OBSTACLES TO TRADE

The Chinese buying spree that Westerners witnessed throughout the mid-1980s has come to an end, temporarily. This pattern of stop-and-go shopping cycles has been seen before. "High technology may be one exception in the 1990s," declares Parris Chang.

The reasons are obvious: a slow recovery in the West and Japan, and the global oil slump (which caused China to lose some $2.5 to $3.5 billion in hard currency in 1986 alone). Also, Chinese are, according to publications such as *The Asian Wall Street Journal*, privately concerned about trade imbalance. In the first 10 months of 1986, for example, imports were about $32 billion, while exports were nearly $23 billion. Since then, imports continue to surpass sales to overseas buyers. The gap in 1988 was nearly $11 billion, with, according to the U.S.-China Trade Council, $26 billion in exports tallied during that 12-month period. China knows it has overextended itself.

The new investment policies following the landmark 1987 Party Congress will shape decisions on both sides of the Pacific for years to come. For example, from now on, the appearance of a Party cadre at formal business meetings is not mandatory. This and other key policy shifts were ratified after a series of major reverses. In essence, joint ventures with foreign firms—the main focus of earlier PRC regulations—will be approved only if technology transfer furthers specific national priorities. As in the 1980s, the goal of increasing exports as a means of bringing in more foreign exchange guides the overall program.

This is a commonsense approach to economic development, but nagging internal disagreements distort economic fundamentals, while they irritate many Western businesses. Repatriation of profits, an array of legal quagmires, and the inability to achieve smooth currency transactions within China itself (in order to obtain needed materials and services) disturb non-Chinese companies. Other obstacles abound. Furthermore, as we will see later on, labor, salaries, and other essential questions often fall into gray areas. Until essential bottom-line factors are clarified, outsiders will never feel completely comfortable in the existing environment.

The legal system, as it relates to trade, has evolved since the early months of Deng's new Open Door. New methods of resolving disputes are encouraging. However, China knows it has a strong hand in dealing with overeager Westerners.

The Chinese step back from an actual agreement and begin negotiations by presenting a letter of understanding that outlines general principles. U.S. managers are often put off because they want to get to details. They're not averse to the rhetoric of preambles, but they want to build a relationship on facts. For their part, the Chinese stress friendly introductions as a way of establishing the relationship. Their rationale is that in laying down general guidelines for all future dealings, they gain leverage that they can use later by calling the partner to task for not abiding by the principles.

When Westerners sign letters of understanding they often don't understand what can happen next. For example, according to *Harvard Business Review* Westinghouse Canada thought that it was well on its way to selling some large steam turbines to the Dong Fang Steam Turbine Works of Chungdu when the company worked out a letter of understanding with a Chinese team visiting North America. What followed, however, was not a sale but two sessions of intense negotiations in Beijing. The Canadians made all the first moves and were then counterpunched by the Chinese, who pressured Westinghouse to live up to the spirit of the original understanding by accepting a lower price. Only after the Canadian team had returned home for a second time was an agreement reached, by telex.

Laws least likely to be altered in the early 1990s cover joint venture deals in the major urban areas. Responsibility for marketing the product is a core issue. Because the Chinese yen is not a freely convertible currency, to balance the foreign exchange account, Chinese usually ask their foreign partner to be responsible for the sale of a portion of total products produced for export. How large this portion is can be a key problem that needs to be clearly settled in the contract.

Registered capital of each party in the joint venture can be contributed in cash, in kind, or in know-how. This, too, should be clearly specified in the contract. The split of net profits between each party is in proportion to each party's capital share. What may be deducted from gross profit in the calculation of net profit also needs to be clearly spelled out.

All Chinese enterprises use a unified wage system; i.e., when a worker moves from one firm to another his wage rate does not change. Actually, Chinese enterprise cannot hire or fire workers without government approval. A joint venture company is usually allowed to adopt its own wage system and hire or fire workers. But, again, Western companies would do well to clearly specify this right in the contract.

Straight buying and selling is still indispensable and makes up a large part of the Chinese trade volume, but a dazzling number of new forms of trade and economic cooperation such as joint ventures, cooperative management, compensation trade, processing, and many other variants have entered the scene.

It's taken hard work on both sides to achieve better results after years of superficial harmony over two-way trade and investment policies. But with the glow off the China market, both sides are beginning to forge a new realism, a new synergy that taps resources, talent, and ideas on the mainland and simultaneously enables selective technology transfer to recast patterns, mores, and entrenched orders forever, building a foundation for Commu-Confucianism.

This synergy aids all parties involved. It is an ideal, but in actuality there will inevitably be unforeseen strains and frictions. The Chinese may at last discover that, without over-promising to the multinationals, their goals can be better synchronized with those of Western investors. After all, while the number of agreements and joint ventures are impressive on paper (nearly 1,000 new contracts were signed in 1986 alone, and many forecasters predicted 6,000 or more joint ventures by the end of 1988), actual results are not. Although some $17 billion was pledged to the Chinese by foreigners since the "Four Modernizations" program was announced in 1979, less than 30 percent of that amount has materialized. The figures for 1987 actually show a decline from the amount of money committed in the previous 12 months ($1.5 billion). Westerners are not the only ones disillusioned with the Chinese market. "The Japanese have not been as active as one would imagine," according to an executive with Matsushita who boasts a decade's exposure to the often slow-moving mainland scenario. The scope of his country's investment remains limited to a handful of large-scale projects. Of about 7,000 joint ventures finalized on paper, only about 2,200 are producing anything at all—and a considerable share of those now in operation are functioning under dismal conditions.

Of several billions in proposed investments to date from the United States, only $1 billion have actually reached this heralded China market. When oil is removed from the "pie," barely $200 million worth of investments have been realized.

The investment total has declined, and in 1988 should reach $18 billion. Of that amount, only a third is actually operative. Oil still holds top place. In the first half of 1987, Beijing reported that foreign investment declined by 12 percent over the same period in the preceding year. That six-month period saw $730 million channeled to the mainland, and the surprising aspect of the data is that smaller totals were tallied for a much larger (450) number of projects. This indicates the effect of multilateral bank programs—especially those launched through the World Bank—in securing medium-sized business ventures aimed at improving fundamental weaknesses in factories, not in the traditional steel and petrochemical complexes or in other massive ventures. Investment trends in 1987–88—and for the first quarter of 1989—reveal some skittishness on the part of EEC and North American investors, with Japan eager to abandon the quest for short-term commercial ties. But, apart from energy and tourism, Tokyo- and Osaka-based multinationals avoid many manufacturing industries as they ponder investment opportunities.

Poor equipment, lack of suitable labor, shortages of supplies, electric power shortages, lack of quality, and other woes plague many of those ventures. Up until now, the scant fraction of ventures that actually came to fruition were guided carefully by a small number of export promotion and government types on both sides. When the zeal is not orchestrated by foreign investment credits—coming from the (U.S.) Overseas Private Investment Corporation, or from its counterparts in Western Europe or Canada, or from multilateral development banks—we will know that enough groundwork has been laid to make for some long-term positioning in the Chinese economy.

Equity joint-venture projects are flexible arrangements, with partners agreeing to proportion shares to be divided. "Risks can be shared, as can the losses," says a manager involved with the American Motors (now Chrysler) jeep venture, one that almost collapsed because of a disagreement over terms. Those equity deals are usually slated for a 15-year term, and the PRC partners, generally selected by state agencies, demand 25 percent in paid-up capital. A new form of deal, the contractual joint venture, is flexible in other ways. It assumes that labor and land can be provided by the Chinese, who are obligated to provide costs for most of the infrastructure. In both cases, regulations governing the foreign partnerships forbid a number of techniques that outsiders think might be useful. Foremost among them is the ban on commissions.

TRADE PROSPECTS

Is the investment climate improving? Views are mixed. A [Northern Telecom] representative from Toronto believes that, in years to come, foreigners will be "highly selective" about which regions of China they choose to deal with, because of the great disparities in different parts of the country. "We stumble about trying to loosen up materials, to get transport ..." he explains, "and it can be very frustrating." Also, some observers conclude that regions that deliver on promises to multinational firms will benefit greatly from exchange programs such as the recent Chungking-Toronto axis.

Some China watchers see new forces on the horizon, developments that lead toward investment diversification. Before 1987, hotels were leading the pack in the non-oil category. While praising these investments at ribbon-cutting ceremonies and *gom-bei!* ("cheers!") rituals, in private, the PRC brass was not overjoyed at foreign travel-industry activities. They acknowledge the value of foreign currency, but they don't particularly care for the "contamination" of their political system and societal infrastructure by outsiders. Second, they reason that the money could be used for projects that build and sustain the post-Mao experiment, not those that contribute to the leisure pursuits of well-heeled foreigners. Yet it is precisely in such (to China) vital sectors that would-be investors encounter ambiguities and confusion over guidelines, timetables, and terms of "turnkey" projects. (Later on, we will discuss those problems, and look at some common characteristics that potential investors would be well to evaluate.)

Apart from the joint ventures mentioned above, a shift in the types of investments occurring—with tourism and hospitality declining in the mix—would signal a real opening of China and more of its many attractive economic sectors for the benefit of all parties. Well over half of the new investments from 1986–88 are coming in textiles alone, an obvious choice, and in services such as telecommunications. But it is in "nuts and bolts" production and light manufacturing that the more recent investments are turning up.

Some of the trends that are paving the road to continuance of the foreign investment component of economic reform—the "Four Modernizations"—are concerned with a new emphasis on foreign expertise and management. Mark van Fleet is Asia-Pacific Affairs director of the U.S.

Chamber of Commerce. "Allowing for decentralization of management is attractive to multinationals, and it shows there is a real commitment towards continuation of reform at its most essential level, that of the factory, where foreign investors' resources are channeled." Others believe that the easing of restrictions on hiring and firing are helping to secure greater influxes of outside capital, as the gloomy era of the 1980s ends. It was one characterized by disappointments on return, and by confusion over terms of agreements with Western manufacturers.

The authoritative *MOR China Letter* tabulated a total of completely or partially foreign-owned companies on the mainland. In the last 10 years, they noted, 10,000 foreign firms were established. These resulted in over $22 billion (a third from the United States) worth of non-Chinese investment. At this stage, encouragement by Beijing, through overseas tours, promotional efforts, and through signals sent by diplomats, are considered the main stimulus prompting continued inflow of capital from abroad.

The relationship of central planes to the cornerstones of reform, the special economic zones, is important. There has been grumbling in the Chinese capital over issues such as disparity of growth (as well as per capita income) in some sections. For example, Guangdong province has achieved more balanced growth, and higher levels of output in most industrial sectors, than has Shanghai. Similar reformist policies are in place in both the province, and in the metropolis, respectively. Yet, policies by the national government mandated high payments to Beijing (calculated on growth within the city's boundaries). This, in turn, made businesses and government reluctant to make many of the all-out strides that would have propelled development further.

The opening of Hainan, a 34,000-square mile island off Guangdong, carries an interesting lesson to prospective foreign investors. In the first phases of that opening during 1984–86, about $75 million was directed by economic planners in Beijing toward restructuring the extreme rural, agricultural base on the island province.

The opening was greeted with anticipation; Hainan's mineral resources, her vast acreage of tropical fruits, and other resources were recognized as having great potential. Within the next two years, corruption scandals sent shock waves across the entire country. Then, officials at all levels were found to be conducting extensive black-market operations. The boom was seen to have its negative aspects (as it might have anywhere in the world, East or West). Then, the inevitable tightening up occurred, with shortages of goods needed to carry on essential secondary phases of development as a key irritant to cadres of foreign investors. Both Chinese as well as foreigners were stung by the pell-mell race to modernize the province.

Last year, a middle ground started to surface, with new guidelines crafted by foreign commercial associations as well as state-controlled planning boards. Free flow of capital in and out of the island was among the welcomed features of the new policy. Quotas on imports and exports were also to be phased out, and—in a move that even outdistanced liberalizations seen in other economic zones—mortgage of land and use of land itself was to be governed by extremely flexible laws. Liang Xiang, who has alternately served in both top political and economic positions for Hainan, asserts that if these pronouncements are matched by stable policies, it will send a message to investors for years to come about how dual systems can work together.

Another major trend to watch is whether overseas Chinese will accept the mainland's word. Taiwan (see chapter 5) is rapidly expanding its semi-secretive investments. Hong Kong-owned businesses now employ a million workers in the PRC. As ethnic Chinese in Malaysia face more difficulty, they may seek to take part in the international mah-jong game that has, thus far, left as many companies ruined as prosperous.

It will take a few years to gauge the impact of this modest burst of industrialization on the as-yet rural, agricultural People's Republic. The most pressing obstacle is the implementation of quality control. It cannot take place anywhere, West or East, without painful steps achieved through time, sound management, solid equipment, and a determined work force. All are in short supply in China, except in a handful of showcase plants. Substantial increases are not likely until the mid-1990s.

Small business from abroad will not fare well in China for years to come, despite the rosy projections of economic attachés from both American and Chinese agencies. For now the vast Chinese market is a long-term proposition accommodating "deep pockets" only.

Many experts believe that, with the exception of certain niche markets that are a high priority for Chinese policy-makers, only a relative hand-ful of those firms classified as newly created small businesses will survive. Rikki Ishak, a New York City-based importer sometimes termed the "king of Chinese joint ventures," is an early comer to the China trade. "You find more people coming [to China] with fewer expectations and high hopes," he says. "The realism will not hurt anyone on either side." He thinks that joint venture profits can be as high as 20 percent a year. "Once people see the hard work that's involved, they appreciate rewards," he adds.

THE STORY OF EASTERN COMPUTERS, INC.

One such niche market was uncovered by a so-called small business based in Virginia. China may have ended its decades-long economic and political isolation, but until recently, communication barriers were still isolating the country's computer users. The problem: how to adapt computers with Roman-script keyboards to the complexities of Chinese ideographs. Several companies have recently developed computer products that will leap this hurdle, including a small family-run business founded by Richard T. Cheng, a Chinese-American computer-systems expert. His company, Eastern Computers, Inc., prospered on Cheng's breakthrough—a Chinese-language character generator.

The device—a circuit board—is no larger than a standard cigarette case. When plugged into the expansion slot of any of several common IBM-compatible computers, the character generator can form up to 30,000 classical or simplified Mandarin characters. (Only 3,700 characters are commonly used in ordinary communication, but that's still an astronomical number compared to the 26 letters in the Roman alphabet.) The keys on a computer using Cheng's device are labeled with both Roman letters and Chinese character strokes. It takes about five keystrokes to form a Chinese character. A computer user follows the same steps used in making Chinese-character strokes on paper, building a character from left to right, top to bottom and outside to inside. Unlike other character generators, Cheng's device stores characters on the circuit board itself. This frees up computer memory and also makes it possible to use the generator on low-memory microcomputers (with only 48K).

While visiting China in 1984 to lecture on computer systems—the first time he had been to the country in 35 years—Cheng related the progress he had made with his generator. Five months later, he signed a contract with the Chinese government for more than $1 million worth of the devices. That helped boost Eastern Computer's sales from $147,000 in 1983 to more than $3 million in 1986. Today, sales are over $6 million.

Many others have entered this arena, bringing other welcome solutions to a field bedevilled by long-standing obstacles. Cheng expects his China business to snowball, especially considering that China bought more than 150,000 personal computers in 1984 alone. "Language compatibility is a tool for us to knock on the door. It is important, of course, but it only leads us into the market," Cheng says. His competitors hold similar aspirations.

Cheng, who has family in Taipei, has been been able to follow a two-China policy in his business operations without suffering any political repercussions. At his Virginia offices, Taiwanese work alongside technicians from China's Ministry of Foreign Trade and Economic Relations. Cheng has offshore manufacturing operations in both Taiwan and China. "Each of them knows what I'm doing," he explains. And both Chinas have come to appreciate the sons and daughters of their common ancestors who, in ways large and small, are forging a new synergy across the Pacific.

MISUNDERSTANDING BETWEEN CHINA AND FOREIGN INVESTORS

Part of the new awareness about what can be realistically achieved comes through realizing just who one deals with in the PRC. All of heavy industry and much of the light industrial sector are state-owned. Most of the country's production, perhaps as much as 80 percent, comes from the 20 percent of all concerns in this group. Despite far-reaching reform, it is Beijing that makes decisions on investments, plant sitings, equipment, etc. Provincial authorities constitute another layer of bureaucracy. "There is stringent supervision of the plants, and of targets for output at those plants," according to Ye Jian, economic attaché at the PRC's Washington embassy. Ye Jian concedes that a slowdown in investments and in bilateral deals is possible, and he is not alone in assuming a temporary shortfall might occur in the 1990s. The revenue downturn caused by sagging oil prices hurt the mainland more than anyone in China admits. A policy advisor at the World Bank insists that even loss of a few hundred million dollars at a critical juncture could have an impact on the overall development plan.

Politics is a bigger factor in the second group—collective enterprises—than China cares to admit. It is here that the new focus on demand, pricing, consumer tastes, and future markets is concentrated, and having its most significant impact. In this category, targets set by the central authorities are being eliminated. Three years ago, the state (through Deng's inner circle) decreed that some vague portion of profits could be reinvested. His is the group that most foreigners would like to work with, but, as a West German with nearly 20 years' experience in China points out, "they [Beijing] put every obstacle in your path, making light industry and the decentralized firms almost impossible to contact in some provinces, let alone work [with them on] … constructive bargaining terms." (A discussion of the new "private" businesses and their impact follows in another part of this chapter.)

A more realistic appraisal of China's potential, and of the real advantages of working there, is essential. "There was a mismatch," says

Dr. Harry Harding of the Brookings Institution. "Companies were willing to give in on lots of issues and on percentages because they felt they could use their base to sell within China, and that just hasn't been part of the Chinese game plan." The PRC saw incoming investment as a means of building up *their* industries to sell to the local market. "They face the same dilemmas and interests as other continental economies," declares Harding.

Ironically, in many cases, the technology transfers and investment will create competition for the very same U.S. firms attempting to tap segments, especially labor-intensive ones, of the "billion-person market." EEC investors share some of the same bitterness and uncertainty as their counterparts in the U.S., Canada, and East Asia.

Confusion and antagonism are a two-way street. Winston Lord, former president of the prestigious Council on Foreign Relations, has served as the U.S. envoy to Beijing. He has publicly reaffirmed the frustration seen since the mid-1980s on the part of Americans scouring the provinces for worthy investments. Those problems are outlined below. "Educated Chinese do not understand the American system," notes the Ambassador, making frustrations inevitable and widespread.

Dr. Harry Harding believes that as the next decade appears, the situation will improve. Dr. Harding senses frustration on the part of Westerners seeking to tap the PRC. "Continued, steady growth—not grandstanding on issues or making wild policy changes on any side—is probably the best way to reduce friction, or prevent it from reoccurring."

John Major, an assistant director of the Asia Society in New York City, and frequent traveler to the People's Republic, notes that "centuries of different ways of doing things are hard to reconcile overnight." That accurately sums up the present status.

Out of this background comes some news that augurs well for improvements in—but not wholesale solutions to—the many dilemmas posed in this fountainhead of bilateral confusion. The latest investment guidelines, dating to the 13th Party Congress, have been carefully analyzed by experts at organizations such as the National Council for U.S.-China Trade and by American agencies in both the public and private sectors.

Misunderstandings can be minimized if broad policy initiatives are allowed to stay intact over time, without stop-and-start edicts from central planners. Foreign-owned firms are officially sanctioned (there were an estimated 130—140 of those on the mainland in 1987). The percentage of ownership in special investment zones changed, granting 100 percent ownership. These zones (see below) are the linchpin of growth in the 1990s, and if sudden swings in policy are avoided there as in the few other favorable regions, a framework for stability in bilateral commercial ventures will emerge. The new policies provide tax concessions, while another kernel of the investment guidelines comes through decentralization. Hiring, firing, salaries, and work rules in joint ventures will be set by the actual foreign partners. In theory, it sounds good but must stand rigorous tests of time. "These things have taken time to work themselves out," says a corporation executive. "What the rules show is that China is finally getting sensitive to the complaints we've aired at forums and in discussion seminars about the broader picture." Customs and mores must be upheld but must also permit a degree of flexibility. This is the greatest challenge before post-Deng economic overlords.

COSTS OF DOING BUSINESS IN CHINA

In 1987, the *Asian Wall Street Journal* reported that costs of maintaining single expatriates ran at $150,000 to $200,000 a year in Beijing. "This does not include office rent," cautions the paper, "which runs from $50,000 a year at the seedy Peking Hotel to $125,000 at the Great Wall Hotel." Little wonder companies are hard-pressed when they make the China plunge. A delegation from the U.S. Chamber of Commerce in 1987 reported back to colleagues in North America that a high proportion of foreign companies were losing money at a rapid clip. "This is why institutions such as foreign banks just can't make money in their short term or even medium term," admonishes Mark van Fleet, Asian Affairs director for the Chamber.

Food, housing, recreation, etc. are astonishingly expensive in this generally impoverished nation. For multinationals seeking to do business, a new policy inaugurated early in 1988 brought about steep increases on duties. The essentials of life for many Western and U.S. executives—items ranging from cars to periodicals—must endure ultrahigh, 200–300 percent duty fees. This could change in the early 1990s, but the policies are justified in the minds of central planning agencies, which believe foreigners will pay any price to gain a strategic foothold.

For companies retaining foreign exchange profits, beginning or expanding industries promoting import-substitution, and for companies assisting in infrastructure (water, sewage, roads, communications), a bevy of rent abatements and tax abatements are offered. In the new plan, companies sending 70 percent of their product overseas—and thus aiding the crucial export campaign—will gain from a list of tax concessions.

In a dramatic reversal, interest-free loans—the ultimate in "soft" borrowing—are now granted to foreigners. This action should solve the problems of obtaining Chinese currency needed to procure materials. For their part, foreigners must deposit hefty sums in the Bank of China's escrow accounts. While companies generating *renminbi* (Rmb, the currency unit) for themselves will benefit, others requiring short-term capital can also take advantage of the plan. Loans are to be issued for periods of up to five years.

SPECIAL ECONOMIC ZONES

"The policy of opening up to the outside world," declared Huang Xiang, a member of the People's Congress, "has become a long-term fundamental policy." Emphasizing "technical exchanges ... and foreign capital," certain "flexible measures" would harness the labor pool and natural resources that are at the core of China's next Great March.

As was mentioned, the underpinning of a 1990s-style "Great Leap" are the special economic zones (SEZs). A little-known, dramatic plan will convert the southern tier, a landmass including nearly a fourth of the country's total population, into a giant foreign-trade zone, complete with many of the amenities found at tax-free sites in other parts of the world (and comparable in some ways to the network of American-based foreign-trade zones). The linchpin of that program is a network of SEZs.

These changes come after mixed track records at the network of four SEZs—and after frustration on the part of many U.S. companies. One vice-president for manufacturing from a California-based electronics equipment maker says that the pieces are not all in place yet—and that "the experience we had leads us to believe that improvements will make or break" the whole zone strategy.

Four zones (Shenzhen, Shantou, Xiamen, Shuhai) were designed to attract needed foreign investment by loosening centralized planning. Some 250 square miles were slated for SEZ development, and neighboring cities are allowed to partake in the new "Open Door." Companies would have greater flexibility in operations, ranging from determining production levels to setting wages. Importing manufacturing technology was, and is, the government's top priority, and the zones were hailed as a way of building a modern industrial base.

SEZs were sited in a relatively small section of China's southeastern corner, but original plans foresaw the SEZs as models for necessary modernization—and forecast extensions of the network throughout a much larger region encompassing much of southern China.

Most observers concede that the dream of building SEZs into mini Hong Kongs is far from reality. Although progress has been considerable and the infrastructure is improving, foreign companies are as skeptical about the zones as are policymakers in Beijing. As was mentioned earlier, only a fraction of the money committed to industrial projects since 1984 has actually reached the SEZs.

Several steps proposed during 1987 by leaders of the PRC are being implemented. They will shape policies into the early part of the next decade. The government recognizes that its curbs on spending foreign exchange prevent foreign companies from importing machinery and other factory gear. Stability in terms of all business dealings—especially joint ventures—is now seen as essential. There is a sense that agreements with foreign companies in China have not been left intact long enough— or are worded too vaguely—to have the desired effects.

Part of the problem in the zones is recurrent stop-and-go, "boom-and-bust" cycles that make planning by companies difficult. For example, one European tire manufacturer reports that the government over-promised on space available for plant expansion, and it took over 18 months to obtain approvals for about half the required factory space.

Friction between foreign companies and SEZ administrators has surfaced over basic differences in outlook. Goals of most of the Western companies actively working in the SEZs differ from those of the PRC. It is now understood that there was never any intention of letting foreign companies produce in quantity for China's domestic market—now or in the future. The PRC's aims have always been to use the zones to import manufacturing innovations through joint ventures and enable China to take rein of production. Learning this lesson may allow multinationals to adjust to real, not imagined, conditions.

Another long-standing difficulty to smooth operation comes from vague policies on employment. Work-force inefficiency plagues companies, but formal contracts issued by the government avoid a satisfactory approach to the problem.

One solution may be coming in the form of processing contracts that allow manufacturers to supply equipment and raw material to their Chinese partner along with detailed specifications for assembly. This technique is a transition stage before full joint-venture status and gives transplanted manufacturers a chance to witness Chinese production methods.

Timely delivery was a serious problem when nearly $1 million of a California machine tool maker's capital was invested in a Shenzhen plant employing 35 on the assembly line. Timetables for processing, assembly, and parts acquisitions—all endorsed by official U.S. commercial attachés on the mainland—went awry. "What killed us in 1986 was the inability of ... suppliers to coordinate schedules with the factory we built." These types of criticisms are heard three years later.

By reverting to processing contracts, the company feels their Chinese partners have a better incentive to synchronize assembly. Mathieson thinks others are using this method, and Ye Jian, of the PRC's Washington embassy declares that hundreds of millions of dollars' worth of processing contracts will be finalized in 1988.

Problems in investments have been widespread. Tod Clare, a vice president at Chrysler Motors Corporation, is another executive who witnessed early disappointments when the automaker (as American Motors) forged a partnership with Beijing Auto Works. "The basic business unit in China is the factory," he notes. "Up to now, factory management has been totally absorbed in meeting production quotas."

Clare insists that liberalizations in the economy are now providing flexibility for SEZ bureaucrats. This, along with Beijing's commitment to train thousands more managers in modern procedures, can eliminate bottlenecks. The problem of quality control remains bothersome. Li Hao, mayor of Shenzhen, insists that the government is working on ways to raise standards and to institutionalize product testing. As for transportation links between economic zones and the outside, more attention is being given to intermodal routes. At least $1 billion in container facilities, rail lines, and acceptable all-weather highways will be spent around the SEZs by 1994.

U.S. manufacturers have been surprised to learn that costs of labor in the zones are much higher than for the rest of the People's Republic (as much as 70 cents/hour compared to 38 cents/hour). In addition, hidden costs for a privileged work force increase base pay. Vincent Cheng, research director for the Hong Kong and Shanghai Banks, estimates that costs may be 75 percent or as much as 80 percent of those in Hong Kong.

Today, most manufacturing in the zones consists of metals, watches, appliances, consumer electronics, and transport equipment.

Beijing is definitely going ahead with plans to make Hainan Island (described above) a fifth SEZ. Ye Jian at the Washington embassy expects the "Open Door" to open wider there. While a "70-30" private/public planning formula exists in the four SEZs, even more latitude will be given zone administrators in Hainan during the 1990s.

There are kindred spirits of the SEZ companies. The (largely) privately owned, privately managed firms found all around the mainland are not all thriving. Only a year after the Deng "reforms" were announced, 130,000 or so quasi-private businesses came into being. The Communist Party publicly proclaimed that, after all, these entrepôt companies would "meet people's needs," and—despite bankruptcies, legal shadowlands, and even corruption—almost 10 million were officially tallied just five years later. In 1985, the figure reached an astonishing 14 million, and current estimates are that, while the growth rate has slowed, absolute numbers hover close to 15.5 million. When price controls ended on many items in 1985, tens of thousands of open markets, farmer's markets, cooperative markets, and local bazaars sprouted. Hundreds of food items and household staples were accorded "free market" status.

Of course, not everyone can join the club, or is qualified to, or has adequate incentives to become a merchant or entrepreneur. Generally, about $12,000 (25,000 or 50,000 yuan) is needed to get approval. In service sectors, some formal education must be proven. And ultimately it depends on the whim of local administrators and Party cadre. Dealings with these millions of shopowners, farmers, and light manufacturers is not really possible for foreigners today, and most believe it will be the mid-90s before handshakes, bows, and contracts will take place at this level.

The State Administration for Industry and Commerce has registered 11.3 million private firms (a decline from 1985 when 11.6 were tallied). Each employs just a handful of workers at the most—fewer than 19 million in total during 1987. About half are trading and bartering. Their salaries are hardly based on egalitarian principles, with managers earning seven to ten times as much as their work force—or about Rmb 1500–2000 monthly ($520–600 at press time). Different sectors offer differing ranges of wages. The highest ones are not limited to light manufacturing. Specialty farmers are bringing in Rmb and yuan; many industrious ones are quite wealthy, and furniture makers have a class of nouveau riche, too.

Yet, impact is substantial. For example, *The Far Eastern Economic Review* estimates that the 60,000 free food markets in 1986 outsold their state-managed counterparts. "Business classified as 'private,'" says Dr. Parris Chang at Pennsylvania State University, "are likely found in restaurants and shopping market stalls than in any other type of activity." He thinks that handicrafts are one large sector for the private, profit-oriented companies.

There is sharp disagreement about the future role of the small businesses. Confined to rural parts of the country, they lack contact with other engines of trade and investment; finances and technical training are nearly nonexistent throughout large areas of the countryside. Yet, the progress to date is impressive. If allowed to expand, they may come to build their own communications systems and solidify building blocks of a reasonably diverse economic base within the fields: Textiles, electronic products, pharmaceuticals, bicycles, motorbikes, furniture, food processing, and a few others are often discussed as having the potential to synergize crafts and guilds free from the dictates of centralized planning.

Most recent changes in the regulations covering private companies specified improved record keeping on the part of the companies. Lax bookkeeping entries probably understate receipts—a problem conceded by Beijing. The solution by control planners came through instituting a mild graduated income tax, 5 percent on Rmb/12,000 annually, ranging to 60 percent on Rmb 2 million or higher.

Wholesaling and retailing aspects of the mainland's distribution system are still controlled by central planners in Beijing. This will delay "lift-off," since those reins on the flow of materials and merchandise prevent the response to market forces that Harry Harding and other experts see as vital in this stage of development. The 18–20 million working in the privately-owned businesses are gaining ground, slicing through red tape and bypassing Marxian tradition.

The progression of this titanic economy is so profound that in some regions it seems to guide macroeconomic decisions by official agencies. The "Iron Rice Bowl"—a term describing the cradle-to-grave relationship between peasant and state in the mainland—will soon crack. It is starting to undergo significant stress as you read this book. The number of workers opting for private contracts soared over the past three years, and today it reaches as high as 4–4.5 million, a startling figure considering the inherent risk to personal economic security. The intrepid few are guaranteed severence pay if they are fired, and since 1987 even unemployment compensation is available in a limited number of cases.

Most analysts estimate that the $70 billion worth of output coming from these companies generates between 5–8 percent of China's tax revenues. According to John Frisbie at the U.S.-China Trade Council, half the building materials, 30 percent of garments, a third of paper products, and most leather goods come out of these profit-making firms whose factories—dominated by antiquated machinery and equally industrious employees—whir and hum beneath the shadow of Mao's watchful eye. One of China's most famous exports, fireworks, is manufactured for the most part by the new breed of quasi-capitalists.

Few doubt that "reforms" announced just 10 years ago, and met by skepticism, did indeed propel winds of change. Drawbacks include lack of trained personnel, uncertain supplies of raw materials, plus ruinous inflation throughout regions where centers of vigorous entrepôt activity is occurring.

The role of the state on another front was also challenged by Deng and his cohorts. A single agency, the Foreign Enterprises Services Company, relaxed many of its controls (and demands for what may be described, without salving euphemisms, as kickbacks), thus giving greater flexibility for companies attempting to hire within China—a task deemed difficult by nearly all neutral observers. By granting companies in favored joint ventures more latitude over salaries, the government is also lowering the exorbitant wage scale paid by foreign companies.

In another landmark event, some companies have been given the right to issue stock. This new shift came after experiments with bonds in 1983–86 saw about 2,000 companies, many of them located in the metropolis of Shanghai, turn to the bond mechanism as a source of revenue. Stock trading was resumed in China after 37 years, and one can expect the number of firms issuing stock (fewer than two dozen today) to swell in the decade ahead. The introduction of stock shares is another major initiative designed to graft inventives onto the economic framework. Shares in the stock of several industrial companies were offered in Shanghai. Details are sketchy, in part because early failures of the program caused embarrassment. What is known is that a few thousand high-salaried workers participated, and that as much as U.S. $75–100,000 was raised for a half-dozen companies. Of course, stringent terms mandate fixed returns in some cases, and rules governing dividends will be in effect.

Few doubt that rise of this quasi-bourse might help transform the country, in large measure by instilling a sense of investment and financial discipline on hundreds of thousands, perhaps millions, of Chinese. Precise terms of stock payments, as well as formulae for their calculation, are not yet understood by outsiders.

FORECASTS AND OPPORTUNITIES

The new Open Door is real. Zhuhai Tours in Hong Kong proclaims: "The grass is always greener in Zhuhai." A young lady clad in sporty athletic attire stands poised, golf club in hand, one hand on a hip, confident and beaming. Is her confidence a look at China's future? "Just 70 miles by Jetcat from Hong Kong," declares the advertisement, "is the Zhuhai International Golf Course. There's a jacuzzi, clubhouses, and the rest. Eighteen challenging holes that spread over pastoral countryside surrounded by verdant hills … if your family needs a diversion while you're enjoying yours, they'll find it next door at Pearl Land Amusement Park … thrill rides, haunted … and elephant shows are just part of the fun."

This is one of the forces that, according to real "China hands," may recast the once-dormant, retroactive economy into the 21st century's bounding Dragon.

Growth requires quality education. Right now, China does not have it, and the potential managerial cadre was decimated during the Cultural Revolution (of 1967 through the mid-1970s). With schools shut down and anything smacking of progress (including intellectuals, artisans, and thinkers of all stripes) imperiled, there was little room for achievement. China is today paying a stiff price for its mini Dark Ages, and the price will be paid well into the next generation, because so much time has been lost. To compensate for past misdeeds, the state is starting to allow students freedom to select courses, and even their own careers.

Too many students going abroad are defecting. When normalization of U.S.-PRC ties took place in 1979, 30 Chinese enrolled in American schools. A year later, the numbers swelled to over a thousand. Most were mid-life professionals of one sort or another, hardly traditional students. Three times as many left for the U.S. in 1980. Europe and Canada report similar evidence of a "brain drain." (Ironically, it is Taiwan that sends the largest single group to the States; China ranks seventh or eighth on the list.) Over the past nine years, about 41,000 Chinese have gone abroad for degrees, but the American Council on Education estimates that fewer than half returned.

Employment, and the relationship between urbanization and jobs, poses problems as well as opportunities. Before leveling off (in about 40 years), population increases, although mercifully modest, should necessitate creation of more jobs. In China, says *The Economist*, during the next fifteen years, 250 million children of today's productive Chinese peasants should enter the job market. The real strain lies in the countryside, where birth control is not practiced as widely as is in towns and cities. Dr. Seiji Naya, at the East-West Center, the Hawaii-based think tank that designed the census conducted in China in 1984, notes that "By 1986, the birthrate reached a high level, about 20.8 per 1,000" and "the rural areas were actually ahead of most large cities" in departing from birthrate policies implemented earlier in the decade. Lee-Jay Cho, a population specialist at the East-West Center who helped design the census, and subsequently analyzed data from that head count, believes that the goal of 1.2 billion citizens (about 200 million higher than is the current population) in 11 years might be off as much as 10 percent. If so, such an increase would translate into unmet expectations. The non-urban regions are ill-equipped to handle additional burdens and demands of available services. Certainly, the 1990s work force is not benefited by human labor; real effects of any strains caused by increased population can only be deduced once the share of citizens over 65, and under 20, are tallied. It is from those groups that pressure for spending programs increases, while they offer scant input into the national economy from which they depend on support.

Demographics are watched closely by experts. In 1986, 37 percent of the population was under 20 years of age. This great demographic bulge is critical when a society is pressed between rising numbers of both the elderly and the young, as those in between must produce more to support their "non-productive" compatriots. Economic strains are inevitable. Looking at the data now, this trend begins to peak toward the year 2015, lasting through about 2030. For the young, more jobs are a necessity; the old require greater health-care and other services. This is evident right now in metropolitan Shanghai, where a sixth of the 12.3 million residents are over 60. (Nationally, life expectancy is now nearing Japanese and Western levels, whereas expectancy was far behind even 20 years ago.) While this is happening, the very family structure, its size, and attendant economic support mechanisms will change. No longer will large rural families provide sustenance for millions. Add to this the mobility factor, plus a radical altering of China's social and economic expectations and an escalating standard of living, and it is clear that new economic blueprints must be grafted onto the present two-tier system.

The rural-urban balance poses other problems, because in the cities, dissidents have access to the machinery that prompts, and often catapults, change. A staggering 100 million people are predicted to leave the farms between now and 1996, seeking better jobs and a more varied life-style in urban centers. How the great cities of China will manage the influx is uncertain.

Serious economic development is not today a reality in much of the countryside. Chinese leaders will be more willing to strike deals with foreigners in order to support construction of plants, and spawn cottage industries, where jobs are deemed necessary.

Apart from the up-and-coming regions of the 1990s, there is excitement in the more traditional spots for investment. "When Beijing allowed Shanghai to keep more of its own income," says Dr. Harry Harding, "this signaled a real change. The city fathers could look at issues like public transportation, housing, and overcrowding." And this soul-searching can produce economic benefits as solutions for maladies are bred at home and abroad. A new, vibrant city administration is pursuing policies to lure better quality investment, with technocrats making far fewer blunders today than in the past few years.

This once-decadent seaport and haven for intrigue already reports a shortage of workers. The growth of nearly 100,000 privately owned and managed businesses has both good and bad effects; the sudden increase in entreprenurial activity saw bottlenecks and inevitable inefficiencies spring up as quick-response production jolted the existing base. According to the Chinese embassy, the number of such businesses will more than double in just three years. Recently unveiled plans call for planned satellite cities of 250,000 or more each and Chao He Jing, touted as a chip production center, complete with U.S.-styled R&D parks, will start to deliver on promises—supplying good engineers and reliable plants—not long after it opens its doors in the early 1990s.

Shanghai provides a good case study of how liberalization in China really does stimulate foreign investment, hence offering some opportunity for those willing to stay the course. In this one city alone, nearly $2 billion must be borrowed before 1999 to fund planned civic improvements. (Overall, China is expected to borrow $30 billion to increase output in industry and agriculture.) Only when this begins will any semblance of Shanghai's contribution toward the "billion-person market" surface, and there is a limited pie in this city, as elsewhere. The city's annual budget stands at $5 billion now. Bridges, harbor improvements, communications, and all the rest will eventually be sought in the lift-off stages; power generation and basics of industry will be other priorities. Foreign companies close to sources of funding can fare best in the 1990s milieu; Shanghai promises that innovative financing and banking arrangements are in store for Western firms.

More emphasis on the interior provinces is in the offing. Today, for example, Hubei, "the land of a thousand lakes," receives little attention. This is a breadbasket along the Yangtze, and is home for 50,000,000 inhabitants. The southeastern province and its Jianghan Plain basks under a 300-day growing season, but a few upstart industrial projects are transforming life there.

Backward, slow-to-evolve regions will not be left out. They should seek their own way of establishing direct links with states and with multinational corporations. Early in the next decade, a few may launch incentive packages on top of the inducements offered by Beijing. One way this could happen is shown by Fujian's outreach—which, according to the best sources (but denied in both Chinese and Taiwanese capitals) includes arch-rival Taiwan. Relying on middlemen and on ties with Hong Kong wheeler-dealers, mutually beneficial sets of trade arrangements are thriving. The province also began an outreach to high-powered financial groups such as Nomura Securities, in order to raise bond financing.

Experts on the scene look at a few select provinces for this trend. Until now, Sichuan was known as the home of the famous pandas and of spicy cooking that tantalizes palates from Tianjin to Texas. The new gourmets are pan-frying a different delicacy for this central China province, in attempts to raise the living standards for 100,000,000 citizens, many of whom earn a mere $100 annually.

Fujian, adjacent to the Straits of Taiwan, has learned much about dealing with foreigners from its years in oil exploration. This province struggled to increase output, and achieved some breakthroughs when over $400 million worth of joint ventures were consecrated in the early and mid-1980s.

All provinces, businesses, and government agencies are now forced to face the issue of corruption. Corruption touches not only the opportunistic entrepreneurs, but trials show that many Party brass at the local level have been similarly tainted. Black market scams, bribery, and financial manipulations surface, and provide a glimpse of how ideologues in Beijing—pragmatic and otherwise—cope with the dark sides of change.

When Hainan Island, the tropical bastion of the south, saw "reforms" reaching it, a pell-mell race toward profits triggered China's first major scandal in the new era. Importing 90,000 autos and nearly 3 million TV sets over a 15-month period ending in March 1985, local agencies resold the merchandise to the mainland. It is still unclear about who gained most—but foreign exchange suffered, and heads rolled (at least figuratively).

The awakening giant will be forced to import a greater variety and quantity of goods from the outside. *China Daily* in Beijing stated in 1987 that over a million tons of plastics are required to fuel the roaring engines of this potentially great economy. Right now, over 3,000 factories turn out 2.5 million tons of those substances, making the PRC the world's largest producer.

All the demographics information quantified right now points to new horizons for Western companies. At some point in the next decade, attention will be given to the handicapped. Hardly a priority now or in the future, at least some portion of the disabled will join the chorus calling for such expenditures as outlays for rehabilitation facilities.

Whether on the farm or in cities, disposable income is growing. A proliferation of sewing machines and washing machine companies attests to this fact. About half the households in Guangzhou Province have washing machines, and nearly 65 percent of the households in Beijing boast this ubiquitous signpost of consumerism. According to some accounts, a third of the households in the top-10 major cities are in step. Numbers of sewing machines doubled since 1978, and number over 80 million today. TV sets have multiplied; the World Bank and others assert that there are nearly 92 million of those in use in China—about 85 percent more than nine years ago. Some 103.7 million radios are found in China.

Omnibus, a Hong Kong survey research company, polled in Guangzhou (Canton) during 1986 and found near-universal use of electric fans, with over nine of ten families possessing a TV. Refrigerators were used by about four in ten, and cameras by a fifth of those surveyed. Imagine the consequences of installing thousands of miles of fiber-optics lines across parts of the countryside, even as today's technological giants remain encumbered by an Industrial Age mode, wiring. China, or more correctly, parts of it, could be equipped with ultra-high-tech techniques while its benefactors still depend on existing infrastructure.

It is not as illogical as appears at first. Satellites are superior to conventional transmission media. China is starting to demand more high, high-tech gear as a prerequisite for doing business. As was true with the postwar German and Japanese recoveries, the defeated Axis powers received modern machinery while for years American manufacturers saw their own factories whir and hum on 1930s-vintage tooling. China is preparing its own "switching" system from analog to digital, and many accounts support the contention that 15,000–35,000 miles of microwave lines are in place. Jane Hurd, an Asian telecommunications specialist at the U.S. Department of Commerce, calls the field "an unknown quantity" with "utterly tremendous" possibilities.

ITT and a handful of companies are planning for yet another Great Leap Forward. This one, which may go forward, concerns that essential ingredient of communications, the telephone. When international telecommunications agencies conducted their own inquiries in the mid-1980s, they found that about 5 million phones existed in all of China, although some authorities dispute these figures as bloated. Moreover, phone service is not of high quality except for some parts of the SEZs. In most cities and towns, if a call is received for a person, someone will run to the rooftops and yell out the party's name in an often futile attempt to reach the intended recipient. Yet commitment to improvements in communications is sincere. "They hope to see about 10–12 million phones in a couple of years," declares Ms. Hurd. "After that period, it's a multi-billion dollar project," which, as is true elsewhere in developing Asia, can provide lucrative contracts for production installation and training. One fact overlooked by ambitious companies here is that the PRC realized that communications is a tiger by the tail, one that could lead to social and political upheaval even as it serves as a catalyst for growth. For this reason, forecasts of market size and gargantuan contracts should be taken skeptically.

Other power sources for the great engine will be needed. More specialized EEC as well as U.S. nuclear technology is sought, although the mainland has successfully advanced to the stage where it currently markets its own reactors overseas. A planned 300-megawatt plant at Haiyan, south of Shanghai, calls for outlays of nearly $300 million, of which $50 million will go for non-Chinese technology and components. Westinghouse is one of the approved foreign companies, and will supply a turbine generator.

Other energy investments should also bear fruit. "China knows energy is the key to economic growth. If they manage this sector wisely," declares Dr. Parris Chang, "they can end reliance on outside suppliers and retain control over their energy destiny." Dr. Mohan Munasinghe, a Sri Lankan who for years has been in charge of energy development loans at the World Bank agrees. "They can escape the uncertainties the rest of the world will face during much of the 1990s, but they have to balance out demand and supply. The introduction of some market force philosophy in distribution would benefit a good deal of China's energy resource picture."

Arco and Occidental Petroleum top the list of leading joint ventures in dollar amounts (both nearing $180 million and possibly higher). Arco is building a natural gas pipeline on Hainan, while Armand Hammer's oil company finally achieved breakthroughs with its proposed Pingshuo coal mine. Some expect a new round of mega-projects to emerge after the track record of this pair is assessed.

Another leg in the nation's growth comes through minerals and mining. The Honolulu-based East-West Center conducted the first study on Chinese mineral resources. In preliminary findings, Center teams reported in 1986 that Chinese reserves in metal elements such as copper, zinc, iron, nickel, and lead are as large as those in the United States. This fact alone would provide hope for regions such as Xinjiang and other long-impoverished sections of north and central China.

China caught the high-tech "bug" years ago, but was incapable of doing anything about it until recently. As we saw earlier, computer buffs who practice a "two-China" policy have much to gain in the battle for a Chinese language generator that can translate the cornucopia of thousands of characters into and out of English. Some, like Minneapolis-based Intech, rely on phonetics in their systems. IBM and other players are racing toward the goal line in a contest that will make it easier for firms to process documents and contracts instantly.

Training technicians will provide tens of millions in revenue, since a large number of the 60,000 or so in the PRC are lacking advanced skills today.

Electronics has rightfully been identified by many experts as being at the core of the mainland's great leap into technology-based, value-added industries. The *baliusan*, a name for the 1986 overhaul of science and electronics, is a rather heterogeneous arena, and its underpinnings range from relatively unskilled subassembly of components to highly sophisticated chip design. In 1983, 24 million integrated circuits were produced, and the figure tripled just two years later. It should surpass 100 million this year.

Is there a realistic timetable for development of an indigenous industry? What is the likely impact of electronics on other branches of manufacturing? Can the Chinese overcome obstacles placed in the way of technology acquisition? One sign that strides toward acquisition are serious comes from the current yearly value of licenses from abroad ($82 million)—four times that of all similar licenses issued from 1978–84. Related to this activity is a $30 billion effort to scrap antiquated equipment in manufacturing.

The battle for higher-end products as well as applications is afoot among the PRC's neighbors. It took five years to produce (in 1984) the once-standard 64K memory chip after that generation became available elsewhere. (For example, Hong Kong and Singapore are basing much of their future growth on ASICS, the application-specific chips.) In view of established producers' (and rivals') efforts, Beijing must select niches that would enable her to maximize real strengths.

Strides in consumer products (i.e., Huachang TV sets and Shawa color units) have propelled the Chinese. Instrumentation, digital circuits, and other devices are appearing on the roster of homegrown items. Although electronics exports amounted to $350 million in 1987, this is a mere 2 percent of all sales overseas, and most items consisted of low-end products. Formidable obstacles remain a hindrance to the quest for a move upscale: lack of expertise in production methods, nagging quality control issues, and shortages of production equipment.

In addition, unsophisticated chemical purification techniques (the cornerstone of quality control and other vital processes) abound; better ones are required to achieve a great leap forward. While technology has been an aim of joint ventures, firms such as computer giant Wang are leery, according to numerous accounts, of close contact at this stage, while shortfalls of hard currency prevented consumation of many deals with the West (especially the U.S.). Organizations such as the China Electronics Import and Export Company are criticized by foreigners because of bureaucracy, indecisiveness, and lack of understanding concerning links with potential customers abroad.

With semiconductor global output now beyond the $50 billion mark and rising rapidly, stakes for the People's Republic are enormous. As the economy opens up, opportunities abound—but Beijing must determine the impact of electronics on societal, political, and economic evolution, which can be transformed into revolution through the special communication and information characteristics inherent in electronics alone. Meanwhile, the torrents of technology itself are recasting electronics everywhere. Chip interconnection and the advent of quarter-micron chips, respectively, are but two of the breakthroughs capable of fostering a vibrant electronics industry. But all of "the right stuff" must be in place. Whereas conflicting data is found on numbers of engineers in the labor pool, most indications are that shortfalls will persist through the forthcoming decade.

The attempt by entities such as universities in Beijing and Quingha to spawn Silicon Valleys are noteworthy. These led to construction (in 1988) of an 18,000-square foot plant that could stand tall in Silicon Valley, Kyushu Island, in European counterparts such as Silicon Glen, or in Canada's Technology Triangle. Impressive blueprints exist for other facilities. Canadian software companies and others are already peddling their wares. A mere 60 microcomputers were manufactured in China in 1980, but the number surpassed the 40,000 mark in 1987. However, according to many sources, only about half are working at capacity.

Japan has discovered yet another market for her declining auto industry. Nearly all the People's Republic's imports are made in Japan, and sales soared from 27,000 models in 1981 to three times as many in 1985. Nissan and Mitsubishi have each sold trucks in lots of 10,000. As is true with other industries and purchases from abroad, China asks for bootstrap-raising methods: transmission technology, factory specs for its own automakers, help with engine manufacturing. Peugeot, Fiat, and Volkswagen entered the fray by the mid-1980s.

There are 750,000 Chinese workers in automotives and auto assembly already. The quest is for a production run of 500,000 autos and trucks by 1990, and for at least a million cars and trucks in 1999. These will likely be used by agriculture and industry, since transit is a pressing concern everywhere. In the past, the military received priority (a consumer would have to forfeit several years' worth of earnings in order to buy a car, since 1986 prices for Red Flag models ranged from $4,000–$5,000 in most of the cities. While bicycles are the preferred mode throughout the land, mopeds are rapidly catching on, and China is striving to attain a goal of 300,000–350,000 for export in four years. Domestically, mopeds make more economic sense, and are in keeping with China's non-ostentatious tradition. Neither climate nor road conditions in most of China today bode well for their use, however.

The first stages of the "Four Modernizations" unleashed China's first major environmental clash. Deforestation, silt deposits, and erosion along the mighty Yangtze's course find enormous amounts of soil washed away along the riverbanks. Some scientists within and without China accuse Beijing of worsening this situation by promoting the Three Gorges Dam. This project, valued at $15 billion or more, stands as the most costly single construction effort proposed thus far and may still hold that distinction five decades from now.

"Building infrastructure and extensive forms of upgrading is what we see as the biggest need in China," according to Pierre Couteaux, chairman of Canada's SNC, an engineering consortium active in Asia. Three Gorges would dwarf the Hoover Dam and Egypt's Aswan Dam, repectively. Views are sharply divided about the ecological effects of altering nature's intended flow along the world's fourth longest river, one termed "China's Fortune." As we go to press, American environmentalists are trying to remove official U.S. sanctions for the project. Beijing is irritated by what it interprets as meddling. The fallout from this protracted battle will at least partially determine just how great a share of other construction projects U.S. bidders will receive.

Other not-so-obvious prospects form the basis of change in the years ahead. The go-ahead for a film industry is one development that translates into an assortment of opportunities for foreign companies. A Brea, California, company, Elicon, sold computer-controlled camera systems to the Beijing Film Studios in 1987.

Other dimensions of China's transition are literally down-to-earth. Over 60,000 construction workers hold PRC passports. There are chopsticks across the globe, held by teams of laborers building bridges, highways, and irrigation systems. From a few foreign-aid projects in Africa during the 1970s, Chinese overseas aid has mushroomed, and we will probably witness a substantial increase in Beijing's foreign investments (totaling $170 million in 1987, according to data at the international lending agencies). With a greater number of Chinese construction companies turning up in the Third World, some support—sales to the Chinese of earth movers, heavy equipment, and assorted consulting packages transposed on other developing countries—will improve U.S. export capabilities.

There is a different kind of export that is more important for Chinese revenue than many imagine in the estimated $2 billion or more in weapons. Most of these armaments, planes, and such are largely antiquated, but clients flock to purchase them. The *Far Eastern Economic Review* in December 1986 revealed that $1 billion worth of jet fighters, tanks, and small arms went to Iran alone.

If the reforms push the nation's momentum upward, as they will in many sectors of the economy, then today's industries must leave behind the low end and specialize. This is happening in textiles already. The importance of textiles is best understood by numbers of workers still employed. In 1987, says the authoritative *Journal of Commerce*, nearly $500,000 worth of deals were concluded at the heralded Paris International Women's Dress Fair. That year, Yves St. Laurent advised the PRC on international fashion, and the 1987 wardrobe consisted of elegant classical garments as well as sports attire.

China is a nation of smokers. Probably a trillion cigarettes are lit there every year—and there's no sign of any health campaign or nonsmoking fever yet. It has not been easy for the U.S. tobacco industry to win an entree to the Chinese market, especially since the PRC produces 2.20 million metric tons of tobacco annually—four times the American yield. Negotiations over production and sales of R.J. Reynolds brands (Camel, Tempo, Winston, Salem) to foreigners through hotels led to a pact to manufacture some 2 billion or so cigarettes in China each year. The U.S. presence in such an entrenched domestic activity did not disrupt the indigenous industry, a lesson that will eventually be transferred to other sectors of the economy.

What will become of the great reforms after Deng, who cannot outlast the 1990s? There is an official view, which is predictably reassuring. Han Xu, China's ambassador to the U.S., was interviewed by the *San Francisco Chronicle* in 1986. the envoy declared that "our open door policy will open wider and wider if there is a change in the leadership." He was optimistic, claiming that the people want continued change. The policies have become law for the most part, he explains, so there will be no reverses.

Tourism should also continue to grow. Official projections call for a 1 percent increase each year through 1992, and steps to double the present number of hotel rooms are afoot. In 1985, over $1 billion entered the country's coffers through tourism, provoking mixed feelings on the part of the Chinese. Tourists bring foreign, often destabilizing, ideas. Yet General Manager Gao Yin of the state-owned China Travel Service anticipates that Mongolia, Tibet, and other off-the-beaten path locales will open up by 1990. The policies "have become law" for the most part, "so there is no need to worry. There will be no reverses." Not everyone agrees.

To get a grasp on the outcome of dramatic changes represented by the Four Modernizations, one must examine a few penetrating questions. Should the reforms inaugurated 10 years ago produce skewed development, and if another outbreak of corruption is witnessed (and acknowledged), it could undercut reform elements. Should rampant inflation continue (at press time it is said to be as high as 20 percent in major cities along the high-growth east and southern coast), there will be clamor for policymakers to apply the brakes.

Deng's passing from the scene may have occurred by the time you read this. Careful steps to assure succession of like-minded champions of the "Four Modernizations" might not necessarily assure continuation of key tenets in the overall plan. Li Yi-ning, a renowned economic and management professor at the University of Beijing, cites "possible damage" stemming from the hurried pace of economic development.

Thorny decisions about pricing policies lie ahead. The degree of market-orientation in prices is an issue that will be contested by factions divided along not only producer-supplier lines, but along regional, philosophical, and political lines as well.

Also, agricultural policy—establishing distribution networks, improving marketability of indigenous farm products, greater use of irrigation and other methods—can ease the transition affecting tradition-seeped areas of the hinterland. Only 12 percent of the land is arable, and conflict over direction of land-use policies and extent of environmental policy is surfacing.

In the drive for foreign exchange, a prerequisite to continued gains in the nation's output, sacrifices are necessary. Tourism has been placed ahead of other needs. This was clear, when, in 1983, Beijing proclaimed a need for amusement parks. While other countries heartily endorse this form of mass recreation, they favor a strategy of building where the population base and transportation links are already in place. Not so in China, where a $1 billion-plus program to construct a dozen Disneyesque amusement parks, most of which are not likely to be revenue-earners for some time to come, is under way. Their location, away from the main interconnecting routes and tourist crossroads, makes them unlikely recipients of foreign visitors (and hence the coveted exchange currencies).

Improvements in infrastructure are essential. Backlogs in the ports have actually sent huge volumes of cargo southward to Hong Kong. The congestion at Tianjin was eased somewhat after phased liberalization was permitted in 1982–84. Other ports—whose 142 million tons of cargo in 1987 should reach 160 million when all data for 1988 is tabulated—think that the commitment of $1.5 billion for over 200 additional berths may not solve this difficulty. The advent of the Kowloon-Canton rail lines provides an important link with Hong Kong; over $8 billion is earmarked between 1985–90 for railways.

There is a possible reaction from abroad to the emergence of China, and especially to the perception of this mammoth Asian nation as "the next NIC." Protectionism would limit potential in some areas where competition is fierce, such as textiles. By 1999, China may likely hold 4 percent of all world exports, according to Dr. Alan Crane at the Office of Technology Assessment on Capitol Hill. This is an amount comparable to the share held by Canada in 1988.

Part of the growing economic clout to be enjoyed by the People's Republic is seen by an overseas presence. China is now part of East Asia's Caribbean trek, through a venture with Hanae Mori, the Japanese fashion corporation. A pair of plants in Puerto Rico are now operating. In two years, nearly 500,000 cashmere garments—estimated at 85 percent of the total sold to apparel purchasers in the U.S.—will be manufactured in the Caribbean Commonwealth.

Last year, China spent $22 million on a Delaware-based steel company that faced financial problems. U Keli, president of Great Wall Corp., a state-owned business that employs 125,000 in the PRC, told the press in 1988 that wholesale competition with Taiwan and Korea in consumer electronics products would be felt before 1990. A midwest base in Tulsa, Oklahoma, is being used to prepare for the import operations of Great Wall and others expected to follow her path westward.

And *The Asian Wall Street Journal* reported that Chinese technology has actually been licensed to an American company. A $1 million licensing arrangement with a mainland firm is enabling use of a "Made in the PRC" magnetometer, a sophisticated instrument used by geologists. Another similar pact has introduced a Chinese device used for recording stress in jet engines to American firms.

Chinese participation in space has captured the attention of Asia's technology watchers. The three-stage Long March rockets, capable of sending a 700-kg payload aloft, have allowed the world's first user of rocketry to capitalize on the malaise affecting NASA's launch cycles. Chinese commercial attachés are active in attempting to sign up more countries to commit to satellite launches. West Germany and France have agreed, and their scientific experiments will achieve lift-off from Gansu, the northwest launching site. In 1992, over $2 billion will be allotted to this unabashedly commercial space program. It brings prestige, and establishes Chinese scientific and technical prowess (as do a few modest projects in superconductivity).

The relationship with Japan has been characterized by many stormy outbursts over not only unfair investment practices and alleged abuse of Chinese natural resources, but by denials of culpability in the Second World War. When Japanese textbooks downplayed, or denied, atrocities, both Chinas joined other Asian countries in voicing sharp condemnation. The two-way trade in 1988 reached $18 billion, with a $3.5 billion surplus in Japan's favor. A possible sore point with Japan in the 1990s will be over ownership of the Spratly Islands in the China Sea. Possible oil finds there threaten to make the little-known isles a flashpoint.

An impressive array of new projects are on drawing boards. China has the advantage of gaining from a comprehensive view of development, which in the wake of concerns over the environment, can spare this most populous of all nations agony in the next century. For example, while a program to bulldoze much of the Beijing suburbs (home for over 2.5 millions) met with enthusiasm in 1988, its large-scale agro- industrial and manufacturing projects, which were said to be attracting $400 million worth of foreign investment, have been put on hold. The reason is that studies pointed to massive water losses from local aquifers, leading to a slow sinking of much of the capital city itself.

As of this writing, a month after the bloodbath in Tiananmen Square, China remains unstable. There is a yearning, at least among some Chinese, for "reform" and "democracy," and the nation's foreign-educated elite have reacted harshly toward the hard-liners in the government. However, at the moment, the ultimate effect of the student uprising, if any, is impossible to predict.

Potential causes of the next Tiananmen Square include: salary cuts in the military, the rise of rival army factions, perception of wide-scale government corruption, ethnic tensions, disparity in regional incomes, as well as the disaffection of the 100,000 university students.

4

Korea: Post-Olympic Marathon

Newspaper headlines pointing to the recent political transformation in Korea obscure another transition taking place in this Northeast Asian country—a shift that is rapidly changing a war-torn, divided, agricultural country into an advanced, industrialized one. That transformation is by no means complete, but observers on both sides of the Pacific marvel at the speed with which Korea—whose work force averages more hours a week on the job than in any other industrial nation—is striving toward that end.

From the harbor at Pusan to the factory complexes at Inchon, this is a nation on the move, mindful of a recent past where poverty was commonplace. The Olympic torch standard hovers over the stadium in Seoul, towering over the jagged peaks that dot the countryside. "The choice of Korea as site for the 1988 Olympics," notes Swarthmore College professor Larry Westphal, "comes just when the country has, in many ways, 'made it' on the road of development."

Imagine a tiny, barren, rocky, inhospitable landscape penetrated by scorching summers and desolate winters, whose only resource is people—millions of them, mostly illiterate. Yet somehow a spirit of hope emerges after years of foreign occupation and deprivation.

KOREA IN THE POSTWAR PERIOD

The scene is Korea, 1945. As a war-weary Asia starts to recover, few imagine the phoenix-like rise to occur in this mountainous land. The title "Morning Calm" belies a savage struggle between survival and

113

hardship in a nation subjected to centuries of strife. Three years later, the nation is once again torn asunder, as Cold War divisions slice off South from North, family from family—and an industrial base is ceded to puppets installed by Stalin. The country's mineral resources are also appropriated. Two years later a southward invasion begins across most of the southern tier, leveling Seoul, the capital, three times in as many years.

It was a difficult road, and a path not often understood in America. Korea was our neglected child, ravaged by foreign occupation for a half century before the onslaught opposed by the U.S. and its UN allies 35 years ago. With nearly all the nation's industry and natural resources located north of the 38th parallel, the infant republic had little to be optimistic about when peace finally arrived.

As the war ended in 1953, an uneasy truce was declared in Korea. The nation is still reminded of the unending peace talks: Its capital is only 20 miles from the North. Impoverished for many years, their resources sapped by Japanese occupation over two generations, a fledgling business community was eager to pull together behind American-educated Synghman Rhee. The outside world lauded Korean efforts but doubted that the measures would lift the populace above the status of serfs. Rhee assumed power on the assumption that serious bootstrapping could at least end rampant hunger and unemployment, which hovered above the 30 percent level throughout the early 1950s. Progress was minimal, and when student demonstrations rocked the capital in 1960, the regime was forced to abandon control.

Restructuring of both political and economic institutions took place after a bloodless coup in 1961, which saw the ambitious strongman Major General Park Chung Hee seize power. Park allowed himself to face voters two years later and received a green light to make economic growth a national priority, if not a state religion. The Park era would last 18 years and irretrievably alter Korea.

"He instituted planning on a grand scale," explains Dr. Laurence Krause, director of the Asian business program launched in 1988 at the University of California, San Diego. He told merchants what products were considered best bets. The plans were treated as informal directives, and businessmen began to mesh their own objectives with the general direction of the national drive. Park and most of his brain trust had little experience in areas such as currency reform and promoting overseas sales of homegrown goods, but they managed to harness not only local skills but also a trickle of outside investment.

The regime institutionalized *chaebol*, or conglomerates formed with the government's blessing and given leeway over different types of service and manufacturing activities. The top 30 or 40 conglomerates usually include up to two dozen companies under a single umbrella, spanning areas such as textiles, electronics, and construction. Each has anywhere from 15,000 to 50,000 employees. Their structure has changed little in the last quarter century, and only in recent months have official reforms curbed their controversial powers and reduced their economic clout.

At the same time, an ever-expanding merchant class responded to what they recognized as major structural changes administered by the Economic Planning Board. Credit flowed through private channels in growing amounts, and badly needed goods from overseas—goods that would fuel expansion for all sectors of the economy—were paid for by selling products in exchange for them. Incentives were attractive enough to give Korean businesses tax breaks and a long-term commitment to their own growth. The government waived ordinarily high import duties on items that could help local manufacturers assemble their own finished products. Generous insurance plans for business were also dangled as lures. All these steps proved quite effective over time.

Borrowing rose to fund the infrastructure required for expanding industries. Ahn Seung-Chul, a leading economist in Korea, notes that over $12 billion was loaned from the U.S. alone during the quarter century ending in 1985. "The direct investment was important, too," he adds. This reached about $700 million by 1985, and the Americans held about a third of the total of foreign investment." Not surprisingly, the United States was the country's leading non-Korean investor. This investment did not work in a vacuum. "In retrospect, Korea's outward-looking strategy, combined with U.S. efforts to promote free trade, laid the foundation for remarkable expansion."

Providing some loose guidelines for local companies proved successful, and by the mid-1960s Park's clique could point to tangible results. Korea's ability to reach GNP growth of 7 percent, 8 percent, and higher gained notice, surprising experts both within and outside the Pacific Rim. Output per person rose as fast as it did in Japan from 1960–83, reaching about 6 percent per year for the period—twice the rate in Germany and France and five times greater than the rate in the U.S. or Canada.

At the end of the sixties, Park's cabal envisioned the need to target certain industries that had the potential for a multiplier effect. Jobs creation was a goal, and the export quest never diminished. But where to place the emphasis? Where to turn the spigots of easy borrowing terms and cozy deals with reigning *chaebol*? While the Taiwanese opted for light industry, a laissez-faire attitude and attention to small companies, her fellow Dragon chose visible, big-ticket items.

If trade dominated the thoughts of commercial leaders, another consideration was added by the late 1960s: nurturing specific industries with export capability. Dr. John Bennett is president of the Korean Economic Institute in Washington, D.C., and he reflects on economic blueprints drawn in those years. "They saw a need to let market forces continue to raise the living standard for most Koreans, but the government still believed in providing direction. They could understand, as could business, how electronics was one of the real winners in years ahead."

Energy-barren Korea stood imperiled as Middle Eastern war clouds nearly brought all industrializing countries to their knees. Other unresolved problems confronted the nation. Political instability was a constant concern, with dissident factions charging that economic gains were not being shared. The level of debt soared—and would hobble other countries lacking solid credit. Yet, Korea recovered from the twin oil shocks of the 70s, and sales from foreign commerce netted stronger advantages than ever. In 1982, when exports reached a staggering $22 billion, the effects of the worldwide downturn caused stagnant growth for the first time in the "miracle's" history. While foreign debt is still projected to be above $25 billion in 1988, the game plan in Seoul calls for reducing it to zero by 1991 or 1992.

Since then, Seoul has consolidated its gains, fine-tuning the tactics that propelled the economy's engines. Advance planning remains a hallmark in the 1980s. Stressing the role of homegrown think tanks, business and government placed thousands of keen analysts in those institutions—and output from futuristic research is impressive.

In 1985, a $4 billion plan to upgrade the successful electronics sector was launched, and observers take Korea's plans seriously. The Leading Edge invasion took personal computer buffs (and everyone else) by surprise, and along with other developments showed that this Dragon is, like Taiwan, capable of offering consumers cutting-edge high-tech products. Dr. William James, a former official at the Asian Development Bank, is a researcher at the prestigious East-West Center in Hawaii. He says, "The traits such as work ethic and commitment to quality will remain, even while labor rates start to rise. I expect Korea's favorable reputation overseas will grow."

Seoul sought early on to cooperate with U.S. companies in meaningful ways—thereby avoiding the trade friction that hinders close American ties with other countries. Never burdened with hangups over foreign policy or forcing allies to decide on a "one Korea" policy, its 1988

Olympics and attendant publicity should generate additional goodwill for years to come. Challenges were as formidable as elsewhere in East Asia, but few who have seen the progress of the past two decades deny that the republic's goal of becoming a major economic force is credible.

Exports for 1988 were rising at levels far above those seen in comparable periods of the preceding year. They may reach the $55 billion mark for last year, when all figures are tablulated. Equally impressive is their composition, with steady rises in value-added manufactured products. For example, about 40 percent of her sales to the U.S. consist of machinery, electrical equipment, and chemical products. A growing share of those sales is coming from medium-sized companies, which had, until recently, been excluded from the games and pains inherent in global commerce. Foreign sales are vital, but signs of healthy domestic consumption are evident—and that is the component of GNP that ultimately assures balanced development. Labor unrest—especially during spring wage bargaining rituals—will be a regular feature of the social and economic pageantry.

THE "NEXT JAPAN"?

Korea is often termed "the next Japan." The suddenness with which her economic trot turned to a fast gallop, as Hyundai's Pony compacts broke past the starting gate (150,000 were sold in the U.S. in 1987 compared to 100,000 for the previous year, and expectations are that 250,000 will be sold in 1988), seemed to confirm that status.

Is this "the next Japan?" Yes, on the surface. Like Japan in 1964, the nation is still reverberating from an Olympiad that accorded Koreans a high degree of respect and visibility. A weak, undervalued currency and the reliance on export sales are two similarities, as are the strong work ethic, emphasis on education, and attempts to utilize low wages as a competitive device. Yet, the global economy is different today from that of the buoyant mid-1960s—a period that saw sharp growth in both developing and developed countries alike. Japan had already been heavily industrialized, and the specter of protectionism was not a feature of trade. Another major difference lies in the ability of all serious economic players to acquire and harness new technologies rapidly. The burden of military expenses (which are currently 6 percent of GNP, far greater than that for European NATO members and five times the proportionate level spent in Japan) is a third unique characteristic of the divided peninsula. While a form of feudalistic paternalism exists—as it does in Japan—the Korean variety is far less benign, imposing no demands on the "boss" side of the worker-boss equation.

Even as Korea nibbles away at Japanese industry, picking up lower-scale segments of heavy industry while her powerful rival retains value-added segments, Korea will soon begin to discover her own vulnerability. The same syndrome is taking place with China and Malaysia, which compete for foreign sales in identical sectors such as textiles, machinery, household appliances, and even consumer electronics.

Exports are far more significant than most imagine. At $45 billion in 1987, they constitute 38 percent of Korea's entire GNP. Japan's worldwide export trade, at $223 billion that year, was only 10 percent of total output. Nearly 40 percent of Korean products reach American consumers, while 18 percent are destined for Japan, and about 12 percent percent are slated for the EEC.

What is usually overlooked about those exports is that Korea purchases sophisticated parts and equipment processed or assembled in Japan, then assembles them and ships finished consumer products from Korean ports. Seoul fairs quite well by this strategy, but she is being forced to shift toward a new set of tactics, ones that avoid sending middleman profits to her former colonial master.

With the top nine *chaebol*, the horizontally integrated quasi-cartels, constituting over a fourth of the GNP, there has been an overdependence on the fortunes of the top conglomerates. Here again, "the next Japan" seems to be quite different from the supposed object of imitation. Because the *chaebol* do not subcontract (unlike the diversified trading companies in Japan), the country's small business sector stagnates.

Japan itself was sort of labor—and instituted robotics as a means of compensating for this disadvantage. "The next Japan," however, must provide more than 400,000 new jobs a year in order to keep employment levels close to the full employment mark. In addition, attention to social goals—sewage lines, roadways, infrastructure, acceptable housing, and the like—confront Korea at the current stage in her ascent, as it did not when the Japanese colossus began to stir. Nor was that colossus confronted with difficult political choices in a society faced with not only rising economic expectations but also increasing political aspirations.

There is one other major difference between the Japan of the 1960s and Korea today. The era of relatively placid world relations—especially across most of East Asia—is over. The genuinely positive relations between the U.S. and Asian countries that characterized the postwar years is no longer apparent, and Korea in the 1990s will probably emerge as a "flashpoint" of future American ties with important allies. The new breed of up-and-coming Korean policymakers views the relationship with America in a different light, and feels a new sense of nationalistic pride. Ironically, the political pressures Americans had put on Seoul to change their political institutions, to democratize, and encourage major reforms, are the ones which could be the most damaging to the goal of maintaining relations along current lines. More than half of the 42 million inhabitants (crammed into the southern tier of the peninsula at the rate of 385 per square mile) are under 22 years old. "They will be tougher to deal with than anyone in a position of leadership was ... before the reform process began," Wheeler says.

THE OUTLOOK FOR KOREAN INDUSTRY

There is no question that the changes that lie ahead for the newly industrialized countries are far beyond the level of minor modifications. They are fundamental, and are rooted in the need to complete a structural transformation along the lines of all advanced industrially developed countries. How will these changes be designed, and by whom?

There is tight control over the general direction of the economy by the Economic Planning Board's (EPB) 500 or so staffers in Seoul, a third of whom were trained at American schools. The Ministry of Finance also has a strong role, and the Korea Development Institute—a think tank with extremely close ties to decision makers in EPB—also provides input. There is no formal division of responsibility among this trio, yet it is generally understood that there is a distinct role for each member of the triumverate. Other players include credit agencies, the Export-Import Bank, and, increasingly, education ministries, which must match education policies with the longer-range technological and economic goals of the nation.

Capitalism with guidance is the mainstay of Korea's vibrant economy. There is no agreement on how to reach consensus, but consensus has been reached in a remarkably high number of instances. The democratization of the country will certainly affect Korea's ability to withstand divisions over economic priorities. Although the general plan for the economy will remain intact (see below), its subheadings and fine print will come only after much contention. This is a nation where such confrontation comes easily, and it is a little-known fact about the country that historical differences and tensions between the southeast and the western provinces have often shaped decisions about the nation's future path. (Few political reports in the Western media made note of this east-west antagonism despite its influence on the ongoing political upheaval. Through the code phrase "balanced economic development" Seoul seeks to remedy the situation, although great progress has been made in equalizing delivery of services since the 1980s.)

Inflation appears to be the major worry ahead. An overheated economy saw money supply increases of 21 percent and of 22 percent for 1986 and 1987. Only rising interest rates, argue some planners in Seoul, keep inflation rates at below 10 percent. Another device in the anti- inflation campaign has been allocating credit so that it is kept from major, *chaebol*-controlled corporations. While this creates some political headaches, it accomplishes a prime social objective, that of modernizing the large, inefficient small- and medium-size business sector.

Very encouraging news continued through 1988: cheaper oil made other industrial adjustments easier to cope with; the appreciation of the yen by 50 percent against the won allowed exports to sustain their high levels. Also, by the end of 1987 Korea's worrisome debt-service ratio plunged, much to the surprise of observers. This means that one of the world's biggest debtor nations can indeed continue to score major gains on the industrial front, pay its loans, use past loans in an expeditious way, and build those investments so as to guarantee growth. Recent data shows that household savings in the republic are continuing to grow, and may now actually be more than 33 percent of disposable income (or more than double that of Japan).

Management of the economy is undergoing a period of transition as rapid as that found in the political sphere. A managerial revolution was already taking place in the latter half of the 1980s before political events ushered in far-reaching changes. The present split between President Roh's Democratic Justice party and his more liberal rivals is a profound one that cannot be bridged easily. Furthermore, traditional means of control, or "guidance," over long-term objectives is complicated by a balancing act between administrative and legislative authority. Roh's control is challenged by the fact that April 1988 elections handed the opposition majorities in the national legislature.

Even when the attempts to set up a form of consensus are well-coordinated, they experience setbacks. Acting on the advice and consent of all of the players, the government set out to add even more tonnage to already glutted shipbuilding capacity in the 1970s. A decade later, a failure to examine more closely worldwide semiconductor prospects led to severe loss of earnings on the part of domestic electronics giants.

Looking ahead, the subsidies that have propped up failing sectors are going to be reexamined. The whole emphasis on heavy industry—steel, shipbuilding, automobiles—is an issue that must be addressed in the context of shrinking markets and rising competition from the second tier of would-be newly industrialized countries such as Malaysia.

The formidable issue of wage policy is one that can slow down the Korean juggernaut. This is readily understood by experts such as Dr.

Kim Chongsoo at Korea Development Institute. While his countrymen total 54.5 hours weekly at $1.38 an hour (the average for industry), Taiwan is just below that hourly wage level. Hong Kong is not far ahead, at $1.78 in 1987, according to sources at the World Bank. Japan's workers are approaching parity with the West in may sectors. "Unit costs," says Dr. Chongsoo, "have been increasing in the Republic of Korea, and to a large extent, Korea might lose its competitiveness when compared with the others [East Asian NICs]." After an impressive record in the 1980s, helped in part by currency fluctuation, the situation might again become unfavorable for his country.

The Korea Economic Institute's Dr. John Bennett agrees that labor settlements are a major stumbling block. "Every spring, you find nearly all of the major wage negotiations taking place. Restraint has occurred in the past, and the government might succeed if there were acceptable calls for moderation on the part of the workers and the bargaining representatives. But you have to remember that it takes a concerted effort to hold back aggregate demand, and that may be the biggest weapon the government has to hold off very big wage hikes.

Working conditions are becoming a part of those negotiations. Base compensation and forms of pensions are now included among the agreements. In the industry association councils and in organizations more closely resembling Western-styled unions, labor forces are making their voices heard for the first time in decades. The Daewoo Okpo shipyard and heavy machinery complex saw 2,700 workers locked out of the site after a two-week walkout in April 1988. Turning down proposed salary increases offered by the *chaebol*, workers instead called for 50 percent across-the-board increases.

TECHNOLOGICAL DEVELOPMENT PLANS

Korea's overall development blueprint depends on foreign capital. To attract that capital, rules concerning reinvestment of earnings by foreign multinationals were relaxed in 1985. Today, the government is moving in different directions at once. While restrictions on repatriation of principal and dividends on foreign investments were eased in the same year, other steps were taken in 1988 that dismay potential foreign investors. Tax breaks for overseas-based multinationals were reduced, and companies exporting half or more of their goods from the Republic of Korea would lose allowances on new equipment.

The scope of foreign investment is undergoing dramatic change. Where some $1 billion was channeled into the country in 1987 from abroad, the best estimates for the totals that come in under technology-related agreements or joint ventures in technology fields (as opposed to more conventional investments in textiles, for example), reached a much higher level than in earlier years, both in absolute terms as well as in proportional terms. They may have topped the $250 million mark.

All across the range of technologies, Korea is benefiting from this quest for 1990s-style economic development. Samsung, the electronics titan, weathered many storms in the late 1970s—Taiwanese competition, difficulty in obtaining licensing agreements from Japanese entities, and other barriers—in order to emerge as an integral part of the nation's telecommunications program. Its semiconductor and telecoms division, called SST, has achieved considerable progress in implementing Korea's ambitious plans for PBX, switching, and digital systems. Even facsimile machines and videoconferencing equipment is to be unveiled before 1990.

Electronics deserves special attention. The major conglomerates have pledged between $2 billion and $4 billion toward refinements of existing plants, conducting internal R&D, and other efforts. Over all, the level of research and development spending is now estimated to be a healthy 1 percent of GNP, or about double what it was a decade ago. This compares favorably with the amounts earmarked by many Western industrial powers. Spawned by the network of science and technology institutes, industry-government collaboration has led to a checklist of some nearly 30 priority projects.

It was in 1985 that the Koreans attained 64K DRAMS (dynamic random access chips), and when the 256K mark was reached by local manufacturers, there was cause for considerable self-congratulation in the country. Chun Hwa Lee, president of Samsung Petrochemicals, describes future objectives of the industry as achieving value-added, with gains of up to 34 percent possibly by 1991.

A special concern is training different types of engineers; the number of technical cooperation pacts signed has increased markedly, making foreign cooperation in specific fields of technology easier. Equally impressive is the fact that, in 1987, over 600 technology joint venture agreements were signed by private businesses.

Among the large-scale research and development projects promoted by the government is one designed to develop technology for a comprehensive utilization of kaolin, a fine, usually white, clay, under the joint cooperation of the Korea Advanced Institute of Science and Technology (KAIST), the Korea Research Institute of Chemical Technology (KRICT), and the Korea Institute of Energy and Resources (KIER). The project calls for the improvement of the grades of kaolin, 26 million tons of which is deposited in Korea, and developing chemical products of higher value-added. Laboratory work needed for the production of piped water purifying agents, desulfurization and dehydrating agents, and detergent additives from low-grade kaolin has been completed. It is thus expected that chemical products valued up to 40–50 times the raw kaolin will be produced from low-grade kaolin.

Another large-scale project is the semiconductor technology development project, in which the Korea Electrotechnology and Telecommunications Research Institute (KETRI), KAIST, seven universities, including Seoul National, Yonsei, and Kyongbuk universities, and several corporations such as Gold Star Semiconductor, Samsung Semiconductor, Korea Electronics, and Hyundai Electronics, are participating. Projects developing technologies for ferrotitanium refining, computer, and basic genetic engineering are also being undertaken.

If Korea is to become a technology-intensive industrial nation under the "technology first" policy, she needs to develop a highly skilled technical work force. The government estimates that Korea will need 150,000 specialists for research and development and engineering in 2001, a ratio of 30 per 10,000 in population. Of that figure, the demand for nuclear research manpower is estimated at 15,760 and mid-level research manpower of 42,760. To meet the demand, the government is taking various steps designed to elevate educational quality in Korean graduate schools, to drastically increase the training functions of the KAIST, to expand training overseas, to induce scientific specialists from abroad, and to establish technological institutes. All of this represents a formidable drive to upgrade the country's science establishment, which was virtually nonexistent until the mid-1970s.

Reports that some $470 million is being allotted for the training of 2,300 engineers over the next two years—with other monies to be distributed as incentives for returning Korean nationals—are considered by some science and technology experts as unrealistic. In 1985, the number of undergraduates working in heavy engineering was 50,000, while another 15,000 were in mechanical engineering. Electrical engineering drew 7,000. Only about 250 were working in applied math and applied physics, and numbers for computer science were seen as minuscule. Only a tiny fraction of Korea's 400,000 scientists and engineers are engaged in research.

There is, on the contrary, a severe shortfall in the number of scientists and engineers, and when skilled technicians and related jobs are added, a neutral observer concludes that the country is well over a million trained individuals short of the type of talent it needs. Yet there is optimism that, just as other newly industrialized countries are seeking the same kinds of personnel, strategies such as joint ventures can bridge the gaps or at least stake out niche markets in these sunrise industries.

Samsung's rise in the realm of computer chips grew out of the joint-venture strategy, and out of a 1987 decision to purchase shares of U.S. high-tech firms. In Silicon Valley, there are 200 researchers working in a state-of-the-art Zymos microchip design plant. The financially troubled California company was eager to strike a deal with the Koreans, who are generally viewed as better commercial allies that the Japanese, and who are perceived, rightly or wrongly, as a more generous venture partner than are rivals in Osaka or Tokyo. Despite positive images about Korean partnerships, the Zymos deal raised many eyebrows, and may have led to resentment over the country's sudden leap into high, high tech. (This was supposedly the reason behind early resistance to Lucky-Goldstar's attempts to fast-track construction of an Alabama factory.)

During the most recent purchasing missions made by Korean corporations in the U.S., the emphasis on large-scale technology buying was evident. Samsung Aerospace—and this sector is one given priority by planners in Seoul—is purchasing a machining center for Rockwell International at a cost of over $4.2 million. Specialized compressors, gas analyzers, and other advanced equipment was bought as deals totaling $400 million were finalized.

Samsung forged ahead in the global DRAM race as a result of a pledge to augment internal R&D with an additional $500 million to $725 million, according to best estimates. Gains are impressive. The Korea Electronics Industry Association in Washington, D.C. indicates that in 1987, 10 million 1-megabit chips were sold by the conglomerate's semiconductor division, but that by the end of 1988, the figure should be closer to four times that number.

One event in 1987 that has contributed to Korea's efforts in electronics proved to be the decision by disk drive maker Seagate Technology to locate a $3 million, 56,000-square foot plant outside Pusan for production of its 20-megabyte hard disk drives. It was believed that Singapore's attempts to attract this facility were a close second to that of fellow Tiger Korea. Seagate's move, like that of others in sophisticated electronics, would help to assure the creation of another mini-Silicon Valley in Pusan, reducing costs of importing the sexier types of electronic devices and components from Japan, Inc.—imports that led to nearly $1.6 billion in expenditures in 1986, and which, unless the trend toward assembling lower-end gizmos is reversed, would cost well over $2 billion by 1989.

Some signs point to a robust electronics industry, one supported by enough R&D outlays and ample profits. The five largest corporations—divisions of Samsung, Daewoo, and Lucky-Goldstar—had combined sales of $6 billion in 1987, for a 20 percent increase over 1986. "It is the profit side," says Dr. Bennett at the Korea Economic Institute, "that could stand for some improvement. The latest figures coming out of Korea show that profits in electronics were never greater than 3 percent for any quarter in 1986," and there were no major increases afterwards.

The contest between Taiwan and Korea is showing both countries at a virtual dead heat in the electronics field. As an underpinning of future growth, electronics is forecast to add $20 billion to the country's coffers in 1991, and nearly four times as much just a decade later.

Sensing Japan's precarious domination of certain realms in high tech, companies like Lucky-Goldstar are intrepidly marching ahead in their campaigns to establish their reputation for new products. In 1986, the number of VCRs manufactured surpassed even the most optimistic expectations, and Korea could achieve worldwide sales of about $600 million by the time final statistics for 1988 are tallied. Nearly absent from markets such as cassette players and stereo equipment, the *chaebol* are nonetheless seizing opportunities. For example, capitalizing on the Olympics, Korean camcorders are light, durable, and inexpensive.

Biotechnology is one of the priorities, and for good reason. Like many other Asian countries, Korea has need for better drugs and pharmaceuticals. Unlike other East Asian countries, with the exception of Japan, Korea has a large enough market to sustain serious, dedicated R&D into those types of products.

Government estimates are that biotechnology could be a $1 billion industry there by the early 1990s. Slowing down biotech developments are questions over return on investment, but helping out the field is the fact that upgrading other sciences in this country's great leap forward has a multiplier effect extending to biotechnology. Korea is earnestly trying to achieve mutually beneficial joint ventures with the U.S. in the area of biotechnology, hoping to sidestep frustration (often directed at her powerful Japanese neighbor) over trade issues. Kim M. Lee is president of the Korea Genetic Engineering Research Association in Seoul. "Within 10 years, we expect to see end-products coming out of R&D," he says. The share of GNP going for R&D is under 2 percent, but this is on a par with developed countries—and is ten times the share devoted to R&D in the early 1980s.

Most of the country's efforts are coordinated through this agency, which chooses companies with a track record to commercialize and distribute products. This system is in keeping with the mixed economic model here, which often directs or suggests opportunities to the private sector.

Samsung, the electronics conglomerate, has given its Cheil Sugar division responsibility for biotechnology. Sales of a genetically engineered hepatitis B vaccine are improving (10 percent of the population carries the hepatitis B virus), and U.S. partners at Eugene Technology International (Allendale, N.J.) provided most of the R&D. Feron, a beta interferon, is marketed locally. An alpha-interferon ointment is one of the leading products.

Korea Green Cross spends about $15,000,000 a year on its own research. Plasminogen activators are receiving priority at corporate headquarters. Products to be released this summer and autumn include reagents for detection of cancer, as well as the vaccine for hepatitis B.

Another company, Lucky Biotech, is based in a science park in Daedok—and a California site provides R&D input as well. Lucky is considered an innovator, and Merck is reportedly working with them on an EIA-type diagnostic kit.

With a growing stock market, it's possible that some of these players can receive more funding. Companies active today are watching U.S. firms' distribution and promotion campaigns in the quest to understand just how consumers and industrial consumers are best reached with new products.

DOMESTIC UNREST

Korea is, on the balance, a Third World country with a heavy foreign debt load—and demands at home are mounting for social spending and improved infrastructure. None of Seoul's moves has taken place without protest at home. If turmoil subsides and tensions ease, the country's track record and visibility with big-ticket items such as autos and consumer electronics exports remaining healthy will allow it to remain attractive to foreign investors.

A change in attitude would take place if power supplies and water were questionable, of if civil turmoil caused transport difficulties. Even at the height of unrest in 1987, there were no signs that export capabilities had been hindered, thus helping to maintain the long- term perceived benefits to Western and Japanese manufacturers.

Looking at current unrest, one should note that when riots broke out in 1980, disorder led to the assumption of power by current president Chun Hwan Doo. American interest in the country as a manufacturing site dropped somewhat, but a global economic slowdown—and reduced overall levels of U.S. foreign investment—were occurring anyway. Therefore, comparisons between events then and now are difficult.

An executive from one major multinational speaks for most U.S. businesspeople in Korea. He believes the current level of disorder is no major concern, but acceleration of civil turmoil will be watched carefully. "After more than a decade in the country, we can assess its problems, and its strengths, realistically," he says.

Unless the situation deteriorates markedly, there is no indication that business is worried. "Business here was looking at whether violence would affect the Olympics and other events" according to a highly placed U.S. official. "If government overreaction takes place, or if the opposition resorts to extreme measures, people will start to wonder." This view is still widely held outside Korea. According to Ronald Danielian, president of the International Economic Policy Association in Washington, D.C.: "They knew that some degree of trouble was in store, so there wasn't the element of surprise that often confronts companies offshore. My thinking is that a slowdown in investment would take place because of fluctuations in the dollar." Danielian agrees with others that the growing Korean middle class is a force for stabilization and con- tributes to a "natural evolution" of democratic tendencies.

Economic performance also contributes to general perceptions of a return to tranquility. Dr. John Bennett, president of the Korea Economic Institute in Washington, D.C., reports that a 15.6 percent GNP growth in the first quarter of 1987 convinced outsiders that inherent strengths of the economy were, if not invincible, resilient. The second quarter of 1987 proved doubters wrong, and both 1987 and 1988 were charac- terized by double-digit growth. Publicity surrounding the Summer Olympics created a favorable impression in many quarters, but other factors far outweigh the Olympiad's glamour. Regardless, South Korea is a long way from being viewed as a pariah state—one where commer- cial links bear a burden for nations with a large investment presence.

Seoul is receptive to reasonable pressures, which may help ease political transitions in a nation where student protests are common. This can keep economic gains afloat. John Williamson, coauthor of a study on currency alignment for the Institute for International Economics, indicates that Seoul quietly acquiesced when an advance copy of recom- mendations was presented to Korean leaders. Chief among the sugges- tions was that Korea run excessive current account surpluses. "That was encouraging, because many countries take very long to respond, once they sense they are on a dangerous course." Williamson feels com- parisons with the pre-Marcos instability in the Philippines is unfair. "The corruption is not there," he explains.

Thus far, competitor newly industrialized countries in East Asia are picking up would-be investors from North America and from the EEC with varied degrees of success. Up-and-coming economies will find it hard to position themselves as an alternative to Korea. Ahmad Salludin Dali of the Penang (Malaysia) Regional Development Authority says his agency's marketing drive is not being altered, but, like others in the Asia-Pacific region, they will review their incentives if violence continues.

OPPORTUNITIES FOR FOREIGN BUSINESS

The dimensions of Korea's buoyant economy are well known to U.S. consumers, who realized that there was indeed an alternative to the legendary Japanese automobile, and that quality needn't be sacrificed. In fact, Hyundai realized the highest first-year sale of an imported product by any foreign company. Korea's "Little Three" automakers, Daewoo, Hyundai, and Kia, are likely to sell some 475,000 vehicles in the U.S. in 1987. Scare headlines proclaimed a rerun of the Japanese invasion. Yet, even Hyundai's big push—with 170,000 cars bought by motorists last year—are not robbing U.S. or Canadian workers of paychecks. Ford is a part-owner of Kia, and GM will be making 300,000 Le Mans models at Pupyong, and what's good for GM—as well as for partner Daewoo—can be good for both countries. Other joint ventures in auto parts are forging lasting ties for small businesses, which are increasingly relied upon as suppliers for the giant automakers. In 1987, Hyundai chairman Chung Se Yung explained to the American Chamber of Commerce in Seoul that only through earnest cooperation can an orderly shift in global auto production occur, and that the Koreans were willing to cooperate in that transition. Most observers outside the newly industrialized countries are willing to take them at their word. (Other experts note that Korea's entry into automobiles was neither a surprise nor an industrial sneak attack. Japan has been abandoning this "sunset" industry for years and plans to shut down nearly all of its car factories in the decade ahead.)

While attention focused on products such as low-cost, high-quality Leading Edge computers (designed and built on Korean soil), news about cooperation has been slow to reach Westerners fearful of a second Japanese onslaught—and often prone to blame all Asia's successful countries for the sins of a few. Ailing Zymos, a California semiconductor company, was bought out by the *chaebol* Daewoo. The result? Custom chips for Korea, and jobs saved for America. "They [Koreans] don't horde all the benefits for themselves," says William James, a specialist at Hawaii's East-West Center. "It's just not their style. There's give-and-take. You have to know how to deal with them, but nobody who does business in Asia … ever accused them of predatory practices."

Foreign joint ventures are sprouting like proverbial Korean mushrooms on the economic landscape. GE and Samsung are exploring medical products, including magnetic resonance imaging. Boeing and Daewoo are building aircraft parts. United Technologies is involved in joint helicopter production. Yet, the potential of these types of alliances has yet to be realized, since attention toward the small business sector in Korea is a recent phenomenon.

Success is creating rising expectations among the populace, and infrastructure projects and social services are being given a new priority. "We were forced to export, to look outward for many years in order to earn money and feed our people," declares Joun Yung Sun, minister for economic affairs at the embassy in Washington, D.C. "Now we will be able to look inward."

Export opportunities to Korea affect North American and EEC companies alike. Telecommunications are critical because phone use will soar. In 1987, only 12 phones per 100 persons were in use; that ratio is seen as growing to 38 before the year 2000. Only a third of all families own refrigerators today, but projections are that this figure will rise to nine in ten by the end of the century.

There is as much opportunity for foreign exporters in the laboratory as in the kitchen. Biotechnology may well emerge as a billion-dollar industry within a few years, simply because of the pharmaceutical and medical needs of a large—and aging—population. American firms like Eugene International are already collaborating on interferon and other products. A continent away from California's famed science research parks, the campus-like park at Daedok is merging R&D from American and Korean teams who design diagnostic kits essential to U.S. health and medicine sales around the globe.

Biotech is not the only "sunrise" industry on the drawing boards. The Korea Advanced Institute of Science and Technology maintains a staff of 1,200 devoted to reaching the goal of 15,000 Ph.D.s in science and technology. Process engineering, ceramics, materials sciences, and electronics are all priorities. Park Pil-Soo, chairman of the Korea Productivity Center, calls U.S.A.-made equipment "essential" if those would-be scientists are to have the technical tools they need to upgrade skills.

Without high tech born and bred in the West, Korea can never achieve its goals. South Korea, according to Minister Joun Yung Sun, lies "in between the status of developing and developed." Low tech, medium tech, and no tech at all appeals to increasingly affluent consumers. The absorption of Western innovations will determine "leapfrogs" in biotechnology, electronics, and other commanding heights of the "sunrise" industries of the 1990s.

Can non-Koreans export to this NIC? In contrast to its era of a close (or controlled) market, Seoul has initiated measures to accommodate overseas traders. Electrical machinery, sporting goods, processed foods, appliances, and household goods are a few foreign-made items now readily available. Under a sweeping plan that opened up 95 percent of all incoming products, over 90 percent of incoming goods are now free from licensing restrictions.

The U.S. alone sells nearly $29 billion worth of products to this vibrant, dynamic society. Ironically, so much of the ultra- creditworthy nation's debt-load is handled by American banks that a healthy share of the red ink evaporates automatically—yet, those billions are not reflected in trade statistics.

Unlike other countries who limit imports to raw materials, Korea years ago sensed that its building blocks would come from friendly trading partners in the West. In 1987 Minister of Trade and Industry Rha Woong Bae flatly declared while on a U.S. tour that his goal is to end, not just reduce, the $5-billion trade deficit. This good news follows on the heels of reforms in copyright and patent protection for export-minded Western traders. Only short-term U.S. protectionism will jeopardize the prospects in Korea.

Korea finds 35 percent of its GNP dependent on exports—three times the level of Japan. About 40 percent of those goods are destined for the shopping malls and corner markets of America. Far from "the next Japan," Korea has a domestic market a scant 5 percent the size of that economic superpower's. Also, 1986 was the first year Korea realized her own balance-of-payments surplus.

Even more dramatic liberalization took place in the past two years. Import tariffs plummeted from an average of 20.9 percent to 16.9 percent. A half dozen native companies controlling most of the $4 billion insurance market cringed as U.S. firms were allowed entry. The $1.7 billion indigenous tobacco industry complained about official steps enabling the Marlboro Man and his counterparts to cross customs.

Sunkyong, a $6 billion general trading company, is one of several major groups actively seeking to "buy American." Seung Bum Oh, manager of its planning division, insists, "We are at the stage, as a nation, where we can increase our purchases."

Meanwhile, one Korean import to American borders will be welcomed. Korea is proving its commitment to forging a partnership through its investments in the United States. Lucky-Goldstar, the consumer electronics giant, has built a plant in Alabama. USX and Seoul-based Posco Steel are using Korea's state-of-the-art techniques in this industry and will channel $150 million into the U.S. by 1991. California is another beneficiary of a boom heading across the American mainland. While Korea has $700 million invested abroad, only $82 million is on U.S. shores. This is changing, and current projects range from TV plants in New Jersey to coal mines in Pennsylvania. To assist U.S. policy aims— and avoid possible protectionism—textile plants are opening in Central America and in the Caribbean.

The Land of the Morning Calm is far from calm economically. She is vulnerable to recession, as the East Asian experience of 1985 proved. Like every other economic power, Korea has stumbled. Its once mighty "sunrise" shipbuilding industry has become a burdensome "sunset" operation. It saw orders tumble from $2 billion in 1985 to under $500 million last year. Overseas construction had been $14 billion in 1981, but declined to $2 billion in 1985, in response to downturns around the Middle East.

Violence across major cities in the Republic of Korea in 1988 did not deter faith in that country's stability. American firms relying on letters of credit and trade-related insurance packages appear confident that deals can continue without interruption. Manufacturers selling in Korea itself have similar assurances that cover any potential losses. America has an $800 million kitty, and according to U.S. Department of Commerce research, a greater return on investment is possible in Korea than in Japan. Benefits for U.S.-based companies go beyond simple equations on labor costs. In 1984, restrictions on repatriation of principal and dividends ended, while rules about reinvesting earnings were eased.

THE SIXTH FIVE-YEAR PLAN

Korea's early plans concentrated strictly on building the economy, in keeping with the nation's desperate need for growth. In the 1970s, however, the plans began to include more social policy tasks, such as health-care improvement, education planning, and housing programs. In recognition of this trend, in 1982 the government adopted the term "Economic and Social Development Plan" to describe its fifth five-year plan. Thus, the importance of social welfare objectives in the overall plan has grown over the past decade, just as the emphasis given to specific economic targets has declined.

This process has continued with the Sixth Five-Year Economic and Social Development Plan, in effect from 1987 to 1991. Concepts and methods employed in the sixth plan have been aired and refined in consultations with business people, scholars, and representatives of citizen's groups, as well as in public hearings. Moreover, the plan's stress on decentralizing government functions will make it more flexible and responsive in operation. "The current plan is really an effort to match up capability with the social agenda," according to Larry Westphal.

The sixth plan's emphasis on efficiency is seen in four major policy categories. The first promotes domestic competition by reducing government involvement and eliminating restrictive business practices. The plan calls for transforming the government's role from one of regulation to one of promotion. It will simplify its procedures of approval, registration, and permission, especially in relation to founding a new firm or expanding an existing one. It will also abolish or consolidate laws that support or promote specific industries, giving market forces and private management decisions the greatest importance in deciding business success or failure. The government may still intervene in cases where a business failure threatens the health or stability of the broader national economy, but such intervention will be strictly limited in scope and duration.

Shipbuilding is an example of the form of mild coercion that Seoul imposes on the reigning *chaebols*. When disastrous losses were faced in 1986 and 1987, guidelines for major conglomerates strongly encouraged several to coalesce their respective activities under a single banner. Others were asked to come up with timetables for shutting down their foreign ventures. The "penalty" for noncompliance is ordinarily a failure on the part of the government to approve transactions, loans, and requests from the disobedient corporation.

For greater efficiency in carrying out tasks that it cannot privatize or eliminate, the government must upgrade coordination of policies between ministries. It must also increase the level of specialized education available to officials, helping them to plan and execute policies more effectively. To end the inefficiency of restrictive business practices, the government will bring Korea's fair trade practices up to a level comparable to those in more advanced economies. Korea's import liberalization ratio rose to 95 percent in 1988 and it will continue reducing tariffs during the period before 1991. The government will employ shock-absorbing techniques such as advance warning of liberalization, and temporary adjustment tariffs.

This is one arena where political squabbling could limit socioeconomic objectives. Steps to appease protectionists in both North America and the European Economic Community, as we discussed earlier, are proceeding. Yet, it is the speed at which they continue, and the nature of those steps—types of products, percentages of tariffs reduced, etc.—that form the kernel of resentment against the republic today. The government will set guidelines for activities of trade associations to prevent them from collusive or market- restricting behavior.

Other fair-trade actions under the sixth plan will include education and training programs to help the government analyze and enforce its laws more effectively. Special attention will go to the small and medium-size industries, which have often suffered in the past from unequal relationships with their larger competitors and contracting partners. Government activities in this area will include strengthening regulations against abuses of economic power by larger firms, improving legal standards for subcontracting regulations, restricting takeovers of smaller firms by larger ones, and ensuring greater access to distribution channels by small and medium industries.

The government's fourth method of promoting a stable economy is to make the best possible use of natural resources. To avoid destabilization from fluctuating raw material prices, Seoul will encourage better demand management and the stockpiling of affected commodities. It will also stress the need to absorb overseas price increases as much as possible.

In the financial sector, this plan calls for raising the domestic savings ratio to 33 percent in 1991. To accomplish this task Korea will diversify savings instruments, promote greater public access to and use of the banking system, encourage firms to retain a higher level of their income, and restrain government spending. Guidelines are being established for achieving and maintaining a balance-of-payments surplus, by encouraging the domestic production of parts and machinery now imported, by encouraging exports by small and medium-size firms, and by supporting productivity improvements by industry.

Under the sixth plan, the government will cut back its involvement in allocation of loans and in executive staffing decisions, making financial institutions responsible for their own management. It will also liberalize interest rates gradually, and continue the phasing out of policy preference loans to favored sectors. To bolster the competitiveness of domestic banks, the government will work with them to find ways of reducing their bad debt burden. It will also encourage more sophisticated financial techniques and more diversified banking functions in order to raise bank profits.

Other steps toward more efficient financial resource management will refine the government's monetary and fiscal controls, with emphasis on the use of indirect instruments such as discount rates and reserve requirements.

The sixth plan aims at transforming Korea's industrial structure, encouraging heavy industry to better attract technology transfer.

Seoul is dealing with the delicate issue of regional development—a sensitive issue in light of historical geographic divisions. In the past, policies placed top priority on dispersing the population of the Seoul metropolitan area, but this approach failed to achieve its goal. Under the new plan, government will focus on balancing development across the nation.

The sixth plan devotes special attention to small and medium-size regional cities, which have tended to show the slowest growth. Local industrial estates will be created in such areas, and the government will work to increase the competitiveness of regional industries. Similar measures will also begin to strengthen local banks to reduce the concentration of financial activity in Seoul.

Korea will make significant progress toward providing a system of welfare protection for its people. Medical insurance coverage will be extended to cover most of the nation's people by 1991. Government agencies will launch Korea's first-ever pension program to go into effect by the end of the 1980s, although on a limited basis at first. (As currently planned, the initial system will cover employees of firms with ten or more workers, with optional application to smaller firms and to farmers.)

The government will work for greater equality in education and for the elimination of discriminatory legal and social standards. The role of women in Korea is in question. There are very strong differences of opinion on this issue, which arises in a society where pent-up aspirations on many fronts are all rising to a crescendo at once.

The new agenda will develop and reinforce environmental protection in Korea. It sets forth a program to improve the coordination of environmental programs, requiring cross-governmental assessment of the environmental projects of each ministry. To achieve this goal, the government will devise comprehensive environmental preservation programs by region, along with a national program for the plan period. The "polluter pays" system of fees will be broadened to deter industrial pollution and raise funds for environmental investment, and fines for infractions will be increased. The government will clarify the criteria for pollutant emission permits and work out more substantial enforcement measures against violators of environmental laws. It will also require environmental impact studies before construction begins on large public and private sector profits.

FUTURE TRENDS

Trends to watch in the early 1990s are those that increase Korea's visibility overseas. The government is beginning to award favored entrepreneurs $50,000–100,000 grants to "plant the flag" where they choose. Some activity has been witnessed in the Caribbean, and it is hardly confined to traditional money-making industries such as textiles.

In 1987, overseas investments topped $200 million, which represented a huge increase form the $137 million reported for 1986. It was the North American investments that saw the greatest single increases, and interest in future investment in natural resources is likely to be witnessed in other Asian countries.

The domestic market will see more vibrant activity in some areas. Insurance, a relatively new field in all of Asia, is, according to *Korea Newsreview* in Seoul, a $3.5 billion market, and should grow substantially during the next few years. This is one of the celebrated service industries that is starting to open up to foreign companies.

Stock-market volumes are modest now, but show signs of advancing rapidly. It will take expertise as well as a readiness to accept some foreign penetration, but those markets withstood the global shakedowns seen during October 1987. No wonder that venture capital in the country appears poised for growth; originally, this was a province of the government, which had channeled about $20 to $30 million into a handful of companies. "We have been watching them closely," observes an official of the finance Ministry in Seoul. "While performance was not always what we hoped to see, I can tell you that they can still bring about the type of technology development which is essential for us." There is probably a total of $50 million devoted to a number of projects in the area.

At the same time, the impact of small business is an issue that has never been effectively dealt with. A surprise during the past year has been the strong measures taken to curb antitrust violations by the top *chaebol*—and even regulations such as antitrust provisions would have been considered improbable a few years ago. Specialized programs attempted since the mid-1980s provide hands-on customized treatment to small businesses selected for this type of assistance. Statistics on government financing and on terms of special loan programs are difficult to obtain since spending is carried out through the bevy of different agencies, but entities such as *The Asian Wall Street Journal* have estimated that spending to be about $200 million. One of the major questions that must be resolved by Korea, but for which there is only now emerging a body of hard research on either side of the Pacific, is how small business can "incubate" commercially viable products, spawn jobs, and make lasting contributions to national economic objectives.

The nation has conceded that housing, transportation, and pollution control are worthy objectives in the decade ahead. Lee-Jay Cho, who has directed a study on the Korean economy under way at Hawaii's East-West Center notes that "a momentous historical juncture" on the domestic issues lies ahead for the land of his birth.

One of the major obstacles to growth in the forthcoming decade will be redefining the social contract—and doing so in a highly politically-charged atmosphere. Many of the new methods of reaching agreement among executive and legislative branches remain untested. Reaching consensus on political decisions will be hardest in the area of social welfare. As the family unit comes under stress in a mobile, affluent society, it will be difficult to maintain the arrangements for family care of elderly citizens. Housing, health care, and forms of social security currently account for about a tenth of all spending by the central government. Larry Westphal and others believe that pressures for de facto minimum wages—not merely the informal company-union pacts that often fail to deliver a minimum wage—could prove a source of acrimony.

The nation need not fall prey to adapting Western social welfare concepts. It may be able to forge solutions more in keeping with its distinct heritage. And, institutional changes have been ushered in without coercion. The ascension of new leadership at major *chaebol* during the latter half of this decade is one promising sign. The first stirrings of a venture-capital market have also shown how adaptable the economy is to non-coercive change.

Korea approaches its seventh five-year plan in 1991. In keeping with the tenets of that blueprint, she is aggressively seeking trade with mainland China, and intends to end some reliance on the conglomerate powerhouses, prompting independent firms to make their contributions to national output. The structural transition that must be undertaken comes in tandem with currency adjustments, but a full 15 months after serious revaluation of the won, exports had not faltered.

This member of the Four Tigers would see exports soar to $230 billion by 1997. The only indicator that will decline, according to planners at Korea Development Institute, is the number of hours spent on the job, which should be 40 per week by the year 2000.

A 6–7 percent GNP growth per year would bring output to the $250 billion mark as the 21st century dawns. Per capita income for 50 million South Koreans by then would fall just short of $5,000, and the country would have achieved the status as the world's 15th-largest single economy. It would be an economy based on industry and manufacturing, with 35 percent of GNP derived from those sectors (compared to 27 percent now). Services would climb to 60 percent of the economy as opposed to 52 percent today. If Korea achieves the goal of converting foreign debt into surplus, it will add greatly to the republic's impact overseas.

The months since the Olympic Games have generated more accolades for Korea. Despite the well-publicized student unrest, and the stress of paying for enormous social, educational, and environmental projects, one has a sense the Korean's destiny will reflect the country's name.

5

Taiwan: Under All Flags

In order to appreciate some of the issues facing the Republic of China in the decade ahead, we have to examine the changing face of Asia itself (particularly the southeast region), the strained but interdependent global economy, and the growing sophistication and market size of Taiwan's industrial and productive base.

The bottom-to-top government planning that contrasts to centralized planning efforts in certain other countries will still be with Taiwan in the 1990s. These are worthy of passing reference because they stand as a prologue for the current and future chapters in the Taiwan saga. That future is generally a bright one if modest ambitions overcome bloated dreams. By 1990 Taiwan will have completed a major transition that will have placed it among the developed countries. In fact, this quantum jump would, were it not for Taiwan's firm ideological stand, serve as a model for Third World and least-developed countries. Components of this "Great Leap" are the key to everything happening around the island today.

American economic aid ended in 1965. Even the near-flawed economic policies suffered some blunders, as when export trade companies (modeled after Tokyo's *soga shosha*) were created in 1982. These organizations have yet to produce tangible results.

Most in the top brass cluster around a belief that more of medium and small business in the economy can be liberalized. A bureaucracy that relishes planning, projections, studies, and assessments of all sorts ("we got it from Stanford and Cambridge," a top economic planner said with glee) is leery of letting go of that planning mechanism too fast.

THE GREAT TRANSITION

When all projections, quotas and blueprints are finally tallied by the 1990s, a remarkable transformation should have been completed in Taiwan.

Building on their past achievements, Taiwan will be able to effect a healthy range of innovations without incurring trial and error costs. Success in this transition rests largely on the triad of electronics, petrochemicals, and machinery. All will depend on greater infusions of technology as the island abandons the labor-intensive mode prevalent during the pretransition years. Taiwan is certain to rely heavily on joint ventures and investments from abroad in the years ahead.

An electronics industry second among the newly industrialized countries to Korea's, the growth of Kao-hsiung as the leading Far East port, and political and economic inroads made across East Asia all secure continuation of the island as an autonomous entity. With the death in 1988 of Chiang Ching-kuo, son of the Nationalist leader, stability was maintained, the island passed a major political test.

Despite strong political rumblings, native Taiwanese—who saw their island occupied in 1949 by Chiang Kai-shek's fleeing forces—are winning a bigger voice in government to supplement the commercial input they were allowed early on. There are uncertainties, however. Taipei's strategy should emphasize diversification of its products, completion of its dozen major construction projects, and the smooth operation of its science technology center at Hsinchu, since adequate training is needed to ensure a labor force capable of mastering the transition. To keep growth rates ahead of inflation, many of the old fiscal and monetary policies will be maintained, but it is high economic development and improved living standards that stand as Taiwan's major arsenal in its goal of outpacing an inflated money supply.

The government is likely to fall short of its per capita income goals by as much as 10 percent when downturns in the Western trading patterns ripple back to the island. Look for an average income of some $5,700 to $5,900 per capita by 1992.

The Nationalist presence overseas was limited to agricultural assistance in the past. In the 1990s we will see medical teams pouring into the Arabian Peninsula and other parts of the world. More Taiwanese will be seen in Yembo and Jubail and other parts of the Persian Gulf, Central America and parts of the Caribbean.

For the first time, government authorities are allowing capital to flow out of the country as foreign travel is being encouraged. These changes symbolize an understanding of the need to reach across the seas that are

Taiwan's lifelines. Investments in other nations will increase halfway through this transition period. Through the oncoming transition, we will find that never before has a nation traded so much with so many yet remained recognized by so few.

Taipei seems to be aware of the new set of geopolitical equations that have been written in the wake of China's ascent, the uncertain health of the world financial order, and recent energy woes. Even a succession of mild downturns worldwide should not disrupt the island's vital export-import activity. Perhaps guest labor from the mainland can be exchanged for services vital to economic development of the People's Republic. Former California senator and world renowned semanticist S.I. Hayakawa is one of those who has made the point that if a true detente between both Chinas were to take place, the mainland could benefit greatly from the type of managerial skills that Taiwan could provide, thereby establishing the basis of truly complementary economies. The Republic of China is a young society, and like the mainland is welded together by morale and a social fiber that has largely disappeared in the West. The Confucian ideal has been a strong factor in past economic development, and that ideal will not be shaken in the next decade by outside intrusions or material gains.

Some of the sugar crop will be slated for gasohol production by the early 1990s. The type of technical experimentation now taking place on the island is very exciting and shows that people in both the public and private sectors in this truly balanced economy are willing to take innovations from overseas and adapt them for not only Taiwan itself but also for their Asian neighbors. This rapport should guarantee that, regardless of events in trouble spots around the globe, Taiwan should be able to maintain its supply of raw materials. The recent discovery of manganese nodules at depths that make mining feasible will also assist many aspects of industrial growth.

After its early success with labor-intensive goods in the global export markets, Taiwan began to give careful attention to its infrastructure. Services, banking, communications, internal transportation systems, and steps to assist businesses were all improved. The most recent lift-off of this economy was in 1977, after recovery from the 1973–74 oil shock. The shift in exports from light to more sophisticated goods, with industrial products making up 90 percent of the outgoing trade, is evidence of a change from raw and processed farm products. Even the textiles sold abroad rely on synthetic fibers to a great extent, and the style of these goods adapted to Western fashion after a textile research center was completed on the island. Today, electrical machinery makes up $3 billion in exports, while metal machinery exports are valued at half that amount.

Taiwan's products, ordinarily ridiculed as copycat knockoffs, have moved out of the five-and-dime category and are now inching along toward Fifth Avenue. This flexibility and diversification were inevitable. "They realized the handwriting was on the wall," declares Joe Kyle of the Washington office of the American Institute on Taiwan, which is the U.S. diplomatic mission to the island. "Even Indonesia and the Philippines were coming up in the picture and starting to produce some of the same items. In Taiwan, there had to be another way for the future."

While the government has stayed in utilities, and will do so through this century, sales of some other enterprises were in keeping with a policy that retained state control over those sectors either needing large cash transfusion or having no potential for short-term gains. The blend of limited government activity plus active private initiative saw production triple and quadruple in metals, chemicals, petroleum, machinery, and other economic building blocks.

The end of Taipei's six-year plan (in 1993) should see an average 8 percent growth rate for each 12-month period, a drop from the 12 percent and 14 percent rates experienced in the recent past. Paramount in the plan are a dozen new projects that essentially consolidate and refine earlier development. An expansion of China Steel Corporation, two more atomic energy plants, additions to Taichung harbor, a round-the-island railroad, and new planned communities are all in store. Drainage improvements and construction of river levees are part of this package, too, and show that the agricultural sector has not been ignored.

In the transition era, the Republic of China will be in a better position to explore the whole shelf of technical advances, even though they will not always pick up the most sophisticated techniques in every sphere. How will this occur? For one thing, greater linkage between economic and commercial sectors will be possible as the processes of tech transfer become more widespread. With small business in dire need of modernization, a beefed up system of facilitating technology transfers, distribution networks, and other features of dynamic, flexible business methods are vital. Reliance on devices such as the fledgling and scandal-rocked bourse have proved insufficient, both as fund-raiser and as an impetus for market-driven development.

The major private industrial corporations already are equipped with R&D facilities and ties to competent academics and technocrats. As a team, they can gauge the demands on both trade and domestic ledgers to assess the costs and benefits of projected products. At the same time, commercial prospects are weighed alongside the technical features of a product. In the decade ahead, Taiwan's serious brain drain may be reversed, with Western- and U.S.-trained scientists returning in substantial numbers to the island.

The Kao-hsiung steel center has advanced pollution abatement equipment that harmonizes growth with respect for nature. In polluted Taiwan, that is important. The environmental price tag on the island hovers in the billions—and is a dark side of recent growth in this congested island. The plant was made possible by technology transfer and assures high-quality, low-polluting production in a time when competitor nations are beginning to grapple with ecological questions.

Industrial giants such as Formosa Chemical and Fiber, Formosa Plastic, Sampo Electric, and Far Eastern Textile also have been successful in installing new designs, methods, and processes that boost overall productivity. Meanwhile, a serene labor picture, albeit enforced by government mandate, circumvents featherbedding.

While most companies lack the ability to maximize use of capital, machinery, and manpower, some strides were seen in the ability to adapt to borrowed methods. The energetic capabilities of indigenous software firms are showing that the island republic may spawn its own R&D, craft its own designs, and best both Western and East Asian competition in selective niche markets. Heavy industry appears, generally, less imaginative, yet the automaker Yue Loong today is willing, and prepared, for Taiwan's own Great Leap Forward.

Taiwan will secure more consulting work from the West in this decade. Bechtel, Westinghouse, and other top U.S. groups will be regular passengers in the L.A.-to-Taipei air corridor. Firms from France and Italy are scheduled for the same destination, streaking to the island from the opposite direction but with similar purposes in mind. As this is happening, Taiwanese consulting presence will be felt in the LDCs; no other pretransition or transition country will be at the hub of consulting input/output. As could be expected, the Republic of China teams will advise other nations on the methods they themselves learned and applied a decade ago.

If Taiwan neglects R&D in agriculture, the error will be grievous. The Asian Vegetable Research Institute outside Kao-hsiung, however, attests to her commitment in agriculture, which was used in the 1950s "land to the tillers" policy as a means of bootstrapping the then-nonexistent economic base. (Certainly, "Made in Taiwan" foreign aid programs have assisted farming ventures in disparate Third World locales from West Africa to Central America.) New medicines, some derived from People's Republic of China-produced herbs presently finding their way into island ports, can be a linchpin for transitionalized agriculture. Here is another field where transfer of innovation is important, since Western drug manufacturing and pharmaceutical techniques lead the world.

There are conflicting reports on the potential of aquaculture, yet a crisis in the world food supply, with a need for more protein from non-meat sources, argues for a stronger research effort. Fish farming techniques have been successful in other nations, and the future in Taiwan should see much R&D in aquacultural experimentation.

Improvements in water, sewage, rural roadways, public housing, health centers, and along the undeveloped eastern side of the island are in store. For this part of the country, livestock breeding, silk, tea, pulp, and fishing are also planned. While industry represents today just over half the economic base, it will grow to over 70 percent during the decade. Agriculture, now a tenth of the economy, is destined for 5 percent of the share; services will remain about the same at a third. Manufacturing, according to recent data, and industrial sectors must grow at about 10 percent each year in the decade, and with foresight, they can. The degree to which the economy, which still revolves around trade, can diversify its products and markets will determine if the various sectors can pull their weight.

Taiwan's location along the shipping lanes that bind America with the ASEAN mineral storehouse and other natural resources make it a good candidate to become a petrochemicals giant. Rapport with Middle East suppliers, especially Kuwait and the Saudi rulers in Riyadh, should secure a steady supply of fossil fuels. If oil finds in the Philippines are substantial, Taiwan's position in this industry will be on an even more solid footing. Petrochemicals received heavy governmental support even during the pretransition years, and will continue to play an important role as an employer and income-producer for the republic in the years ahead.

Taiwanese leaders envisioned electronics as a major industry during the 1960s, but they were unclear whether to concentrate on one type of product, such as portable television sets, or a multitude of products. The consumer electronics empire built at a special economic zone at the port of Kao-hsiung during the 1970s attests to both the strength of policies innaugurated by the Nationalist regime, as well as the potential of export-driven strategies during that era. But, the years ahead—characterized by surpluses, competition among the East Asian Tigers (or, Dragons), and the lack of potent engines driving the economies of (Western) customers for "Made in Taiwan" goods—could all disrupt linchpins of the island's development.

FOREIGN INVESTMENT

Taiwan is following in Japan's footsteps and committing vast sums in direct foreign investment to construct factories and textile plants, and purchase technology-based industries. This recent trend marks Asia's second major thrust into North America after Tokyo-based multinationals began their headlong rush to invest billions in factories in real estate during the mid-1980s.

Although small by comparison, the Republic of China is turning its unique dilemma—cash reserves as high as $80 billion—into an opportunity to forge new relationships with its often-reluctant American ally. Those new relationships are as much political as commercial. By creating goodwill in the United States, this prosperous—yet diplomatically isolated—island neutralizes some criticisms about formerly closed markets. Taiwan tallied a $15.8 billion trade surplus with the U.S. in 1986, and final figures for 1987 were over $18 billion. In any future showdown between the two Chinas, support from America would be critical to Taiwan's position.

The scope of this investment surge includes textiles in Georgia, facilities owned by China Steel, Tatung electronics plants, and electricity-generating projects by the utility Taipower. There are 10 moderately sized Formosa Plastics factories. Petroleum industries in North America are being considered as candidates for infusion of cash. Across the stretch of Maquiledora "twin plants" from Arizona to East Texas (where manufacturing is divided between labor-intensive Mexican plants employing 300,000 and automated plants in the U.S. side), Taiwan's presence is also felt. Sources in both Washington and Taipei confirm that there is now upward of $1.25 billion worth of direct investment in the United States.

That amount will grow. The reason is that a parade of states, and some cities, touring Taiwan will bypass Japan as they seek investment from the Pacific Rim. Jimmy Lyles, president of the Corpus Christi, Texas Chamber of Commerce, believes his city's growing bilateral ties are "a natural evolution." In order to promote economic development, Lyles and the Chamber began an outreach effort last summer. "Tangible results came pretty soon," as we shall see below.

Other states are following the same tactic, and not all are recovering from depression in the Oil Patch. The roster of states with headquarters in the towering Taipei World Trade Center includes Arizona, Colorado, Oregon, Washington, Maryland, and Illinois.

The Maquiledora strategy gains Taiwan valuable political points. Labor costs in electronics in the Rio Grande Valley are $4.27–$5.19 an hour, about double Singapore's $2.32 and over twice as much as Hong Kong's $2.02 in comparable industries. Yet, when electricity rates, rent, and freight charges are added in, savings range from 1–10 percent over those three nations and over Taiwan as well. Ironically, the increasingly affluent East Asian nations are losing their low-wage advantages rapidly. The "touch labor" factor is not as important as it was before recent strides in automation, yet by producing in North America, future protectionist statutes can be avoided.

At the American Institute on Taiwan, some expect the equivalent of upward of $1 billion to be channeled into the U.S. during 1988. Taiwan's liaison offices in the U.S. say that high-tech items and goods Taiwan doesn't produce at home receive priority. Petroleum industries are being considered.

Another alternative for cash-rich Taiwan is to order more purchases during its regularly scheduled U.S. buying missions. The 1987 mission resulted in $600 million worth of orders, and the annual event is considered good politics—with sensitive states targeted—as well as a means of reducing the protectionist clamor in America.

At the same time that Taiwan is increasing its purchases of U.S. goods, it is attempting to foster long-term company-to-company relationships that can assist in forging joint-venture projects, especially in technology-related fields. Since 1979, some $10.5 billion worth of made-in-U.S. goods have been purchased in official "buy America" missions. "As Taiwan makes more concessions on copyrights and liberalizes to allow American companies to invest on reasonable terms," says Mark van Fleet, director of Asia-Pacific affairs at the U.S. Chamber of Commerce, "her investments here will grow."

The impact of some investments is substantial. For example, one Taiwanese project is Corpus Christi's Project Bullwinkle—the world's largest offshore oil rig. Dr. An Wang, the computer magnate, has inaugurated a $500 million investment pool whose purpose is to investigate solid sunrise industry possibilities in both countries.

A recent government spending package earmarked $8–10 billion for domestic projects. "There is demand to spend on 'quality of life' issues," says America's long-term envoy in Taiwan, Joseph Kyle. Infrastructure, pollution abatement, and completion of a subway line for congested Taipei are needed.

Taiwan's foreign exchange surplus is an embarrassment of riches. When it reached $40 billion in 1986, outdistancing West Germany's tally, it prompted many trading partners to clamor for currency realignment. This stash of foreign reserves could pay in 1988 for 24 months' worth of imports; by comparison, Japan's reserves would pay for 10 weeks' worth of purchases.

New Taiwan Dollars (NTD) are currently valued at 34 to the U.S. dollar. The official line in Taipei is that it is being appreciated, but U.S. government spokespersons insist that efforts to move that ratio to 29:1 must be stepped up. While America's balance-of-payments deficit with Taiwan is soaring above the $17 billion tallied in 1988, the foreign reserve horde in this East Asian country could prove to be a negative. In an embarassing attempt to lower the trade deficit with the U.S., Taipei began to purchase large ($1 billion-plus) stores of gold. She is prepared to engage in other tactics which, on paper, will reduce surpluses with other friendly nations, whose goodwill is vital to her continuance as a nation-state.

Both situations give Washington a heavy stick in negotiating with Taiwan for further currency realignment. Taiwan resists immediate action on several counts, insisting that tight curbs on money leaving the islands were necessary. The Central Bank argues that inflation would take off unless controls are tight. Further appreciation of the NTD is expected in the medium term. New regulations allow banks to send foreign currency abroad and have enabled U.S.-based credit cards to be used with few limits by the island's 19 million inhabitants.

ISSUES FOR TAIWANESE MANAGEMENT

The managerial revolution sweeping the Republic of China is a microcosm of the larger whirlwind sweeping companies across the region. Contrary to the image held by their counterparts in North America, East Asian managers make mistakes, suffer setbacks in attempts to implement "just in time" manufacturing techniques, and are constrained by the quarterly report syndrome. "They are facing issues like training and control of departments," says Steven Carroll, a former consultant with Black and Decker in Taiwan. "To some extent, relationships among managers at all levels are undergoing fundamental changes."

An array of new issues confront even the most successful Asian companies. Steward Veel, division manager for international affairs at the American Management Association, was in charge of the association's programs in Taipei. "These countries are coming to realize that certain employee backgrounds are not always appropriate for administrative tasks," he says.

The advent of automation and more recently, of office automation, is having a profound effect on issues such as worker motivation and on the regrouping of existing corporate hierarchies, especially where family-owned businesses have held sway. A tight reign over internal practices (as well as over the flow of information) is evident.

Consider the extent of change now surfacing in major manufacturing companies in increasingly affluent, export-minded Taiwan. The old guard is disappearing, while more U.S.-educated mid-level executives are coming to the helm. Companies are becoming internationalized. As East Asia seeks value-added products, their dealings with Western and Japanese transnational corporations must increase. "These managers have seen the work force in several countries," says Veel. "They have a better understanding about motivating employees."

Multinationals like Philips, Seiko, and Hewlett-Packard are leaving their imprint on Taiwan and on her fellow Tigers, since the four newly industrializing countries require massive infusions of foreign expertise (and automation equipment). This, according to W.S. Lin, president of Tatung, the Taiwanese electronics giant, is leading to "some blending" of East and West. "Improved working conditions are becoming more common," he notes. This "blending" emphasizes quality circles (born in the West but more widely used in the East) with greater acceptance of women in authority, for example.

"It will take us time to adjust to the way that Eastern and Western styles are coming together," declares "Eddy" Tao, president of Taiwan's Nova Marine Industries, one company that opened operations in the Caribbean. "In many ways, our company, and other companies looking at international business, were unprepared for these changes."

While Tiger-based companies ponder ways of implementing computer-integrated manufacturing (and are at about equal stages of implementation when compared to counterparts outside Asia), office automation is just beginning. Even in Japan, most memos and business correspondence are handwritten. Numbers of word processors and similar electronic gear were compiled in 1987 by Hong Kong-based Office Automation Asia, a consulting firm. Singapore and Malaysia have only 15,000 or so electric typewriters each. Hong Kong has about 20,000 printers linked to office computers, and that number will increase. "More responsibility is given to our office professional staff," says Boo Kheng Hua of Singapore's Applied Technologies, a robotics company. "In the office, staff must learn to make more decisions on their own."

While these Tiger economies are free-market oriented, all with the exception of ultra laissez faire Hong Kong rely to varying degrees on government direction. Resulting red tape has contributed to a reluctance to adopt automation, according to many experts.

One common thread in Taiwan, as in the other three Tigers, is that outside consultants are shunned. Whether in the office or on the factory floor, calculating return on investment is a perplexing problem. "None of their companies have all the match down," says John Barry, director of The Forum, automation specialists in Milwaukee. "What they have is a sense of simplicity. While the U.S. sees complexity" and its managers respond by computerization, "Asians are willing to see the same complexity and try to simplify the problem."

In the foursome, simply identifying key people to manage strides toward computerization and computer-integrated manufacturing is difficult. What helps many companies in the transition is the sheer number of hours all workers spend on the job—and the dedication that prompts weekend shifts at no overtime bonus.

Executives at Taiwanese companies receive guidance through a network of automation centers that seek to overcome lethargy on the part of tradition-bound family businesses. "What helps them out is the fact that there's a very high proportion of advanced degrees in engineering," says Stewart Veel at the American Management Association. Estimates are that in machinery, electronics, and a few other sectors, automated equipment spending per employee is nearing the $2,000 mark—a huge jump from 1984–85 levels. In Taiwan, two factors will continue to aid automation. These are the notion of planning before production and strict adherence to the target cost concept.

Company initiatives are assisted by R&D matching funds, tax credits, and government loan packages. "Downstream of engineering commodities and upstream high tech are goals that … justify individual company efforts," says Jia-Ming Shyu, executive secretary of the automation committee at the Ministry of Economic Affairs. Here as elsewhere in the region, Western and Japanese guidance is counted upon to help firms pass through early stages of automation and inventory control.

W.S. Lin, president of consumer electronics manufacturing giant Tatung, is promoting "autonomous management" among fellow Taiwanese corporation leaders. So-called "quality control/quality thinking circles" are the cornerstone of his philosophy. Tatung is an employee-owned corporation, but Lin feels the concept is years away from general acceptance in his country.

THE QUEST FOR HIGH TECH

Diplomatically isolated yet commercially intertwined, tiny Taiwan continues its march toward a post-industrial society, aiming for a place in the planet's high-tech sun. With limited space under the sun's rosy glow, many nations hope to shine in the radiance of tomorrow's industries, and failure to earn a spot could bring economic eclipse.

In the type of global economy we are entering, high tech is an ambitious goal for Taiwan—but a quest essential for survival. While the island has performed miracles in the past, this drive requires a higher degree of cohesion, entrepreneurial verve, bureaucratic savvy, and sheer luck. Pitted against the Republic of China are an array of competitors—most likely Korea and Singapore, and possibly Hong Kong, despite the uncertainty over its status. All three countries, like Taiwan, have prospered through an export-driven economy. Should Taiwan's capitalistic neighbors take too big a share of the "Third Wave" prizes, she will not be posed for a transformation from the industrial to the post-industrial era. In successful, highly competitive East Asia, that would be disastrous.

Steel production is on the upswing, and the China Steel facilities that Taipei controls are at full capacity. Although only about 3 million tons are currently produced, a billion-dollar modernization plan will expand capacity until 1990. Production per employee rivals the level seen in Japan. Pechiney, the French metals group, may buy Taiwan aluminum, which should give the Republic of China greater access to European processes—and an infusion of know-how to bolster an unspectacular operation. A number of events show that the Taiwanese are seriously planning their great leap into the next century. For example, a $400 million World Trade Center opened in 1986. Located in Taipei, this ultra-modern 30-story, 3.5-million-square-foot facility will house exhibit areas and other space for exporters and importers.

Officials in Taipei hint that their goal is to transform their island into the transshipment center of East Asia. To this end, shipping and airline activity will increase, with existing Pacific transportation links improved. The new International Investment Trust Company will be a vehicle for opening the stock exchange to foreigners and raising funds for high-tech firms. The market has an estimated $7–10 billion in capitalization, but has experienced reverses, which point to a need for closer oversight to assure accurate and honest accounting procedures.

Hsinchu, a 2,000-hectare science and industrial park some 80 km from Taipei, is an important cog in the high-tech scheme. This planned community environment patterned on the Silicon Valley model is directed by Dr. Irving Ho, a former semiconductor R&D specialist with Hewlett-Packard. A five-year tax holiday is granted to companies, and can be granted within the first nine years of operation. (After the holiday, a 22 percent ceiling is in place.) Materials science, precision instruments, and even aeronautics are given the red-carpet treatment. Hsinchu is paying off in big dividends already. IBM, Hewlett-Packard, Digital, Qume, Wang, and other high-tech firms have set up shop. The park, the first of its kind in Asia, is part of a master plan to place the island in first place among the Four Dragons in computers.

Hsinchu saw over U.S. $100 million invested in the park since 1983. A scant $8 million worth of products were exported in 1981, but five times as much was exported a year later. The figure reached $100 million in 1983, and in 1987, nearly $900 million in products were shipped from this mini Silicon Valley. Foreigners are drawn to the site by what Dr. Ho sees as a desire to carve out East Asian markets and prospects of joint ventures with Taiwanese groups. Even bioengineering and futuristic projects such as electric autos are taking root at Hsinchu.

Steps to improve training include a doubling since 1977 of the number of advanced students enrolled at special centers in engineering, biology, chemistry, and physics. Last year, 460 left those centers, having completed their highly technical training. A cadre of over 200 students is on campus abroad—half in the U.S., where the "brain drain" takes its toll, and about 40 more are in Western Europe. In addition to Hsinchu, there is a precision instrument center and geothermal power plant on the East Coast. In 1982, over 8,000 graduates on the island were awarded advanced degrees in electrical and electronic engineering, twice as many as in the other three "Dragons" combined. By 1986, that figure rose to over 21,000, with the island still holding a comfortable lead over its rivals.

Electronics made up nearly $4 billion worth of exports in 1983, and computers (hardware and software) tallied $500 million. The island is a leading terminal and monitor exporter already. By 1989, this sector should be a third of an expanded electronics export pie (of $14 billion). Taiwanese computer parts and peripheral equipment cost a third less than the U.S. price tag, and salaries for engineers are about a fourth the U.S. level in most categories.

Computer clones abound. *The Far Eastern Economic Review* reports that Compaq's new 32-bit desktop was cloned by local firms in two months. The U.S. Department of Commerce asserts that, while a scant $5 million worth of products and peripherals were sold abroad in 1980, the amount surpassed the $3 billion mark in 1987, for a 600-fold increase in just six years. Over 40,000 direct jobs are not stemming from the computer industry, with Multitek, Mitac, and other byproducts of new venture capital arrangements surviving Asia's high-tech wars.

There are problems confronting Taiwanese high-tech companies. Aid from government and banks has been limited, R&D is criticized as inadequate, and barely 1 percent of GNP goes for science. Compounding matters, a proliferation of small firms tends to fragment the industry. Yet, the Republic of China has overcome many hurdles to emerge as a titan on the world trade scene. "It is a very challenging period for us," says Kwang Shih-chan, chairman of the China External Trade Development Council. A breakthrough on Chinese language capabilities would boost the industry.

A limited domestic market mandates exports in software as well as in peripherals. Kao Chao-hsun, president of the country's Software Association, feels that the best strategy is to concentrate on software for personal computers. "That market is big, and software is easy to make, so programs for these machines can pioneer our exports," he explains. Computer exports reached U.S. $205 million in 1983, double the level of the previous year. The figure for 1990 should exceed $3 billion.

Taiwan is able to stake out a share of the integrated-circuit market, but Korea is close behind in identical products. For example, recent government investigations in chip and in semiconductor design firms may yield paybacks once the appetite for chips expands in the 1990s. By 1992, according to Dataquest, the domestic need for these "smart" devices will nearly double the $1.25 billion worth consumed in 1988. Some early plans for an assault on the global computer markets were scrapped. One idea was to develop hospital management software for export, but it was dropped after a realization that varying managerial schemes would make for radically different software—and mandate extensive research into differing national conditions. Wang Chao-ming, vice minister of economic affairs, believes that some foreign companies will agree to joint ventures, tapping consulting experience as well as the lower wage rates in Taiwan. "The Western companies have sales networks, and working with a reputable firm would show that our products have assured quality." Another plan is to develop interchangeable operating systems, thereby enabling Taiwan to reach a truly global market.

Copyrights on software and related products and on published materials will be respected, assure Taiwanese authorities. One government official claims strict policing began in 1985 and that arrests are taking place. If these efforts are unsuccessful, retaliation from the U.S. and Europe for continued piracy will hurt Taiwan.

Taipei views its high-tech quest as a culmination of R&D efforts in several fields. "We are not hedging any bets," a cautious computer company executive says, "and we have to move rapidly in each of these in order to reach a level for growth for strategic industries." One program covers design, research, and manufacture of integrated circuits and their applications. Numerically controlled machine tools are receiving attention, while an experimental small-scale distillation column has been installed as part of a project on process-control applications of microprocessors. In that program, design of a modified software system flowchart is a priority item. Semiconductor devices were developed in Taiwan recently that resulted in a new type of bipolar transistor.

Conditions on the island are ideal for electric vehicles. Road conditions are such that few stretches of highway allow for high-speed driving (which electrics do not hold up well to), and motorists are not in danger of being stranded far from charging stations for great distances between towns or cities.

A project to lift electrics off the drawing boards has been under way since 1978. Dr. Ru-yih Sun, a Ph.D. graduate in solid-state physics from Purdue University in the U.S., leads the drive. "Electric-powered cars are one possible option for not only our country, but for others in this part of the world," he says. He may be right.

Prototypes were developed by 1980 by Tsing Hua University teams working with scientists from the metals industry. Their proving ground was the Science and Technology Park at Hsinchu. Telecommunications and postal vehicles are already using one model, the THEV (Tsing Hua Electric Vehicle) IV. This car seats four, with additional space for cargo. With two passengers 225 kg of cargo can also be carried.

Specialists opted for use of lead-acid batteries rather than nickel-zinc batteries. "We found," says Dr. Sun, "that nickel-zinc gives three times the energy density, but decided to emphasize life-cycles to achieve longer battery durability." The batteries can be recharged from 300–400 times, and a range of 100–120 km is possible at speeds of 70 kmh.

Taiwan hopes to produce 20,000 of these vehicles next year. Already, hundreds are on the road, and most use a system of eight 96-volt batteries weighing 292.5 kg. They turn a 90-hp motor at a maximum speed of 6,000 rpm. A four-speed transmission is featured, and acceleration from 0–56 kmh takes nine seconds.

THE FUTURE

The thrust into high technology is producing other tangible gains in this egalitarian society. (As far back as the 1960s, the top fifth of the population and the bottom fifth had less difference in wealth than was found anywhere outside the avowedly Marxist bloc. Per capita income rose by nearly 20 percent from 1986–87, when the level reached $4,000.)

The similarities between Korea and Taiwan are apparent: both have sizable domestic markets; both share a common geopolitical stance; both are forging ahead under the Confucianist-capitalist brand of economic development. Yet the difference between the two countries comes through the divergent paths adopted in the 1960s and reinforced during the 1970s. Taiwan chose a small-business, light-industry strategem while competing Tiger Korea decided on the heavy-industry formula, with autos, steel, and shipbuilding forming a far bigger core of growth, under the guidance of major conglomerates.

Some of these factors strongly affect relationships with joint-venture partners from the West. The financial infrastructure is stronger in Korea, and that country is not bedeviled by complex diplomatic constraints, which will see Taiwan remain isolated through most of the next decade. Countries within Asia and outside the Far East still pick the mainland over Taiwan, for obvious reasons. Beijing imposes a one-China policy, and none dare offend the Chinese. Equally significant is the apparent loss of loyalty from the potent community of overseas Chinese, whose ethnic communities span Europe, East Africa, and the Western Hemisphere.

Just as in the case of Hong Kong and Singapore, the island republic is seeking application-specific chips. A small band of new entrepreneurial companies are working feverishly to perfect their own designs because U.S. and European businesses are reluctant to work with Taiwanese firms, which have a reputation for copyright theft in technology. There are a few large assembly plants, with clean rooms and state-of-the-art facilities, where the kernel of advanced semiconductor production is to germinate. Probably $1.5 billion worth of plant construction since 1987 will house homegrown companies that seek to be in the vanguard of the next high-tech waves. More is planned, including a $200 million hard disk assembly plant.

Apart from Hsinchu—where 70 technology-based companies are active—there is the old port of Kao-hsiung, which gave birth to the household consumer-electronics products boom of the 1970s. Across the island, incentives are being streamlined in order to draw more Western companies that can contribute to the incubation of indigenous companies. One exciting sign that the Taiwanese are shifting away from cloning to true innovation came when plans were unveiled in 1986 to construct prefabricated plants, comparable to Japanese-built "floating factories."

To secure the transformation through the 1990s, Taiwan still needs massive infusions of technology and capital. Cheap labor is no longer a feature of economic life there. The other Dragons are competing vigorously in order to compete for foreign branch plants and factories. Another competitor, of course, is the People's Republic. China believes it can always dangle contracts or otherwise tantalize foreigners, and thereby take a considerable share of industrial expansion away from Taiwan.

The "pie" of foreign investment is shrinking, making these contests far more critical than in the past. They are also more critical because of the force of rising economic expectations on the part of all of East Asia's population. As we saw in the first chapter, the evidence suggests that what was formerly a torrent of direct foreign investment has been reduced to a trickle, in response to conditions of modern manufacturing and other trends in global production. The island is involved in a protracted war, or rather a pair of protracted struggles. One is internal, and involves the contradictions that underlie formation of the self-proclaimed "Republic of China," in essence imposing a benign occupation upon the native populace. The second involves an ongoing struggle against mainland Chinese objectives, an effort to retain a political identity. Investment and trade are inexorably connected with both struggles.

New domestic investments are continuing in order to upgrade products. For example, one plan calling for a total investment of $2.5 billion to develop Taiwan's chemicals industry in the next 10 years has been drawn up by the industrial development advisory council of the Ministry of Economic Affairs. If implemented, the scheme will allow the island's chemicals makers to produce value-added, specialized chemicals for use in the electronic, automotive, and information industries.

The key points of the plan include: listing chemicals that are assessed as productive for incentive industries; making investment in certain chemicals eligible for benefits extended to government-designated strategic industries; and encouraging manufacturers of petrochemical intermediates to move their factories to nations with abundant oil and gas. With a third of the total output concentrated in petrochemicals, this new plan is important.

Trade is highly dependent on special arrangements—or the perception of them—on the part of the U.S. In May 1988, a scandal rocked the Washington diplomatic community when it was learned that the government in Taipei sought to reduce the trade deficit with their American allies by purchasing vast stores of gold, possibly as much as $1 billion worth, and then use the purchases to distort actual export-import data. It is with the EEC that the island places much of its faith for future growth markets. In 1987, a 70 percent increase in commerce was seen with Western European nations. West Germany accounted for nearly a third of that two-way trade, and other industrialized nations on the continent brought the volume of trade to $11 billion. Although South America and Africa were once hailed as markets for the Taiwanese, the ever-expanding debt crisis prevents Asians from making serious inroads to either region.

The Taiwanese, who will number 23.5 million in just 11 years, will see their lives changed in countless ways as the great transition continues. Despite their affluence (and per capita income is seen as being in the $8,000–9,500 range by then), serious quality-of-life issues confront the island. A 54-mile subway system in Taipei is desperately needed now, but will not open until 1993. With 1,400 people crammed into each square mile, pressures have forced many to support the first rumblings of an environmental movement to protest plans to construct more refineries and nuclear utilities.

The liberalization of the economy, and steps to end government ownership of monopolies in energy, plastics, steel, and other industries, comes just as Western Europe and the U.S. are succeeding in demands for major currency realignment. Social forces are stirring, too, as years of intense relationships with the West usher in a yearning for women's rights. The political succession of 1988, a de facto abandonment of the Three No's (no talks, no contacts, no compromise) regarding the mainland, and the vanishing of a Republic of China mythology are all overwhelming changes that come just as fundamental restructuring is occurring on Taiwan at many levels.

Taiwan must now grapple with new problems, the problems of success. She is in the position of being too advanced to take advantage of remaining opportunities in labor intensive industries, yet too far behind in the technology pool to leapfrog competitors in Singapore or in the Republic of Korea. She is largely a captive of whims of many foreign investors—all of whom eagerly eye post-Deng reforms on archrival China.

A large number of her highly-trained, well-educated students are overprepared for actual jobs that await them. An enormous bill must be paid to undo the effects of long-standing pollution. A determined environmental clean-up program would spare the republic as a dumping ground for greater infusions of hazardous wastes. (Recall its chemical and petrochemical economic foundations of the 1970s, a legacy that may prove to have yielded short-term gains with substantial long-range social as well as economic costs.)

And, with a growing population, and the diplomatic setbacks encountered since the 1970s, she must seriously consider a rapprochement with the former foe (who would gain mightily from Taiwanese strides in every industrial and scientific sector). "The two may actually build a natural complementary arrangement," admonished S.I. Hayakawa in 1982. (At the same time, the rulers in Taipei are faced with strong sentiment on the part of the native Taiwanese movement. The Nationalists allowed natives to rise in finance and business, thereby satisfying a demand for some degree of autonomy. Taiwanese are fearful of annexation by the mainland, and deeply resent the specter of any "foreign" occupation.)

Other political hurdles remain if the great economic transition can be realized. The Koumintang, or KMT, allowed considerable liberalization and democratization to take place, and was praised in 1987 for fair nationwide elections. Another round of accolades followed last year during the transition that came after Chiang Ching-kuo's death (he had been son of Chiang Kai-chek). But voices for even greater reforms are rising. "During the 35 years or so the KMT held Taiwan in authoritarian sway," noted *The Asian Wall Street Journal* in 1988, "the connections between government and KMT enterprises were talked about only in whispers. But as democracy takes hold ... the KMT financial network is becoming an embarrassment." That "network" spans several monopolies—and provides rewards for 7,000 functionaries as well as 400 community centers.

How close will the two Chinas become? What chance for synergy is there in the decade ahead? Will peaceful resolution take the place of conflict? Three decades ago, artillery bursts roared across the Straits of Quemoy. These were replaced by canon blasts—with propaganda leaflets, not shells—in the 1970s. "You may find pragmatists on both sides working quietly, slowly, to form a solution," notes Dr. Parris Chang at Pennsylvania State University. Chang, who is among the few with access to the very top political leadership in both countries, thinks that "the changing of the old guard in both countries" is a healthy sign, and gradual improvements in relations are likely. "There is still a faction on the mainland ... with the goal of creating another special region, modeled after Hong Kong," he concludes, "but how far they go depends as much on events, such as exactly how strong political ties are with the United States, if those ties are still in effect in any meaningful way ... in East Asia itself."

Cautious relationships were established between the two Chinas. Dr. Frederick Chien, until recently Taipei's envoy to the United States (where Taiwan is recognized not a political entity but as a quasi-geographic one), once proclaimed his people ready to supply military aid to support any insurrection on the mainland. Ten years later, this attitude has disappeared from top levels of the Nationalist regime.

Two-way trade between both Chinas was as high as $50 million in 1982, but has risen to some $1.5 billion in less than five years. Some of the complementary commerce envisioned by Hayakawa, while then a

Senator from California, took place in 1988 when the state-run utility, Taipower, purchased 20 million tons of Chinese coal.

Economic challenges ahead include assuring a vibrant small-business sector, ending dependency on the U.S. market (where 45 percent of exports end up), and devising a formula for privatization (about a tenth of the GNP is the province of government corporations). Social mores, too, are intertwined with the pace of development: Women are becoming a force in the society, and, as is true in Hong Kong, their real opportunities are increasing. Whether Western cultural values are transposed too quickly and whether women's ascent can be reconciled with tenets of current Confucianism are questions to be answered as the dawn of the Asian Century approaches.

6

Hong Kong: The Challenge
Before 1997

There is no other place quite like it. Bustling brawling, cosmopolitan—with all the dangers and opportunities that befit great
cities—exotic, a town frantically carving out new niches for itself and
seldom content to rest on the laurels of bygone days. Will this dynamic
character change when Hong Kong is formally ceded back to China in
1997. The citizenry has been taking an emotional roller coaster ride since
1982, when the People's Republic unilaterally announced the shift.
Initially, guarantees about the economic system, press freedom, and
other issues seemed to assure continuation of the territory-cum-colony's
status. However, uncertainty has arisen, largely because of shifting
policy on the continuation of free elections. Yet William Dorward, until
this year Hong Kong's commissioner for North America, is buoyant.
"The old argument that China won't disrupt things still holds. Hong
Kong is too valuable for China's own trade, for her own advancement
into the next century."

There is another question to be asked of Hong Kong's future, the same
question asked in developing and developed countries alike: Will Hong
Kong be able to remain competitive in a world where product life cycles
have dwindled from years to mere months and in which technology is
transferred in seconds not in decades?

Some experts also wonder about Hong Kong's own thrust into the
postindustrial economy. The colony was guided by a zealous determination to master trade, and it succeeded well, developing into an unrivaled
center of commerce—but it may not be preparing for the coming great
shifts in the Asia-Pacific economy. The unabashedly non-interventionist

approach to business has worked well, but the transition from ultra-small small business (most are launched on under $1 million in capitalization) requires a new synergy, with some degree of guidance from central entities able to gauge the demands of an ultra-customized global economy.

Hong Kong's manufacturing base has prospered well on a get-rich-quick philosophy that provides global markets with prompt turnaround on consumer items. But without strides toward automation, and by delaying development of more sophisticated industries such as precision tools, continued high-growth rates are in doubt. While serving as "the gateway to China," Hong Kong has seen much potential investment—in fields such as in biotechnology—drift to the mainland, bypassing her own far more skilled work force.

Many influential men and women in Hong Kong concede that the question of such structural change may dwarf even the question of what will occur in 1997. To understand the challenge ahead, consider the progress the congested territory has made in a short time.

She was destined for trade. Hong Kong is comprised of 200 islands scattered about the stormy southern Chinese coast. When China was closed to outsiders, Hong Kong could serve as a listening post.

As a result of three separate treaties with Britain (1841–98), she lost her sovereignty. Few in Great Britain recognized the port's potential, yet the territory served various European masters ranging from Portugal to Holland, in their respective quests for the often-elusive China trade. Chinese immigrants found shelter from political chaos at home. The 33,000 people tallied in 1851 mushroomed into nearly a million before war clouds covered the Pacific in the late 1930s.

The British legacy—a reliable communications system, a solid infrastructure, a bilingual tradition, plus a network of credible educational institutions—was useful in achieving tangible growth in the postwar years. A talented, industrious work force and limited taxation were powerful enticers for Western companies seeking a presence in this strategic location.

GNP increases have hovered in the double-digit range for much of the past two decades, and the port proudly ranks as America's 17th largest market (and it is unfettered by protectionist obstacles, as officials in the city-state constantly remind some U.S. Congress members and members of the Japanese Diet). A third of China's exports to the U.S. pass through its gates, as do about a fourth of all American sales to the Chinese mainland.

Some 800 U.S. companies have a presence on Hong Kong, and half of the manufacturing investments there originate in the United States.

When all U.S. $4 billion-plus worth of foreign investments are added up, the U.S. share reaches $1.5 billion.

Can its entrepôt legacy steer this venerable port toward a comfortable postindustrial transition? What conditions are necessary to continue the "miracle"? Views differ on not only the answers but on the questions themselves. Trade, manufacturing, and other industries have fared well in the current equation: good location, scant regulation, reasonable wage rates, a diligent work force. The future equation will be different, and will be shaped by factors outside Hong Kong itself. Around the Asia-Pacific region, competitors are poised to assume components of Hong Kong's current economic base, as rivals stake out their own claim to growth. It's of scant comfort that others of the Four Dragons are trying to portray themselves as banking centers, for example. Hong Kong's old standby, electronics, is flourishing in Malaysia, and several other countries position themselves as would-be havens for assembly and manufacturing of those items. Other countries in the region are now adopting deregulated, promarket environments to service firms that once flocked to Hong Kong. What was once a torrent of offshore manufacturing is slowing to a trickle, as Japan and the West limit new branch plants and choose instead to automate domestic factories in an effort to shave production costs.

Yet, several years before the historic Chinese annexation is set to occur, the surface is calm. The Hang Seng stock market index is soaring, a treasury surplus exists, and GNP is growing by about 9 percent a year. Protectionism still looms on the horizon but has abated slightly. Groundbreaking for a $3 billion new airport should begin months before the return to China in 1997, and Queen Elizabeth herself recently opened a sprawling state-of-the-art convention center.

DOUBTS ABOUT TRANSITION

All this comes during a rebound by Hong Kong after a four-year slump that began in 1982 as word of the Sino-British accords shook public confidence as well as corporate balance sheets. Margaret Thatcher assures the world that "the free and dynamic ... environment which has attracted large numbers of businessmen for years will continue to flourish"; yet there are doubters. She has reiterated, as has everyone else involved in the negotiations, that the colony, or territory as natives call it, will remain "a going concern with a future stretching into the next century and beyond." And Chinese Premier Zhao Ziyang has repeatedly admonished that it is "in the common interest" to implement guidelines of the ratified accords "without interference." Even leaders from across the globe are involved—George Shultz asserts that the agreement built "a solid foundation" for "Hong Kong's enduring future and progress." As far back as October 1985, George Bush, then vice president of the U.S., proclaimed that the terms of the pact led to a "bright future."

What are those terms, and why is there such doubt within Hong Kong itself? The exodus of thousands of middle-class men and women, the flock to Canadian embassies and to other consulates to obtain high-priced visas ($2,000 in the Dominican Republic alone) and the trek made by pregnant women outside the colony to secure citizenship for their offspring are all signs of a nagging sense of insecurity.

Gyrations of a number of financial indices and economic barometers followed on the heels of China's unilateral, surprise announcement in July 1982, which went unchallenged in London.

Terms of the annexation are confounding to those in Hong Kong because of constant reinterpretations and because of what even neutral observers insist is an uncompromising, intransigent, posture taken by the People's Republic on key issues.

China's reclaiming of the territory was a rude shock, and came as Hong Kong was recognized as a rapidly advancing, increasingly affluent entity. "It had achieved its own cultural identity, its own form of constitution, and its own customs," notes Professor Michael Oksenberg, dean of the Asian studies faculty at the University of Michigan in Ann Arbor. "Of course, the Chinese insisted that they had long-standing claims to the area, and, just as in the case of Taiwan, or Tibet, it was an integral part of the Chinese nation." Still, he points out, "the suddenness with which the Chinese announcement reached not only Hong Kong but the rest of the world was surprising."

For 20 years Peking has treated Hong Kong as already being, for all practical purposes, within the Chinese realm. Peking has acquiesced blithely—even during the Cultural Revolution—to its legal separateness, and has for many years used the profits from the relationship to pay all the costs of its very substantial food imports. Deng's Peking has even allowed the dynamism of Hong Kong's highly competitive industrial, commercial, and financial system to spread out quite publicly into its adjoining neighborhood—into Guangdong, into Guangxi and Fujian provinces, and further.

China's logic in assuming a seemingly intransigent position on Hong Kong is based on its history with regard to European colonialism. When terms were set for China's quasi-annexation of Macau in 1987, many official organizations on the mainland proclaimed an end to the last vestiges of foreign rule that had divided the Chinese people for a century and created artificial political divisions. To Beijing, the colony/territory represents no more than such an enclave. Europe, especially Britain in the 1980s, never challenged this assumption. "China has had its mind made up for some time," asserts Dr. Oksenberg. "They view the creation of an 'autonomous region' as not only inevitable, but as a way of repairing past wrongs ... and the injustices of foreign, namely European, rule."

Beijing's do-as-it-like attitude in each case has prompted observers to reevaluate the possibility that the 50-year self-autonomous region plan will actually work. The first issue involves democratic reforms. London has moved to institute some fundamental changes in Hong Kong's system of government to give it the autonomous status promised in the Joint Declaration. But it is now clear that Beijing has the final say on whatever London proposes.

At the top of London's list of changes is a shift toward a fully elected Legislative Council, the law-making advisory body that currently has 24 indirectly elected members and 32 appointed members, of whom 10 are senior officials. This proposal quickly ignited intense debate on whether Hong Kong should have one-person, one-vote direct elections to the Council, as in a full democracy.

In November 1985, however, Beijing accused the British Government of "deviating from the Joint Declaration," a clear reference to Beijing's displeasure with British attempts at unilateral political change in Hong Kong. The accusation was made by Beijing's representative in Hong Kong, Xu Jiatun, director of the official Xinhua News Agency's Hong Kong branch. The low-key British response left many in Hong Kong with the impression that Britain just wants to transfer Hong Kong peacefully to Beijing and has already given up on the battle for a truly representative government.

The second issue involves the drafting of the Basic Law. Because the Basic Law is expected to function as a mini constitution for the Hong Kong self-autonomous region, China claims that the drafting process is an internal affair. This gives many Hong Kong residents the distinct impression that their views will not be represented in the BLDC.

There is a growing lack of confidence in China's willingness to abide by the Joint Declaration. Martin Lee, an elected member of Hong Kong's Legislative Council, indicated this concern in an *Asian Wall Street Journal* article when he asked: "What can be done to ensure that what has been promised in the Joint Declaration will not be taken away by the Basic Law by which Hong Kong will be governed after 1997?" His answer was that Hong Kong needs democracy to protect its own identity and its political traditions.

A third issue that raised popular response from Hong Kong residents involves the controversy surrounding the construction of the Daya Bay nuclear-power plant. Located 30 miles northeast of Hong Kong, the facility—before as well as after Chernobyl in 1987—gives residents the jitters. However, a petition against construction of the plant signed by 1 million Hong Kong residents in 1986 was ignored by Beijing. Even more distressing to colony residents, China has yet to produce adequate evidence to support claims of plant safety, and Beijing even signed agreements with contractors before receiving a safety evaluation of the plant design. According to Lee Yee, editor-in-chief of *The Nineties*, a Hong Kong monthly magazine, the Daya Bay incident has taught Hong Kong that it has next to no influence over decision making, even concerning those issues that have the greatest impact on its residents' lives. Meanwhile, government officials demonstrated an unwillingness to confront Beijing over local issues, leading Lee to conclude that the autonomy Beijing pledged in the proposed self-autonomous region after 1997 seems a partially empty promise.

Since 1979, Hong Kong's trade exchanges with the Chinese mainland have risen dramatically; they are, today, roughly a third or more of Hong Kong's foreign trade turnover. Since that year, exports to mainland China rose 18-fold and imports fourfold.

The bank of China has become an increasingly influential presence in the city, slowly displacing the established (and mostly indigenous) Hong Kong and Shanghai Banking Corporation. Beijing money has also propped up the failing, locally founded Ka Wah Bank and bailed out Conic Investments Ltd., a major manufacturer of TV sets, radios, and electronic components.

Beijing's China Resource Holding Company has invested heavily in Hong Kong businesses and now controls more than 300 firms in the territory, encroaching on the preserves of traditional British *hongs* such as Jardine Matheson and Swire Pacific Ltd. Mainland China has a substantial interest in the newly founded Dragon Airlines (chairman, Sir Yue-kong Pao), which competes with Swire's Cathay Pacific Airways and intends to cash in on Beijing's projected takeover of Hong Kong's Kai Tak Airport.

Beijing has also invested heavily in the territory's real estate market. It owns some choice properties on downtown Victoria Island, including the site for the new, 70-story-high Bank of China building, designed by I.M. Pei.

Hong Kong investors have been active in mainland Special Economic Zones. Already, Hong Kong's economy is being restructured away from the traditional export industries and redirected from its cosmopolitan orientation toward mainland China. In a sense, the city-state is reverting to its traditional role as an entrepôt and a conduit for China.

American companies are increasing their presence in the Colony, and some of the concern about Chinese intentions has lessened. Trading, light industry, original equipment manufacturing production and sub-assemblies have thrived—and continue to do so. These are not capital intensive, and they helped build Hong Kong's reputation in electronics (which constitutes 28 percent of total exports) as well as in textiles and toys. The Hong Kong economy is truly small-scale, despite the $50 billion in trade it registers annually. About 90 percent of all businesses there employ under 50, and frequent job switching is another characteristic of the type of flexibility that keeps the export count ticking on. The attitudes that flourished in the walk-up garment factories and multistory buildings that intersect crowded inner-city freeways are still prevalent today. Many companies have had little reason to change their ways. "They don't think about future expansion," says Alice Lai, deputy director of the Industry Department. "They just think about survival." And, since many businesses are family-owned, the concept of venture capital—which would threaten control of a company—is difficult for many to accept.

The traditional economic base may be slower to change than its leaders would like to think. What worked well in the 1960s and 70s may not carry this island chain of 5.6 million along a high-growth, more technologically driven path.

FOREIGN TRADE AND INVESTMENT

Hong Kong is still considered Asia's second financial capital after Tokyo, and remains the world's largest exporter of toys, garments, radios, and watches. The rising prosperity of the city-state is evidenced by the fact that $1.5 billion worth of textile *imports* were tallied in the first quarter of 1987 alone, a period that also saw $910 million in electrical appliance imports and purchases of nearly $600 million worth of telecommunications and electronics equipment. "If ever one needed proof of the notion that trade is a two-way street," says Dr. Seiji Naya, a ranking economist at the East-West Center in Hawaii, "you have only to look at the way that Hong Kong buys foreign goods, and remember that they have a virtually open market to those products."

Naya is correct. While the volume of trade was rising by as much as 40 percent in the first quarter of 1987 over the preceding period the year before, European and Asian countries found no barriers to imports. "They seek to increase levels of more upscale products," says Dr. Naya, "but they do not interfere with sales of competing product lines entering ... their own border."

Little wonder Hong Kong decries evidence of protectionism elsewhere. The colony is the world's third-busiest port and is considered the gateway to China as well as to other parts of the region. Today, 700,000 expatriates from around the globe reside there, contributing a cosmopolitan ambiance generally found in major world cities such as New York, Paris, London, and Tokyo.

The city-state linked its currency to the U.S. dollar in the 1970s. With the greenback's sharp decline since 1985, Hong Kong exports have soared—just as America's own have risen appreciably. In 1987, for example, sales abroad jumped by about 30 percent, to $18 billion. In 1988 they continued to grow. Some 40 percent of those exports are U.S.-bound. Hong Kong's sales to Japan increased by as much as 60 percent in the same period. From now until the 1990s, any deterioration in the American economy would cause a severe downturn across all of East Asia. Ultimately, as restructuring and upgrading of the economic infrastructure proceeds, it is sales to North America, to Western Europe, and to a lesser extent to Japan, that determine the GNP rate.

While investment from the EEC has not increased significantly since the mid-1980s, it is Japan that is making use of the colony/territory to a surprising degree in the wake of the rising yen. In 1985, according to government statistics, some 127 Japanese-owned plants were located in the colony, with new investments carrying a value of $365 million. A year later, 200 Japanese plants and factories, representing $600 million in foreign development, were churning out plastics, textiles, metal products, electrical products, and watches, employing nearly 20,000 workers. C.L. Chu, a specialist in the Hong Kong Department of Industry, estimates that by the end of 1988 there may be another 75 factories and possibly an additional $200 million worth of direct investment by Tokyo-based multinationals.

K.Y. Yeung, director of the Department of Industry, noted in a June 1987 speech that Japan's total foreign investment pie was $3 billion. Hong Kong is competing for slices of that pie with fellow Tigers Singapore, Korea, and Taiwan to attract identical types of DFI, with the possible exception of textiles.

Hong Kong's re-export trade with China has been significant since the late 1970s. Then goods imported from China were retained; now the majority (60 percent) are re-exported. These are products assembled and reassembled in the colony, as imported parts are crafted into products that line shop shelves worldwide. Or many are simply transshipped by way of Hong Kong. In 1987 they rose by 50 percent over 1986, and reached $16.58 billion. In 1988 they surpassed $20 billion.

There is concern now that the stock crash of October 1987 has caused belt tightening on the part of consumers who buy toys, clothing, electronics, and Hong Kong's other products. As Mark van Fleet, director of Asian-Pacific affairs for the U.S. Chamber of Commerce points out, "Any lack of momentum in the newly industrializing countries [including Hong Kong] now can slow down future progress." Without sales, jobs are threatened, and although trade balances have been healthy in the past, continuous accumulations of hard currency—especially in U.S. dollars—are required to fuel the economy in the years ahead.

Foreign businesses in Hong Kong complain about a few things. Rapidly increased labor costs—and the high labor turnover—draw fire. So do a lack of pure tax holidays and of long-term land leases.

When the Industry Department surveyed over 500 local firms in 1987, they were particularly dismayed about one feature of the foreign investment experience. Over a third of the companies felt sales growth was not satisfactory, and some 20 percent had the same impression of their profits. Over 40 percent believed that both sales and profits were probably going to be bad, or uncertain, in 1987, owing to costs and competition in their product lines from other Asian producers. Some also cited a shortage of technicians and rising costs of materials and parts as reasons for lackluster performance.

Low taxes, the communications network, lack of exchange controls, and excellent port facilities are cited most often as pluses for foreign investors, and these should continue through the 1990s. Reginald Kent serves as senior marine officer of the port. "Capacity wasn't enough, considering the very strong growth in tonnage. This problem will be resolved by 1989, with additions of some berthing capacity and handling space. We could become first, ahead of Rotterdam, when our sixth terminal opens [in 1989]."

The attractiveness of Hong Kong to foreign companies will continue for some time, if steps are taken to maintain a competitive posture. The existing base is substantial; Japan's presence is growing, and China's own direct stake in major service and industrial enterprises is on the rise. The United States holds 37 percent of all foreign investment in manufacturing, which gives American interests a $1.03 billion stake in the colony. In 1987, over $440 million was held by American electronics companies—a 10-fold increase in that sector alone since 1982. All told, there are 39,000 inhabitants drawing paychecks at 170 U.S.-owned facilities on the islands. Fred Armentrout at the American Chamber of Commerce in Hong Kong believes that the absolute number of American businesspersons living in the territory may have surpassed that of Britain (each has bout 16,000).

However, the fact that Americans (or others) have not announced plans to vacate Hong Kong before 1997 does not mean they intend to reside there through the 21st century. As for services and banking, a few taps on a keyboard at Kowloon and capital can instantly be transferred to havens in Singapore, or halfway across the globe in Barbados, or to proposed offshore banking sites such as the one Taiwan is quietly planning.

Many observers believe that, if the numerous American business executives in Hong Kong were surveyed, most would state that their respective companies will continue cautious expansion through 1990, then adopt a wait-and-see approach. Dr. Stephen Cooney, vice president for international affairs at the National Association of Manufacturers, speaks for a range of experts on both sides of the Pacific. "You can't pinpoint the numbers of branch plants or whether the numbers of dollars will go up or down" before 1997, he says. "Companies are looking at the other newly industrializing countries very carefully. Everyone who invests offshore has different reasons for doing so, different sets of deterrents that make one place look better than its competitor. Hong Kong has the potential to attract more of the technology-based firms it needs to spawn jobs with spinoffs—and with a future—but they run smack into competition from the other NICs."

And, in may ways, the trio of fellow Tigers is doing more than Hong Kong is to greet the postindustrial era. Their respective governments are independent in spirit, have been giving direction to local business, and are coordinating the general direction of private companies.

INFRASTRUCTURE IMPROVEMENTS

The commitment to large undertakings is taken seriously in Hong Kong (it was in 1984 that the costliest office building in the world, the 41-story Hong Kong and Shanghai Banking Corporation structure opened, with a price tag as high as $980 million). Massive investments in public housing are proceeding afoot. Nearly half the population today lives in high-rise citadels jutting out of the rock, which seem to spiral defiantly upward from the plush green carpets covering the rolling mountain slopes. Since the city's population will reach 7 million by 1999, a year when its work force could include half the population, upgrading living conditions is critical. The New Towns program, a $17 billion project that will house 970,000 residents, is on schedule and should completely transform the Tsuen Wan section by the mid-1990s.

Transport links are vital to the territory's successes. With Singapore's race to best Hong Kong's 13 ½-hour turnaround times, easing congestion is a cornerstone of the overall competitiveness strategy.

In 1987, Hong Kong overtook Rotterdam as the world's busiest container port, with over 3.5 million tons tallied in that 12-month period. For these reasons, when major transport projects are planned in this city-state, the worldwide shipping community takes notice.

Over $15 billion is slated for improvements in air and water transport alone. The focal point of these plans comes through the Port and Airport Development Strategy, or PADS. A new airport will replace the antiquated Kai-Tak facility. At the same time, continued land reclamation will add more harbor space.

Increases of 20 percent in the quantity of goods transshipped are expected because the largest container terminal, Kwai Chung, will double its current volume by 1995. In addition, significant railway connections to the People's Republic will be completed within the next few years, while infrastructure spending on internal highway routes continues apace. A $250 million tunnel from the Kowloon section to the New Territories, on China's border, is one such venture.

Another form of transit is in the cards for the city-state. A group associated with unspecified European telecommunication firms announced plans to explore construction of a fiber-optics network that would link Hong Kong, Singapore, London, Tokyo, and New York. Fiber optics, one of the "miracle" technologies of the decade, has the ability to transmit enormous quantities of information at lightning speed; as many as 60,000 simultaneous phone calls could be handled at once on the hair-thin, static-free strands. Another player, Cable and Wireless in the United Kingdom, is interested in the project, and assumes it would take $500 million or so and 18 months to complete the task in several stages. Facsimiles, video transmissions, voice, and electronic data would reach Seoul, Taipei, and other Asian cities instantaneously via the new system. Sir Eric Shapre, chairman of Cable and Wireless, is enthusiastic, and Japanese firms such as Dai-Ichi and Fujitsu have publicly expressed interest in participating in the project.

More improvements of the port are needed. Capacity was strained in 1988, and delays have irritated shippers. While 8,000 oceangoing ships reached the harbor a decade ago, the figure was closer to 15,000 in 1988.

Reginald Kent, director of the harbor, acknowledges that a $20 billion master plan extending to the year 2005 would cover not only the port but adjacent facilities such as highways and tunnels. A spokesman for Neptune Orient Lines sums up the prevailing view: "The industry is watching to see how fast they can catch up with demand now, and decisions for long-term commitments would be based on the sincerity with which the territory actually goes ahead with port expansion, berths, container facilities."

Airborne cargo accounts for more traffic than was projected in the 1980s. Intermodal transport will be more important in the future. A project suggested by several international construction firms calls for bridges to connect Lantau Island by land, therefore making it possible for goods to reach East and Southeast Asia far more quickly than is possible now. The master plan for transportation—which includes a $5 billion replacement of Kai-Tak, the notoriously crowded, but tastefully designed, international airport—is considering many ambitious projects, ranging from subway expansion to highway interchanges.

THE NEED FOR LOCAL R&D

Hong Kong's economic foundation also requires retooling. Electronics employs 107,000, and some $4 billion worth of those items were sold outside the territory in 1988. Ms. Lai believes that early strides toward semi-customized circuit boards can give Hong Kong a foothold in application-specific integrated circuits. "We could handle certain 'mature' areas in integrated circuits in 5–10 years," she asserts, "and are going to support the training of some engineers overseas to help us along."

K. Y. Yeung, director of the Department of Industry, is not alone in believing that production carried out by simple assembly work (or other labor-intensive business) has no future. The challenge facing the city-state is to carve a niche for itself. Yeung declares that "more complex processes and higher value-added products would move away from Hong Kong to countries more technologically advanced." Simply being in the middle is no longer safe.

Hong Kong's $4.5 billion electronics exports is a base far more fragile than most imagine. Samuel Fang, general manager of General Electronics, the colony's largest electronics company and a subcontractor for Coleco and Radio Shack, points to a trend that will affect electronics' future. "Low-cost manufacturing bases are being set up in China by our own local people. It's happening slowly, but in time, more will join. They will have to," he says. And only through what he describes as "flexibility" can Hong Kong master markets in electronic toys, high-tech entertainment systems for home and for other purposes, as well as in video games. By "flexibility" here he means the ability to shift production lines quickly, to retrain workers, to respond promptly to foreign tastes, etc.

S. K. Chan, director of the Hong Kong Productivity Centre, is one who monitors not only the indigenous developments within electronics but compares them to what is taking place at the nerve centers of technology on three continents. "We're at the crossroads," he said in 1987. "We have reached the stage where we are manufacturing compact discs, videotapes, and those types of products. It shows how far we have gone along, but there are not that many doing this kind of work now, and also a couple of companies employing maybe 15 or 20 people each went broke. ..."

"Then there is the fact that most of the electronics companies here are still looking at currencies, looking at trade, things like that ... traditional patterns [in electronics] won't continue ..." and a true local industry, born and bred in Hong Kong, with its own ideas—not just performing roles (albeit capable roles) as order takers for Europe, Japan, or the U.S., does not exist.

The companies are managed by older men. They have a different time line and think on a long planning horizon. They are not accepting change, argue some observers—and the same syndrome turns up in other sectors that form the industrial base. According to one official, the electronics makers are closely knit, and many know precisely what their competitors are doing. This can be an advantage when it comes time to adopt new technologies, or prompt others to conduct research— a hitherto unexplored topic.

So, the challenge may be to place much greater emphasis on R&D— and a frank recognition that merely filling orders for the multinational OEMs (original equipment manufacturers) cannot guarantee earnings in the ultra-competitive era of shortened product life cycles and instant technology transfers that lies ahead in the 1990s. Samuel Fang and others wonder whether the research and development component will start to emerge.

To develop more of this type of local R&D, some improvement in job skills is necessary. Vincent Cheng at the multi-billion-dollar Hong Kong and Shanghai Bank notes, "Sometimes industry itself isn't really sure about the kinds of jobs they need, and we cannot always plan ahead to train without guidance." A government official candidly calls this situation a "dilemma," but believes that vocational-training boards composed of business and government can fill some of the gaps. In 1987, the government launched a pilot program to grant financial aid for overseas scholarships, to help engineering candidates and electronic engineers obtain a leg up in the ever-changing field of high technology.

Another aspect is technical education and the need to provide for continual worker training. This problem is faced by every industrial nation and is especially important to the Asian newly industrializing countries, which—without the benefits of a large, thriving, diverse internal market—must rely on exports to drive their economies. A $58 million training-center complex, completed in 1987, is located at Sha Tin and can accommodate about 4,000 students. Lee Wai Lee Technical Institute receives high marks, but needs to expand its facilities to accommodate more than the 1,500 students there at present. A pair of new technical institutes have recently been completed in the territory, and a new institute for computer-aided design and computerized drafting has begun to accept a modest enrollment.

Worker training is needed for as many as a quarter of the 870,000 employed in manufacturing. The 600,000 in retail and trade and service industries are proceeding at a better pace, taking advantage of in-house programs to upgrade vocational skills.

As people climb the skills ladder, products must follow them. Another new development is the completion of a Standards and Testing Centre, headquartered in Tai Po Industrial Estate. Its chairman, John Lo, indicates that product testing in chemicals, pharmaceuticals, and other fields will be carried out by ultra-modern laboratory equipment. "We expect to conduct over 10,000 tests every month, on everything ranging from shoes to packing materials," he says confidently. "Now any remaining doubts about standards and quality controls here will be ended forever." (China could certainly enjoy great benefits from such a facility in the colony/territory.)

As toys have become increasingly complex, their importance to Hong Kong—where they constitute $1.5 billion in export sales and could reach the $1.9 billion mark by 1990—is such that the testing concept must be readily accepted by more local producers. Apparently it is. This is good news, since Hong Kong toys have sometimes been criticized for not meeting international standards. With China already spawning its own toy industry, Hong Kong has to be on the alert. Alice Lai, a specialist at the Industry Department, says that "the traditional manufacturing methods have come to integrate high standards, and the reputation of our industries is a vital part of future trade." Especially since, as she notes, "apart from China, other countries can easily pick up a major share of our toy industry."

THE OUTLOOK FOR HONG KONG

Such steps by industry and government recently demonstrate an attempt to cope with the need to upgrade, but a major structural shift is years away. It boils down to producing more value added and spawning homegrown engineering design.

For Hong Kong, merely climbing steadily up the ladder isn't enough. Worldwide economic forces and the spread of technologies force all nations to increase their pace. The grand strategy is to seek value added. "We are moving to upgrade quality and increase productivity," says Ms. Lai. Beyond that, the structure of industry must be transformed beyond simple fulfillment tasks. "Hong Kong could start by developing application-specific integrated circuits. Our engineers will have the skills to compete with the postindustrial nations, and certain advanced technologies would become 'mature' in five or ten years as we move into customized chip production." A new electronics and data-processing center is trying to promote the benefits of automation for Hong Kong businesses, but proponents discover that obstacles such as cost and lack of information inhibit the move to advanced production techniques.

Hong Kong has to play catch-up. The foundations of manufacturing—which still employs a third of all workers—need upgrading. Although she is able to tap rich agricultural and herbal raw material for biotechnology, few steps have been taken to promote this critical sunrise industry. Dr. Walter Ho at Hong Kong University speaks for many experts. "We could have more support from business, because we have the talent here to capture niche markets in biotech. But, the businessmen and investors here are waiting for news of some breakthrough before committing their own financial resources, and it doesn't always work that way."

Hong Kong's previous role as a gateway to China is less certain than once assumed, because of the stop-and-go attitude toward development taken by the People's Republic itself. In theory, the goal of farming out labor-intensive operations to China while keeping high-end, value-added aspects within the colony is practical for years to come. Hong Kong's best leverage against any intrusions—inadvertent or otherwise—in its unique economic base.

Hong Kong is expanding its ties with China through various mechanisms. The network of Chinese entrepreneurs and barters operating in Taiwan have used the colony as a conduit through which to ship goods to China itself. This trade, while officially unsanctioned, has grown from an estimated $50 million in 1981 to nearly $1 billion six years later. It is officially and technically outlawed by both sides, and, according to a Chinese commercial attaché in Amsterdam, "Both sides will probably look the other way, until formal diplomatic ties are established"—which may not be until the next century.

Hong Kong is home for Taiwanese looking offshore for business expansions, as the cost of running factories and the cost of labor increases markedly in the Republic of China. Most of the products are in the same categories accounted for by other countries trading with China: electrical machinery, chemicals, and finished products needed for manufacturing.

What is even more surprising is that Chinese exports to Taiwan, sent through Hong Kong, are increasing at an equally rapid clip. They may amount to $125 million today, according to C.J. Chen, long-time Taiwanese diplomat and director of the Taiwanese commercial offices in Washington, D.C. If that figure is accurate, it is double the amount for 1986. A railway link from Kowloon sends freight to China in growing volume, and as mentioned above, new rail connections are on the drawing boards.

Of course, foreign investment will play a major role in steering Hong Kong through its transition. The U.S. still holds the lead, but China itself is now third, partially to allay fears about its own intentions toward the laissez-faire economy after 1997. Japan ranks second and, with the United States, accounts for about $1.2 billion in trade, or half the total. China holds under a fifth, but her $370 million is a huge increase from a zero base in 1983. It is the investment pool from all three that accounts for a rise in joint ventures. Those operations may hold the key to the ever-heralded "China market," with Hong Kong companies acquiring some skills needed to exploit the giant north of their border. As a newly industrialized country, Hong Kong can serve as a true conduit. "We have a complementary role in China's modernization program," insists Ms. Lai.

The foreign investments are helping the colony in other ways, too. More of the foreign manufacturers are installing some quality control, and as many as a third may have the capacity to conduct in-house R&D. Significantly, electronics leads the way in the recent influx of capital from beyond the colony's borders.

In response to the host of new challenges, Hong Kong has embarked on a plan to build a pair of industrial estates—"free zones" with special incentives further reducing taxes. Called Yuen Long and Tai Po, they are sited along the New Territories region, which is far from the maddening crowd of the heavily populated downtown corridor. The parks' space totals some 420 acres, and most of the $130 million cost was for civil engineering. The companies setting up shop in the parks are concentrating on microelectronic motors, videotapes, photocopier parts, and packaging materials. Continental Can and Carlsberg Brewery are also among the tenants. Chips, appliances, and heavy machinery are being made at the sites as well.

Dr. Vincent Cheng, chief economist at the Hong Kong and Shanghai Bank, asserts that the new industrial estates are an "important showcase" for the colony/territory. "We never had anything like a true R&D office setting for international or multinational companies." He emphasized the importance of creating campus-like settings for foreign businesses pampered by the "high-tech–high-touch" ambiance found in California and elsewhere. The parks are the centerpiece of the city-state's drive to remain competitive.

The parks are in effect a pair of planned towns, about 45–60 minutes from the central city, by car or bus. Today, the rates vary from $130 to about $155 per square meter. Tai Po is on the Kowloon-Canton Railway rail link to China, but Yuen Long has a large housing complex adjacent to its factory shells.

Those not wishing to rent factory space in the multistory structures or the pair of new industrial parks can purchase land through auctions, with contracts running for 75 years and covenants pledging to guarantee rights of ownership after the 1997 changeover. Companies offering substantial gains in technology are being given greater consideration for scarce space over other types of businesses. The same preference applies for companies bringing in natural resources, or providing a great many jobs.

With much industrial research around the globe financed through venture capital, some attention should be focused on this mechanism. "The lack of an institutional source of venture capital is a serious constraint to the development of technology-intensive enterprises," notes S. K. Chan, executive director of the Productivity Council.

Product development is not easily achieved anywhere, and the venerable family-owned, family-managed companies in Hong Kong are often slow to adopt new ideas. Other "Dragons" may slice into Hong Kong's electronics "pie," in part because they devoted resources to R&D years ago. Mr. Chan finds electronics at the crossroads. "I'm told we now have companies manufacturing products like videotapes and compact discs, and so forth. But those companies are exceptions, rather than the rule." The old formula of filling orders, albeit with panache, has not spawned indigenous industries.

Some companies understand this point. Irene Lee is manager of Design Computer Products, whose toy robots are in the forefront of upscale (and pricey) exports. The colony is trying to look past the heady days that saw 150,000,000 Rubik's Cubes churned out of its factories. "Profits and losses still teach us a lot about marketing abroad, because for many Hong Kong companies there are always new lessons to learn." Her firm suffered some reverses after it missed out on the critical U.S.

buying cycle. "Value added in products like our educational, program-mable robots is a good way for the companies here to keep up the momentum," she declares. Her company was launched less than four years ago in a typically Chinese way, with $16,000 in pooled family capital. Nearly a half-million dollars' worth of orders are expected to come in each month.

The drive to take products upscale is happening in other quarters. Textiles, for example, is taking this route, using top-of-the-line designers and European fashion leaders to lend their names and patterns to local firms. Clothing and apparel employs 380,000 and is a $6 billion export item. There are signs of automation and computerization taking root in some factories, but dyeing and spinning are lagging in adopting new innovations. Management skills are not keeping pace with demands in an industry that finds low-cost countries (which Hong Kong is no longer) rapidly assaulting the lower end of the market.

The colony is at last shaking off its image as a low-end producer of cheap goods. Visitors today would be hard-pressed to traipse through Kowloon in search of a tee shirt for under $10. This fact has been communicated to overseas buyers, and now prestige names like Armani, Abercrombie & Fitch, and Christian Dior rely on the Crown Colony for their own output. Stylists and trendy designers are aiding Hong Kong's assault on upscale fashion.

Recent steps to transform textiles and leave behind last vestiges of the cheap labor "sweatshop" image are coming through more widespread use of computer-aided pattern design, a technique introduced in 1986. For an industry whose exports near the $6 billion level, this is a major stride.

Improvements in production processes in other industries are becom-ing evident. Stung by failures of Coleco, the U.S.-based toy maker, Hong Kong's industry (now a $1.6 billion export earner) seems eager to try market research of its own, either through an association effort or through joint ventures.

The need to move upscale rapidly is understood by some in the computer industry. When IBM transferred 60 staffers from its Tokyo offices to transplant its Asia-Pacific division to Hong Kong, indigenous electronics firms—until then isolated and self-confident—realized that merely being close to the IBM operation could have payoffs, and that the relocation would, in itself, help introduce new ideas.

By 1990, it is expected that over $200 million in new venture capital funds will be channeled to deserving enterprises. But, the successes of venture capital are based on many factors. Meshing this concept onto the business culture, known for a reluctance to share control with outsiders, may prove difficult.

As it looks ahead to the 1990s, the territory knows that it must contend with a pollution problem that has been allowed to fester for decades. Probably four-fifths of the factories are unregulated; lack of pollution abatement equipment may cause severe health hazards soon. (In 1988, many beaches were officially closed because of debris and high levels of contamination from industrial wastes.)

With as many as 40,000 additional professional men and women taking leave overseas in 1988 (an increase of 50 percent over 1987), a clearer understanding of Chinese intentions is needed. Recent confirmation of an arrangement to keep business and financial systems fully intact for 50 years following the beginning of the Special Autonomous Region in 1997 was not met with universal praise. China pontificates admonishing observers that a few modifications (such as a mere switch from driving on the left side of the road) will assure smooth transition along the road to 1997.

An $800 million EXPO is planned to coincide with unification, and while its precise theme is uncertain right now, this quasi-World's Fair would be one effective means of allaying fears, as well as creating long-range goodwill upon Chinese within and without Asia.

London's diplomatic efforts to secure a mild public statement from Beijing guaranteeing the terms of the 1997 accords were, a month after Tiananmen, to no avail.

7

SINGAPORE: FATHER, SON, AND HOLY GOH

To Victorian colonials, it rivaled India as the star jewel in Britain's far-flung Crown. To Japan in World War II, it was a stepping-stone toward India. When Sir Stamford Raffles glanced back to the coast from his schooner on a wintery day in December 1816, he wondered aloud about whether it would hold any value at all. That question must have been posed by others since, but today there is little doubt as to its answer. Within a decade Singapore's inhabitants may achieve the world's highest per capita income.

This renegade nation, a breakoff from the Malayan Federation, stands poised for an encounter with the next century. It launched a program for its citizenry that provides incentives for its best and brightest to reproduce. Its population will soon be fully connected to a sophisticated videotext system. It is ahead of even the Persian Gulf sheikdoms in a plan to decrease its dependence on a thriving oil- refining industry—the world's third largest—and to diversify its potent petrochemicals base.

The city-state boasts perhaps the world's finest airline and plays host to an indigenous shipping and merchant marine fleet that may well rank at the top of the roster. Singapore in 1985 became the first financial futures market in Asia, with a 24-hour hookup with Chicago, the foremost financial and commodities futures center.

Singapore, on the rim of China's ancient invasion routes, offers much contrast to other East Asian settings. Her relatively open markets can hardly be compared to the social control that permeates her society.

When the Japanese occupation forces rounded up Singaporeans for shipment to labor camps in 1942, a teenager jumped off the truck and escaped his captors. Less than a quarter-century later, he would rise to the post of prime minister, a job he still holds today. Lee Kuan Yew's unique brand of one-man rule has taken the unforged core of a tiny nation and brought it through the fires of a social, political, and economic blast furnace—with his constituency emerging as tempered steel. Today the prime minister prepares to transfer the reigns of power to the new generation of leaders, including his own son. Let us explore this very unordinary place which, although it is seldom featured in the news media, plays such a pivotal role in fostering the Asian Century.

HISTORICAL BACKGROUND

Small trading settlements sprouted in Singapore along the Straits of Malacca in the mid-1770s. The prize for Dutch and British adventurers was great indeed, with tin uppermost on the minds of many.

London was quick to seize an opportunity, especially after many in that world center were startled at the Dutch acquisition of Indonesia. Hoping to gain a toehold along the strategic Straits of Malacca, Stamford Raffles, a Crown agent in the Pacific, proved more forward-looking than most of his contemporaries. He admonished the queen to negotiate a purchase of the harbor and a lone offshore island some 170 years ago.

The constellation of events that surfaced in the mid-19th century saw Singapore rising from a collection of insignificant fishing villages to a major harbor overshadowing rivals such as Penang on the west coast of the Malaysian (then Malayan) Peninsula. Some 35,000 residents were tallied in the 1835 census, with as many as half the population being Chinese.

Situated midway between China and India, Singapore might have suffered from an assault by the Malayan provinces or from other European expansionists. It achieved a reputation for tranquility, one that allowed it to absorb diverse cultures and foster an entrepreneurial drive. Tamils, Bengalis, Chinese, and Malays were the first waves and enjoyed their status in a relatively open society. British rule maintained a degree of harmony, as it did in other possessions populated by disparate ethnic groups.

By 1890, over 200,000 people lived in Singapore. The vast array of commodities in the region and a good harbor made the area attractive as a small-scale banking center. Before long the colony became a major Asian port. Poems were written about Singapore, songs rhapsodized over her, and a popular (and potent) bar drink, the "sling," favored by a legion of literary titans, paid homage to her glories. Before World War II, a fairly sophisticated infrastructure was transforming the jungle, with the city-state emerging as an important railway center for Southeast Asia.

While the ceiling fans in the lobby of the much-celebrated Raffles Hotel spun around, the world seemed relaxed and prosperous. During the heady days of 1941, few could imagine that war clouds hovering above the Pacific would ever threaten Singaporeans or their life-style. Colonialists and colonial alike were satisfied and apathetic as the Japanese prepared for invasion at the close of the year.

The war saw the demise of the Rising Sun as well as the sunset of the British Empire. When plans to forge a Malaysian Federation were approved in the mid-1950s, the dream of one multicultural nation, bringing together Malays and Chinese, took shape. (Until he was 40, Lee Kuan Yew, already by then a local politician, referred to himself as a Malayan.) After independence in 1957, race riots in the Malaysian capital of Kuala Lumpur saw festering antagonism aimed at the Chinese. Much of it was over the alleged control of money and the economic institutions by that group. Singapore would go its own way, but would give the Chinese a homeland of their own.

The break saddened visionaries of all persuasions. The Indians, argue most observers, were more comfortable with the Chinese merchants than with the rural-oriented Malays still uncomfortable with white-collar chores. It seems unreal in retrospect, but the indefatigable nation-building energies of Lee and fellow founding fathers were to pay off. They ultimately succeeded, but by 1965, Lee and his allies had set about founding their own republic.

Within Singapore's officially recognized racial groups—Indian (7 percent), Chinese (74 percent), Malays (15 percent)—great diversity prevails. Of 2.6 million in all groups, most are able to direct their energies toward a cohesive posture. Most nations have a single recognized language. Singapore has four. Malay is the national tongue, English for administrative purposes, while English, Malay, Mandarin, and Tamil are all official. All citizens are encouraged to be, and all schoolchildren expected to be, at least bilingual—fluent in English and one other official language.

In 1986, Singaporeans held the second highest per capita GNP (over U.S. $7,200) in all Asia, after Japan. Another indicator of well-being is housing, and two-thirds of Singaporeans in public units hold title to them, compared with one in 10 in Hong Kong. Continued growth at yearly rates of above 15 percent assured division of wealth on a Confucianist, capitalist, egalitarian model. Singaporeans are the world's top savers, a fact assisted by compulsory programs instituted in the 1960s. All citizens and residents must contribute over 20 percent of their salaries to the government-managed Central Provident Fund. Employers match the worker's contribution with another 25 percent. This vast pool had a balance of $4 billion in 1985.

Fully two-thirds of Singaporeans are part of the service economy. Of the 1.4 million in the labor force, 28 percent hold jobs in the city-state's 4,000 factories. By 1990 it is expected that 80,000 of them will work for government agencies. Those agencies direct, plan, and manage to a degree not seen elsewhere in the region. A planning mechanism, while allowing for market forces and entrepreneurism to flourish, prohibits strikes (no major ones have surfaced in a dozen years) and restrains wage demands. It directs a handful of successful subsidy projects, while export agencies such as the Economic Development Board (EDB) set strategies for luring foreign multinationals to new industrial parks.

In the 1980s industrial promotion became relatively selective as the goal of full employment was achieved. Emphasis was on value added, with better quality products and jobs the goal of tax incentives and financial-assistance schemes. As a means of accelerating the growth of technology-based industries, emphasis was placed on upgrading equipment. Manpower training was intensified. Foreign technical and skilled personnel were allowed entrance more freely than ever before.

However, the global recession following the oil crisis of 1973 prompted an adjustment of promotion plans. To sustain economic growth and employment as investments declined, labor-intensive operations were again admitted. Investments were attracted by various favorable conditions, including lower wages compared with Hong Kong, South Korea, and Taiwan. However, problems of inefficient utilization of labor arose. World economic recovery brought labor shortages and somewhat hampered progress. The dilemma, then and now, is that admitting foreign (mostly Malay) workers can destabilize a delicate social and political fabric, which national leaders insist rests upon strong, undiminished allegiance.

New incentives came in 1979 to encourage automation and computerization. Selective industrial promotion was announced with emphasis on capital, technology, and skill-intensive industries, and products less vulnerable to the protectionist measures of the developed nations were targeted. To temporarily alleviate the labor shortage, more foreign, non-Chinese unskilled labor was also admitted.

During 1979–84, Singapore's economic performance continued to be strong. Real growth averaged 8.5 percent a year; unemployment remained quite low; and investment continued to increase—peaking at 47 percent of GDP in 1984. Meanwhile, the government continued to run a budget surplus; the external current account deficit fell steadily after increasing somewhat in 1979 as a result of the second round of oil price increases; and inflation averaged less than 5 percent annually, helped by the appreciation of the Singapore dollar against most other currencies.

Underneath this performance, however, a number of adverse trends were beginning to emerge. Perhaps the most important of these was the gradual loss of cost-competitiveness in manufacturing over the period. In 1979, in response to concerns that Singapore's relatively labor-intensive industries would face increasing competition from other newly industrializing countries, the authorities decided to accelerate their policy of upgrading the labor force and promoting high-technology, high-value-added industries.

To this end, the authorities carried out several "wage correction" efforts during this period. Under this policy, wage increases were granted that averaged 13–14 percent per year, considerably higher than either productivity growth or inflation. The authorities hoped that these wage hikes—together with substantial increases in indirect labor costs, notably employers' contributions to the Provident Fund—would encourage employers to economize on labor and concentrate on capital-intensive production.

The wage correction policy formally ended in 1981. However, with workers' expectations of high wage increases aroused and the labor market still tight, substantial wage increases were also granted in each of the next three years. As a result, unit labor costs in manufacturing rose by more than 40 percent; in fact, when adjusted for the appreciation of the Singapore dollar against the currencies of Singapore's competitors, unit labor costs rose by some 65 percent relative to other countries. Moreover, the levels of corporate and property taxes in Singapore remained high.

Profitability in manufacturing fell sharply, with a corresponding decline, beginning in 1981-82, in foreign direct investment and in investment in machinery and transport.

At the same time, while investment reached historically high levels, an increasing proportion was allocated to construction activity. From 1979 to 1984 the construction industry enjoyed an unprecedented boom in response to soaring property prices in the early 1980s, inflated expectations of tourism growth, and—especially from 1983—the acceleration of the public housing program. Construction activity nearly tripled over the period, and in 1984 construction investment was equivalent to almost three-quarters of gross national savings.

However, by late 1983, it was becoming increasingly clear that the expectations underlying the property boom were unlikely to be fulfilled and that the current level of construction activity could not continue.

With construction and related activities accounting for almost one-third of GDP growth, the growth rate was likely to fall sharply when construction activity began to decline.

In addition, growing economic difficulties in neighboring countries—partly resulting from the weakness of world markets for primary commodities, especially rubber and oil—dampened demand for service exports, especially tourism (although in 1983 and 1984 the negative effects of these developments on combined exports of goods and services were more than offset by a sharp increase in exports of electronic components and office equipment to the United States).

All these unfavorable trends came together in 1985, as real GDP fell by 1.8 percent, led by a 13 percent decline in investment. This was largely the result of a collapse in construction activity, which plunged by 19 percent. Investment in machinery and transport equipment also fell by some 6 percent, reflecting concerns over the deteriorating economic situation and the erosion of international cost-competitiveness over previous years. External demand also weakened, owing both to worsening economic conditions in neighboring countries and to the shakeout in the computer industry in the United States. This resulted in a sharp fall in exports of electronic components, which had been a mainstay of export growth in 1983 and 1984. These external forces, together with the weakness in construction and the continued depression in oil refining and ship repairing, resulted in a 7.5 percent decline in manufacturing output.

As the recession took hold in 1985, employment fell by 8 percent for the year as a whole, with the job losses concentrated in manufacturing, construction, and commerce. Initially, retrenchments concentrated largely on foreign workers, but by the end of the year the unemployment rate among Singaporeans had increased to 5 percent, the highest level since the early 1970s.

As we shall see, recovery by 1987 enabled the city-state to retain its established base while securing a niche in technology-based sectors.

THE QUEST FOR SPACE

Measuring a scant 41.8 km long by 22.5 km wide, Singapore never enjoyed wide, open spaces. Inadequate housing supply and the need for more living space necessitated a massive, two-pronged plan, which is realizing considerable success. One is land reclamation. The city's Housing and Development Board (HDB) is aware that speedy action is needed to avoid catastrophe; already, a backlog of 100,000 people are on the list awaiting public housing. In a massive, island-building venture, new land will be created where dunes and marshes now exist. Settlement of nearly a million inhabitants will take place to accommodate rebuilding, renovation, and construction. The price tag on that venture, through a six-year period ending in 1995, is placed as high as $10 billion.

Housing construction is another leg of the quest for space. A growing population (now 2.5 million) threatens a crisis of congestion. In addition, other pressures have arisen, with turf battles over which areas are allotted for new construction to house the offices, port facilities, and other structures that befit this bustling city-state.

Loh See Hong, chief planner for the city, explains that Singapore's land-use issues differ from those of other Asian countries: "The scarcity of land makes it vital that all use and development be carefully monitored and coordinated. Our most serious problem was how to resolve, satisfactorily, the conflict between demands of an expanding economy, given our fixed area of land."

Financing new buildings is difficult for any national treasury under the best of conditions. Even affluent Singaporeans shudder at the cost, but are aware of stratospheric rental fees that can hardly be expected to decline. If more families could own their residence, it might have many social benefits. Some have turned to the Central Provident Fund as the solution. With nearly 400,000 housing units now under the jurisdiction of the Housing and Development Board, HDB is landlord for three-fourth's of the city's population. The Fund is set up take land from the government and allocate housing in parcels. It establishes a savings system that the government can draw from. Workers and employers contribute a total of 45 percent of the workers' salaries, with a maximum of $600 a month. Interest is accorded each account, and these deposits are used to purchase housing. The city concedes that not everyone comes out ahead in the plan, but is satisfied that this is the most cost-effective approach. A three-room, 60-square meter unit goes for U.S. $21,000, and a more spacious (five-room, 135-square meters) alternative costs $76,000. HDB is the agency entrusted with the reclamation venture, whose current phase in land-hungry Singapore is costly. Each square meter carries a price tag of between $60 and $100—up to 10 times what land in shallow waters used to cost, where less fill was required. Another 126 hectares will be added to the landmass along Singapore's eastern coast. In this phase, engineers examine water depth, quality of the seabed, and obstacles such as existence of soft, unstable clay deposits.

In another project, a pair of Dutch companies, Ballast Nedam Far East Pte. and Boskalis International B.V., are to merge two tiny islands off the coastline. This unique project will create new petrol-storage capability on what will be a 50-hectare isle.

Half of the new Changi International Airport is on reclaimed land, and that 700-hectare spread will be joined by additions on the facility's northern and southern borders. Korea's Hyundai construction group is dredging offshore soil to develop five km of beach, and additional reclamation work proceeds by the East Coast Parkway. Another 600 hectares is slated as the homesite for new industrial and manufacturing buildings at the Jurong Town section.

Slum clearance is given attention in a new master plan recently announced. The advent of mass transit should assist the city-state with its drive toward an attractive, workable environment. Mr. Loh explains: "An earlier plan saw growth taking place in new towns insulated by other green belts and agricultural areas. Now, major growth along the coastline is encouraged, with a ring-shaped form being extended in different directions." Urbanized areas are divided into self-contained groups of between 250–300,000 people with industries and social amenities. A scaled-down green belt idea was incorporated into the plan.

OPPORTUNITIES FOR BUSINESS

The EDB has charted major new directions for the years ahead.

Computer services is one field with enormous growth potential. The region needs a center for specialist software skills and customized chips. Singapore plans to fill that need by keeping one step ahead of other newly industrializing countries.

In aerospace, there are good prospects. Firms engaged in helicopter distribution and repair, aircraft-parts machining, engine maintenance, and airline service can prosper.

Telecommunications is also receiving attention. (In 1984, hardware sales totaled $60 billion, and that figure grew by 50 percent to $86 billion in just four years.) Failure in this arena would place Singapore toward technology-oriented gateways far into the next century. Singapore seeks to consolidate its position as the telecommunications center for Southeast Asia. This is bold gamble, a significant move for many reasons. Nearly all telephones in the country are push-button models. Following on an extensive fiber optics program in the 1970s, the republic may now proclaim itself as a bastion of truly instantaneous global "one touch" communications.

Bilingual skills found in Singapore might give some of its technically-minded citizens an opportunity to cash in on the nascent telecommunications translation industry, which designs software to process messages and interpret them across national or continental borders. A surprising amount of computer-graphics work is being carried out in

East Asia, and Singapore may use its ascent to the "information era" as a vehicle to spawn related businesses. Certainly, the banking and insurance sectors will benefit from the transformation.

The U.S. helped design a videotext project that links major businesses, offers "at home" shopping, and provides tourists with numerous kiosks around the city. It was a support team under Dr. Godwin Chu in Hawaii, financed through the U.S. Agency for International Development, that scored breakthroughs on technology and videotext applications. Today, Chu is "surprised" that Canada picked up where bashful Americans left off, and used their own marketing savvy to gain contracts to implement the plan.

Dr. T.C. Yung, director of the Singapore Office of Telecommunications, points out that the infant information age is growing up fast. The cashless age in Singapore is "four or five years away," he says. Already bills can be paid by transferring funds via the phone lines, but the banks still have to develop an electronic clearinghouse. The Monetary Authority is urging them on. Further ahead are smart-card passports and computerized medical records. Pocket change in Singapore may be a stored-value card, which, when it runs out of credit, is charged up again at a bank's automatic teller. In keeping with Singapore's traditional practices, once the new technology can be utilized—with tangible gain expected—every effort will be made to do so.

THE OUTLOOK FOR SINGAPORE

Vincent Yip sits at his desk at noon on Saturday. Like 2.6 million fellow Singaporeans, he is about ready to close down the work week. He recalls days spent at the University of Southern California. "O.J. Simpson was at the school back then, so I know something about running around blockers and fullbacks. And that's not too different from what Singapore has to do to stay ahead." The game is economic competitiveness.

The analogy may strike sports enthusiasts as imprecise, but Dr. Yip's opinion counts for plenty in this Southeast Asian city-state. He serves as executive director of the Singapore Science Council. "We are planning for the future, and carefully thinking about ways that science" and what he terms "new tech"—not high tech—"can be part of the overall economic plan."

Singapore is at last showing signs of coming out of the slump that saw conditions deteriorate in 1984–86. That period was a bitter pill for this high-flying member of the "Four Dragons" to swallow. Construction, property, and tourism—three foundations of a buoyant economic base—slumped. Her GNP actually declined after nearly two decades of double-digit growth. Not only had per capita income soared during the 1970s, but the tiny (617 sq. mile) country had a sound reputation as one of Asia's—as well as the world's—most dynamic economies. No lesser sage than John Kenneth Galbraith described the experience of this one-of-a-kind port as "a lesson of what a modern metropolis can be."

A tiny manufacturing base of only $120 million in 1960 exploded into a $4.3 billion behemoth a quarter-century later. Today, 20 percent of the $17.5 billion GNP is made up of services and finance, and as much of GNP falls in manufacturing. A telecommunications system is universally hailed as among the most advanced anywhere. And, high tech is taken seriously, as shoppers in this "shopper's paradise" will discover when confronted by batteries of videotext machines at department stores. The scant $80 million in exports tallied in 1980 soared to $12 billion in 1987, of which $1.1 billion was in electronics. By 1990, the amount should surpass $1.4 billion, according to specialists such as the (U.S.) Semiconductor Industry Association.

Can the miracle continue? If so, how? It's the same question that the other "Dragons" ask themselves, as does their powerful neighbor Japan. What looms on today's economic horizon may be almost as formidable a challenge for the citizenry as was that invasion. Despite her refineries, her port, her foreign investment, her financial services, her state-of-the-art telecommunications system, and other features of her first-class infrastructure, obstacles stand in the way of Singapore's quest for post-industrialization.

Times have changed since the boom years of the 1960s and 70s—when foreign (chiefly U.S.) investment, spawned by low wages in labor-intensive manufacturing—propelled a buoyant economy. Today, and through the mid-1990s, companies are producing for global markets with short product life cycles. The old rules no longer apply, and the traditional reasons for setting up factories in newly industrializing countries are not as valid as they were as recently as the early 1980s. Singaporean wages are about 60–75 percent higher than those of fellow Dragons Taiwan and Korea. In a situation with severe labor shortages (some 100,000 foreign workers have been imported since the mid-1980s to fill job slots), productivity "is our main concern in manufacturing," according to Economic Development Board (EDB) director Yong-Sea Teoh.

Half the population is under 25, "and our workers are willing to learn new technologies," insists Wong Kok Seng, a director of the EDB. That fact may be crucial in propelling the economy. In fact, the boast of a skilled labor pool is a cornerstone of Singapore's drive to lure more companies to its shores, and tens of millions of dollars are now spent on upgrading those skills to accommodate new technologies. Old incentives—the traditional tax holidays and low- cost space for multinationals—are being played down, with job training receiving emphasis.

Now European and North American companies are told that Singapore will help them boost their own competitiveness by offering them a base for regional operational headquarters. "We just couldn't keep selling ourselves as politically stable anymore," explains one highly placed official, "although this is completely true. Are we any more stable than New Jersey, or Texas?" Yes, it's American companies that are targeted in the main, although the EEC is receiving attention and it's obvious Japan has a stake in Raffles' old bastion. U.S. firms—as part of the new tenet of high-tech manufacturing— aren't moving offshore in the way they once were; there is a retrenchment. This makes Singapore's selling job before multinationals crucial, as the highest value-added factor is sought in both service and manufacturing companies. Needs of both types of foreign firms must be met quickly in a drive to satisfy ultraflexible, "quick response" manufacturing, reckons Singapore, if companies will continue to set up shop within its borders.

TRAINING FOR HIGH TECH

To make itself competitive over the medium term, Singapore is sponsoring industrial training in a way that makes it easier for firms to find the needed talent pool—and to tap the engineering base. Nixdorf, Philips, Hewlett-Packard, and other leading-edge companies appear pleased with these arrangements, and are pouring in vast amounts of money in state-of-the-art factory-school settings.

The German-Singapore Institute was established as a result of efforts to tap West Germany's strides in robotics—as well as to counter labor shortages projected for the next three decades. Dr. Ooi Inn Bok, its director, says 5,000 students will be trained next year at his institution alone, and this number will increase markedly in the years ahead. The operation is charting an unabashed high-tech course. "We are building flexible manufacturing cells and integrated systems," he declares, "to conform to what industries that can compete successfully in Singapore will need." Other alliances such as Dr. Bok's Institute are needed, and Singapore is quietly working to secure them in microelectronics applications of automation.

James Ling is director of the Automation Applications Center, which runs a no-nonsense leasing and consultancy operation for companies exploring robotics and automation. The Center is a joint venture of EDB and others, and its showroom features the latest robots from top-notch brands like Sweden's ASEA and America's Gould. Some multinationals are already using computer-aided design in Singapore itself to improve consumer electronic items, and if the trend continues it will help "the Lion City" prove its moxey.

Singapore is serious about its efforts to advance beyond the newly industrializing country stage, and the city-state is turning its sights on a broad plan to automate the factories that turn out much of East Asia's electronics components and consumer goods. With a shortage of labor as well as the recognition that an upscale move is necessary to best competition from future members of the growing newly industrializing countries club, the quest is important in a mid-term strategy that extends into the 1990s. "Many of our engineers and scientists understand the true nature of competitiveness," declares Dr. Vincent Yip, chairman of the Science Council. "While automation in factories was not acceptable to them even two or three years ago, it is felt today that advanced manufacturing concepts will pay a bigger role than ever in several of our established industries."

Singapore already starts with a sophisticated base for its industries. Its armaments production is highly automated and earns high marks from many experts around the globe. Restructuring of the economy has transformed Singapore from a low-wage "sweatshop" to a high-cost, ultra-cosmopolitan center, with shimmering high-tech citadels dotting the skyline. "Our small size," notes Philip Yeo, chairman of the Economic Development Board, "is both a weakness and a strength. We are vulnerable at external events, but are very flexible to changes. Automation is important for us because we make goods for a world market, and everything produced here must be competitively priced as well as the highest quality."

A plan to bring multinational corporations into the national drive for automation was launched back in the early 1980s. So far, it has been highly successful, and shows the degree to which Singaporeans are preparing for "Third Wave" manufacturing. Philips, the Dutch electronics giant, is one of several West European, American, and Japanese firms that are active. A West German executive insists that some foreigners are hesitant about these types of bilateral relationships, but "here, they already proved there was a base to work with … the funding was made to give workers tools they needed," which has been a bargain for this giant corporation—whose top brass make no secret that they regard Japan's competitive edge as a menacing factor.

With 45 engineers per 100,000, Singapore believes it is capable of eventually spawning homegrown technology in order to conform with rapid design and product changes. Application-specific chips are a possibility, and wafer diffusion is a technique that began in 1988. The island state ranks as the world's leading center for production of Winchester disk drives, and work-force skills could readily be upgraded to match.

There are over 800 research engineers and scientists in businesses around the island, and a network of polytechnic institutes and training centers are serving as meccas for them. In the new plan, CAD,CAM, CAE (computer-assisted design, manufacturing, and engineering), integrated circuit, and tool and die design is emphasized. Microprocessor software development is another priority.

EDB's applied technology group can show results from both man-power training and from the array of courses provided in this technical/high-tech education network. CNC press brake controllers, automation controllers, automation vehicles, and mass-storage systems for personal computers are coming off assembly lines. The new investment package offered to foreign companies includes generous incentives for those working in automated production of circuit boards, and for precision-fabricated metal products. EDB Chairman Yeo insists that tool-and-die mold making and specialized, customized die production has pleased U.S. and Western European companies locating or expanding in Singapore. "Our CNC centers are now able to produce micropulleys, special sockets, and components like rollers and pins for (computer) peripherals."

Some 19 foreign firms are taking part in a manpower-training program that Ooi Inn Bok, director of the German-Singapore Institute, thinks will carry the republic toward its goal of a diversified, technology-driven future. More than 5,000 engineers retrained in 1987 could double the amount in 1988. The Institute is only one of several facilities for this type of hands-on, no-nonsense instruction. In some cases, the government pays as much as 90 percent of a student's costs. No fewer than 15 laboratories and facilities are working on a partnership basis with multinationals. Secondary-school candidates are apprentices, then serve for two years on the job at selected companies. "Nearly three-fourths of the time they spend (which is over 4,400 hours)," declares Bok, "is in factory environments." The most popular certificates earned are for mechantronics engineering, industrial electronics engineering, and for instrumentation and control engineering.

The test will be whether Bok's goal of turning GSI into "a platform for technology transfer to industry" is met. Counterparts at other institutes are forging ahead on the race to transform Singapore's economic base. The types of robots, and functions such as materials handling, are targeted—in keeping with long-standing practices in this East Asian newly industrializing country to target carefully according to assumptions about which industries can benefit most from techniques (and which will still be on the city-state's economic menu in years to come).

The interface between work at the Institute and its counterparts is not easily transmitted to recipients in business, according to some analysts. Singaporeans are experiencing the same handicaps found elsewhere as world industries attempt to retool for the new era that is already upon us. "A major disk drive manufacturer wanted to install robots," says one manufacturer of automating equipment. "We did the studies and complied, but when an inspection and follow-up was conducted later, we found the robots idling, and workers in other parts of the production process had nothing to do, either."

One who agrees that overpurchasing is a problem is James Ling, director of the Automation Applications Centre. "Middle management here needs to see that their own education on this is important. Too many still think that robots are a solution to their overall problem."

Ling's company is a joint venture that includes the Economic Development Board, so care is taken to offer independent advice in facilities planning, WIP/inventory control, control software, special purpose machines, storage and retrieval, and other comprehensive elements of manufacturing. "We tell a lot of people who seek our help that, after seeing their (financial) books, it may not do them any good. They may have no future in that product line." And, for the ones who can succeed through automation, unless steps are taken to train maintenance staff and inaugurate MRP or JIT, productivity goals will still never be met.

In the past two years, textile, metalwork, plastic, chemical, electronic and precision-equipment firms have all responded in varying degrees to the message from Ling and others. About half are truly "small" business, with under 50 workers and less than $2 million in sales. Moderating wages will be necessary to sign on other firms—and to please those among the Fortune 500 contemplating expansion or continuing operations.

Apart from limiting pay increases, several other strategies hope to reverse the present slump and carry "the Lion City" through this new era of manufacturing. One is a long-term biotechnology program. First discussed years ago, a serious timetable for the program is emerging, and observers look upon the project as more viable than previously imagined. A knowledgeable researcher at DuPont calls Singapore a "sleeper" that has a good shot at scoring in some biotechnology niches.

What share of the biotech pie can the city-state pick up? In a quest for value-added industries, researchers at the newly inaugurated Science

Park foresee work in cloning and in plant-cell-tissue culture as tied to Asian agricultural needs. At least three companies are hiring staff in roots, tropical fruits, and other horticultural species. The aim is superior varieties. A handful of companies are concentrating on areas of biotechnology R&D where niche markets can be conquered. "We're not going to have any Genentechs," says Yip, "but we have to build a groundwork." Spinoffs can help other industries, so the $15 million invested in four biotech firms carries more weight than this figure—or the scant $2 million in output—would have one think. A government-sponsored Molecular and Cell Biology Institute has opened its doors, and is being managed by imported talent.

Coordinating research is a hurdle in this fledgling "sunrise" industry, as it is throughout the world. Bioprocessing—the techniques for production, commercialization, and automation—pose as many headaches for Singapore-based companies as they do for their counterparts in the U.S., Japan, and the EEC. The first few steps have been taken to launch joint ventures and begin collaboration necessary to propel this important sector of the economy.

Dr. Nga Been Hen is in charge of the National University's biotechnology program—one that allows graduates and postgrads to comingle with the handful of active companies, as part of the overall skilled-labor program. "In looking for these niches," he says, "we're going to the U.S. and Europe, and to Japan, and looking over what's there and what we can realistically do. By looking at advanced technologies, we can take one plus one and make more than two.

Dr. Tank Kok Kheng at Evergreen Biotechnology Ltd. has seen his staff grow to 70, and the shiitake mushrooms he is cultivating through high-tech systems are now marketed in the U.S. "This is a billion-dollar industry," and something that Singaporeans can handle without extending themselves into the stratosphere, where Japanese and U.S. firms compete for the "sexy" breakthroughs. The government's new incentives plan includes "pioneer" status, meaning generous tax abatements and other financial support for costs of trade fairs and overseas travel. Yet, a lack of venture capital and tight government funding for start-up money could inhibit others.

Plantek, also in the Science Park, is another example of how niches can be identified. This company is using tissue culture R&D—as well as joint venture agreements with a Utah-based firm—to harvest "super" tropical fruits, disease-resistant cxdrops, genetically altered coffee beans, and "designer gene" flowers. After just 18 months of operation, the staff is nearing 60.

TOURISM

Other pillars of the economy are also getting attention as the EDB contemplates its competition edge in the 1990s. A tourism project is channeling $500 million into improvements over the next few years. As in other arenas, there is stiff competition from Asia-Pacific neighbors and the city-state can market itself only as a stopover point to other "exotic" locales.

For the moment, this affluent Asian city-state, which is pinning much of its hope for the future on tourism, had been adrift in a sea of unused hotel space during 1986 and 1987. To fill that space, the Singapore government has embarked on a five-year, $500 million program to boost tourism revenue by attracting more tourists—and getting those who come to stay longer and spend more. There were 3.7 million visitors in 1987. The tourism program calls for expenditures of $200 for each of the 2.5 million Singapore citizens. That's fairly low compared with other Asian destinations. Hong Kong figures on spending $290; Tokyo, over $500 per capita. Only Kuala Lumpur, Malaysia's capital, is lower, at $190. The plan could help keep more than 15,000 service jobs and would also spin off benefits to the sagging fortunes of a construction industry that suffered a prolonged slump in 1986.

The average tourist visit to Singapore lasts just three and a half days. "Even a half day more for conventioneers," says Dui Tui Leong, deputy director of the Singapore Tourism Board, "will generate tremendous income." If the goal of adding a half day to each visitor's itinerary by 1990 is reached, it would bring in nearly $400 million in additional revenues.

With hotel overbuilding continuing this year, room rates are in their second year at bargain levels. The 19,000 hotel rooms available during the recession year of 1985 have mushroomed to more than 24,000, and 2,000 more are on stream. Occupancy rates in 1986 were as low as 25 percent in some major properties, causing serious financial losses.

"We aim for about 7 percent [in occupancy increases] this year," a confident tourism official declares. That would result in 400,000 more room-nights.

A spokesman for the Mandarin Hotel group speaks for many in the hospitality industry. "Losses since 1985 ... have put a lot of us in difficult times. But there is a lot that can be done here, if we position ourselves differently to keep up with competition" from other parts of Asia.

Mr. Leong points out that for the Japanese—who made up 400,000 of the 3.2 million visitors in 1986—the British colonial image has appeal, as does Singapore's reputation for safety. Shopping discounts attract North

Americans. A growing number of visitors are coming in from neighboring countries in Southeast Asia as well. And the Tourism Board believes that most visitors want Singapore to keep its "Asian" appearance despite the skyscraper boom and Westernization of some areas.

Other aspects of the tourism overhaul call for developing upscale shopping districts. Haw Par Villa, the celebrated Tiger Balm Gardens, will be renovated by 1989 to include a theme park. The highlight will be a Disney-styled underground ride through an Oriental fantasy setting, complete with dragons and demons.

PLANNING FOR THE FUTURE

Despite all its many indigenous strengths, Singaporean leaders realize that they have little chance of building their own homegrown economic base. "To an extent, we are an anomaly," says Tan Puay Chuan, a vice president of Intraco, the city-state's $400 million integrated trading company. "Other countries can bask in the sun and use a large population as one way of selling domestically. We cannot. Another country might feel comfortable with a higher percentage of foreign capital, if it's secure, and just follow the lead of some multinational. Here, however, we never have the luxury of sitting still. We have to make a really big leap forward, and end dependency on foreign corporations.

"Mind me, we like them here, and we have a lot to offer. But they are making decisions on what's best for them. We know this. We don't blame them for this. They are as vulnerable to a worldwide trade collapse, or to energy price fluctuations, or other things that may be coming on the horizon."

He is not alone in pointing out that the successful marketing trips launched by EDB—whether they are to Europe, to the U.S., or even to Japan—will not necessarily produce long-term jobs or long-term spinoffs vital to continuing growth and to avoiding a perilous shrinkage as was witnessed during 1985–86.

Singapore needs that foreign investment, but must prepare for the era when it will shrivel up. Multinationals in the developed lands of "the North" now seem to prefer siting close to their own markets. The real downturn in overseas investment could be in the early 1990s. (Only Japan is boosting its offshore siting, and doing so now because of a currency realignment.) The narcotic of foreign investment is dangerous, especially when Japanese and other outsiders are not concerned about long-term commitments. (The port, for example, is desirous and could be very much so after 1997, but that is not a certainty.)

So, the city-state needs a form of investment that provides for the creation, or incubation, of domestic industries with some potential for competing in Asia, if not elsewhere. And, while its base is potent, it is small—small in numbers of people, in comparative capital resources, and in physical space to house incoming plants.

The Lion City cannot survive without foreign capital and outside technology. It knows that other East Asian newly industrializing countries are staking out claims: "gateway to China," "your distribution center for Southeast Asia," the "best port," "qualified labor," and so on.

To set itself as attractive, and apart from others in East-Asia, the minuscule republic must aim ever-upward. Land-scarce, population-short Singapore has no other direction to travel as it seeks value-added products and a true postindustrial economic base—one with enough talent to respond quickly to the twists and turns in the 1990s world economic maze. The high living standard and high wage structure make it necessary for Singapore to attract industries with wealth-generating spinoffs.

The Lion City justifiably tires of contract work for multinationals— "OEM" (original equipment manufacturers) production. "If we want to stay ahead in this game," declares Dr. Yip, chairman of the Science Council, its cornerstones in telecommunications and services, and a thriving, advanced electronics sector must leapfrog. Hence, Singapore's competitive luster will remain. Major multinationals are fickle, can move quickly (as in textiles and toy production), and subcontract little to help support local companies. The problem (shared with other Dragon neighbors), *The Far Eastern Economic Review* estimates, is that Philips relies on suppliers based in Singapore for only 4 percent of its equipment purchases. And, says Boo Kheng Hua of the Applied Technology Group, "most companies doing well are just subcontracting," which he finds "could change without much notice."

To bypass the subcontracting route, the city-state needs modifications in its base. It is facing up to this reality, through a number of aggressive campaigns supported by business and charted by government agencies whose continuous contact with the private market assures some ability to act on reasonable, feasible plans. (Yet, as we saw in the area of automation, it is not happening that quickly in most cases.)

In addition to the strong competition coming from Taiwan, Hong Kong, and the Republic of (South) Korea, others in the industrialized world are grabbing for the same high-tech and services "pie." As nations leapfrog each other, and advanced countries in Asia move upward on the skills ladder, the battle to position oneself as attractive become more difficult. Only those countries destined to produce sandals and batik through this decade have enjoyed the luxury of complacency in the global fight for foreign investment. Today, even these pronounced less-developed countries are yearning for some respectable share of a technology base during the years ahead. They are fully prepared to "give away the store," sadly, in many cases, in order to get a handful of visible projects that can produce tangible economic wealth—and hopefully lure other multinationals onto their turf.

Agreement was reached among top-level Singaporean government bodies in 1987 to recast the development strategy. Henceforth, the city-state would be portrayed as a regional headquarters for North American and European companies. This is a riskier and more difficult approach than more conventional strategies, which aim for only branch plants and factories, but if successful, it will attract senior management and administrative expertise, and will introduce an assortment of sophisticated equipment. It can also bring in considerable revenue through types of upscale spending that occurs when executives form the cadre of a multinational's offshore siting decision. Beyond that, possibilities for major warehousing and marketing divisions of the multinationals are bright—if the "regional center" concept is accepted. In addition the multinational's Singapore inventory would provide business for the port and would allow the island nation to make cost-effective decisions on other forms of infrastructure needed to accommodate expanding white-collar business. As one official joked, if enough corporations accept the premise, "we can pay back the [new] subway long before schedule."

The regional center concept will be marketed as the 1980s draw to a close. Singapore's traditional strengths—the port, infrastructure, location, work force dedication, job training programs—form the kernel of the new promotional push.

To add to existing incentives, reductions in the contributions by employers to the Central Provident Fund—the pool used primarily to construct housing—are seen as reducing labor costs by 12 percent annually for multinationals with over 20 employees. The government estimates that manufacturers can save 3–5 percent on total yearly costs through this single measure. Further reductions in the corporate tax—from 40 percent to 33 percent, were implemented in 1988. In addition, property taxes were lowered by 50 percent, and income taxes dropped substantially.

R&D must be bolstered, but this is difficult to do. "Pure research is out of the question," says Dr. Yip at the Science Council. "We place our hopes on the … National University." Small wonder many technology firms are clustered close by, and that the Automation Applications

Centre under Dr. Ling is adjacent to National's campus. Yip believes that some creative incentives can stimulate local companies to direct more resources and personnel into applied, if not basic, research.

Government constitutes about half of the (1988) $140 million R&D expenditure "pie." Engineering is a big share of both government and private R&D funding, while electronics makes up 60 percent of private research spending. Health sciences and medical fields account for much of the balance, and while all R&D rose from a base of just $35 million in 1982, it must perform better to capture vital niche markets in product lines of such sectors as biotechnology.

Shared R&D with multinationals is essential in the more promising sectors of Singapore's 1990s economy—machine tools, medical equipment, aviation and aerospace, and some areas of electronics. According to the Economic Development Board, markets for electronic products and sophisticated testing equipment will grow from $200 million in 1988 to nearly $250 million a year later—and organizations like the German-Singapore Institute are determined to mesh their plans with those of foreign manufacturers.

To try to secure some research and product development in aerospace, the city-state imported over $500 million in equipment, most of it from the U.S. It understands that Singapore Airlines can no longer depend on its high-quality service reputation alone and that the aviation industries, now producing some $450 million worth of GNP, can increase each year by 4–6 percent through 1999, when it would become a $700–800 million colossus.

Despite some impressive jumps in outside investment, R&D still lags. In 1987, $585 million of direct foreign investment (DFI) reached the Lion City, and electronics again saw significant increases; in fact, DFI in this single sector has grown by at least 12 percent annually for the past decade.

Of the DFI reaching Singapore the U.S. and Japan each have $220 million, giving the two together nearly 80 percent of all DFI for 1987. A good chunk of that DFI is still coming into the Jurong Town Corporation network. The *Christian Science Monitor* reported in November 1987 that JTC plans to build five more 20,000-square foot factories, with leasing rates ranging from $1.80–$4 a square meter. They are expected to add another 40,000 to the quarter of a million workers already employed at JTC sites.

Where is the new investment surge headed? In November 1987, Toshiba announced that it would increase audio production from 800,000 units to a million units. Aiwa's recent plans to greatly increase Singaporean production translated into a threefold increase in output over 1986, boosting the level to $175 million in 1987. This Sony subsidiary has been plagued by financial losses, and with the rising value of the yen, was determined to cut costs in manufacturing. According to sources at Aiwa, Singaporean plants run at the JTC sites result in a 15–20 percent cut in production costs, thereby allowing the company to compete cost-efficiently. Sony is building a $22 million precision parts center in the city-state, one that hopes to be a springboard for the technical support required in other Southeast Asian markets in the years ahead.

AT&T is rumored to be ready to take up vast space allotments at the new Jurong Town development. Philip Yeo, Economic Development Board chairman, says that this may be the most significant success for his agency's 1987 efforts to attract DFI. "For AT&T, it gives a chance to have a solid base from which to expand and review markets in the ASEAN region," says Mr. Yeo. An R&D staff of 40 is expected in the new facility by 1989, and product development—a focus of the new value-added campaign in the city-state—is getting top priority from this one AT&T operation. Yeo was pleased for another reason: U.S. tax-law overhauls in 1986 made the desirability of foreign offshore plants questionable for a number of important American industries.

Another expansion may be seen as General Motors, which makes 4.5 million integrated circuits a year in the city-state, talks about expanding its plant there. Control Data, which suffered losses in the hundreds of millions during 1985 and 1986, bought the argument that a site in the Lion City would save costs and possibly open doors elsewhere in Southeast Asia. The Minneapolis, Minnesota-based firm invested $50 million in a plant that opened its doors in 1988, with projected savings of 20 percent on the million-plus disk drives that will be manufactured there annually.

Hewlett-Packard is actively involved in technology transfer through operations such as the automation centers and the network of automation and robotics institutes across Singapore. Fiber-optic components, keyboards, a range of peripherals, and terminals are assembled in the city-state by the California-based firm. Faced with some of the same problems shared by other technology-based corporations during the protracted electronics slump (1984–86), Hewlett-Packard was faced with options of cutting back or expanding. "We look at Singapore from a strategic standpoint more than anything else," says a spokesman in Palo Alto, California. "If they (Singapore's EDB and other agencies) were serious about plans, we could fit right in. But if we thought they would take a turnabout and couldn't deliver, it would jeopardize our relationship."

After the firm had expanded, Singapore was hit by the recession, "and we got caught in the squeeze," according to the same executive. Instead of retrenching further or instituting layoffs, the firm offered employees the chance to work on flexible hours—something which Singaporeans were not accustomed to, and which raised many eyebrows around the city-state in the lean recession years. Results were encouraging, since productivity increased dramatically and a few hundred employees actually put in 20 percent uncompensated overtime. The worker-employer contract will not be altered, but this experimentation proved that multinational partnerships can have constructive ends—and salvage the fortunes of participants on both sides of the equation.

The shape of multinational investment in the 1990s will mirror this type of activity, according to many experts. The priority for EDB and its quasi-planned forecasts point to an irony: Continued large influxes of foreign capital are the only means of letting Singapore shake itself free from fickle multinational corporations in the mid-1990s.

Just as the whole concept of economic development, and of making one's nation attractive to investment from the West, has changed, so has education. Singapore prizes education. In 1988, a new program, dubbed WISE (for Worker Improvement through Secondary Education) hopes to upgrade retraining and vocational education and forever ease doubts about the quality of the school system. In private, EDB officials confess that the nation's no-nonsense policies often impose a puritanical standard yet fail to make the universities as responsive as they must be in order to adjust to rigors of technology education.

When, in the summer of 1987, the prime minister publicly called for a policy to encourage more intelligent people to have more babies, it was seen by some leaders as a gaffe—a response to studies showing that many people, perhaps 600,000 (or half the work force) did not enroll through a ninth year of formal studies. The call for such drastic action, whatever its merits, points out the seriousness with which the situation is viewed.

While over 6,000 university and polytechnic graduates were tallied in 1987, that is a mere 4.8 percent of the student population. (Taiwan, by comparison, scores a little higher at 7 percent, but the figure for Europe is 28 percent, and for North America 40 percent.) Dr. N. Narendram, director of research for the Singapore Science Council, asserts that the percentage of workers in professional slots, or holding jobs in technical fields, must increase by over 5 percent before 1995 if the goals of having a fifth of the total work force in that category are to be met. "Right now, we have pushed our young people … they respond well, they score well on tests, and they work hard, but we need many more of them," he says.

As the above shows, there are unique problems found in population-short Singapore. In addition, the whole matter of allowing schools to foster an entrepreneurial spirit—which one large faction of educational observers note is essential for the sorts of creativity that breed innovation—has been addressed only in study reports thus far.

The current recovery from the last downturn is evident in many sectors, but the traditional base—construction, services, and trade—had been bogged through 1988. Overall, the GNP gained and manufacturing displayed a promising increase of 9 percent in output. Commerce, including tourism, many services, and trade, fell by nearly 1 percent in 1987, and construction tumbled by 25 percent. Clearly, the massive tourism project outlined above would improve conditions in two or three ailing sectors, and foreign trade has increased as economic conditions around the region and among Singapore's trading partners have improved.

In 1988 and 1989, the U.S., Japan, Malaysia, and the EEC remained the country's major trading partners. Exports to America and to Western Europe grew slightly, while sales fell to Japan and to a Malaysia just emerging from recession. The nation gaining most proportionately from import- export links with the Lion City was West Germany; the Federal Republic jumped from 11th place to 6th place among trade partners worldwide. In Asia itself, Taiwan and Korea both showed robust 20 percent increases in two-way commerce with Lee Kuan Yew's democratic fiefdom.

Singapore is rightfully concerned about Asia's energy future. With production at her refineries running 650,000 barrels daily (in the second half of 1987), groups like Shell, Exxon, and Caltex are confident that the old days of refining—when over 750,000 barrels were processed daily—might return. Price increases around the world would contribute to a sounder base for refining, and Indonesia's plans to increase her level of petrol exports are seen as benefiting Singapore.

Experts agree that OPEC's decision a decade ago to play a larger role in refining is having an affect everywhere in the non-OPEC world. Once China becomes a major player in the world oil market, (and this is an event which could take place by the mid-1990s), Singapore may battle with others to take on Chinese production in order to increase refining capacity. If Japanese interests win out, the Lion City's daily refining loads would fall to 450,000 or so barrels.

Looking ahead to the 1990s, the city-state must prepare to upgrade itself in other ways. Recent trends that suggest that the port is about to overtake Hong Kong as the premier (measured in tonnage) harbor are impressive. Yet, productivity at Jurong has been criticized in the past. A series of programs by government agencies have made it possible to handle large amounts of cargo. Last year, the *Journal of Commerce* reported that quantity at about 600 containers in a span of seven hours, with "a smaller, more efficient workforce" than was found at corresponding Asian ports.

Yet more modernization is needed. The port is far more than a visible prestige project. Transshipment is playing a greater role in world commerce, as intermodal transport systems take root. Container ships will likely be offered discount rates in order to keep the tonnage up, and if cargoes from oil-rich Indonesia and Brunei enter in growing numbers, the loads will continue to grow.

A journey to the harbor today finds laser scanners, electronic weighing bridges, and computerized data-billing systems functioning around the clock. In San Francisco, a spokesman for Singapore-based Neptune Orient Lines indicates that port expansion is considered such a high priority the ceiling on improvements may be $700 million over 1989–93. Neptune Orient—which is planning major new routes to North America in 1988—substantiates rumors that a major new container terminal is likely in the early 1990s, with another $200 million or so going to the project. Feeder berths and perhaps three or four container berths will be added.

The much-publicized 24-hour stock-futures-trading hookup with Chicago has not proven to be the roaring success its planners projected. For one thing, telecommunications at other exchanges, including Tokyo and the recently opened market in Osaka, are drawing business from Singapore. Another less-than-spectacular success was the financial- services plan. Originally, the plan, whose origins are traced to the advice of international consultants and even multilateral financing institutions such as the World Bank, saw the city-state positioned as the only viable financial center for Southeast Asia. Taiwan's plans to set up an offshore banking center were not taken seriously, and Korean efforts to develop a vibrant stock exchange were not seen as serious competition. Richard Hu, currently minister of finance, thinks the plans at least "brought us to the point ... of thinking about world finance, from the standpoint of Singaporeans as playing a real role in it, not just acting as intermediates for the world's bankers." He understands that another competitor, Tokyo, is its own special case, and that other contestants such as Sydney, Australia, are too far away from the hub of East Asia to be considered "the financial center" for this region.

Even though plans to set up a large-scale, autonomous, electronically oriented banking structure floundered, a cadre of highly trained professionals have come out of the plan. So the manpower is there, to be tapped for related crafts. In the late 1980s, a number of events will make it possible for the country to harness skills of this fairly large (1,000–3,000) cadre. Foreign companies will be listed on local stock exchanges, in spite of objections by some members of Lee Kuan Yew's own People's Action (political) Party. The brokerage industry within Singapore is likely to be able to accommodate foreign firms, and while a pell-mell rush to handle transactions is expected, the first and second waves in this trend will lay foundations for other arrivals.

Another factor will play a decisive role in the emergence of board-based private capital markets in the city-state: the call by officials to at last privatize. Even in this bastion of private enterprise, the government controls a healthy share of the economy. In March 1987, the final report of a study panel, which spent over 14 months investigating supposed benefits in releasing the megacorporations to buying and selling, made its recommendations. Three billion dollars worth of shares would be offered in 40 state-managed corporations, including Singapore Airlines, Intraco, and Hitachi Electric Devices. The panel indicated that another 20 percent could be added to market capitalization should these sales occur, and that an "orderly" process of putting percentages of the companies on the market would allow most of them to adjust to macro-economic conditions. "The government here is still too powerful," according to one vice president of a shipping firm. "We are unable to adjust rates as we wish. We play catch-up to the rest of the world, because some bureaucrats think the status of having national carriers far outweighs economic considerations. That will be accepted here, but you can't tell people outside Singapore that some edict is more sensible than supply-and-demand forces ... at work."

The report praised past actions of the state-run enterprises, which propelled growth in the postwar era. As industries "matured," however, conflicts between government goals and realities of the marketplace necessitated change. It emphasized the fact that interlocked companies would need time to adjust to any phased-in privatization. For example, the Development Bank of Singapore controls 16 percent of the giant horizontally integrated trading company Intraco. Changi Airport Services, Inc., is largely owned by the Port of Singapore Authority. Sembawang Shipyards, Inc., is 70 percent government-owned. Takeover bids have already surfaced in Singapore, and disputes among different factions in the loose confederation of public-private combines are more numerous than ever.

One of the more controversial sections of the 1987 report was a call for privatization of Telecoms. The enormous communications and telecommunications market in this advanced, affluent society make the scope of any moves to open the market astonishing. These efforts in regard to the bourse will be accompanied by actual foreign holdings of shares in these sectors.

All these factors sift into the equation that will make the next few years a challenging period. And no one can be certain what the tea leaves read for 65-year-old Lee Kuan Yew's future. The prime minister—often criticized even at home for his special brand of mild, benevolent authoritarianism—will probably step down before 1990 after more than a quarter century at the helm of the nation he created. There is the 1997 question in fellow newly industrializing country, fellow Dragon Hong Kong, where flight capital or a "brain drain" could surface, adding immeasurably to the Singaporean economy, while turmoil in neighboring Malaysia will send an exodus of Chinese to the Lion City.

As planners look at the period through the mid-1990s, they eye niche markets in aerospace (including servicing the large network of air carriers traversing the Pacific in ever-expanding numbers). Marine and oceanographic engineering equipment is seen as a promising industry. The technocrats at EDB—regardless of who replaces Lee Kuan Yew (one recent joke has been "the Father, Son, and Holy Goh," referring to the Prime Minister's son and a top politician as possible successors)—intend to make only slight modifications in the form of centralized planning which has directed growth.

"Most of our businessmen are very supportive of this form of decision-making," says an executive at Intraco, a leading trade company which, like other industrial giants, has recovered from the dark days of 1985–86. "We feel we have flexibility to move around the key spots in Asia, and close to our doorstep," including the People's Republic.

EDB style of targeting is, of course, geared towards science-based industry. And, national security in an uncertain world takes precedence in future plans; whether in beefing up armaments productions or in providing security through agricultural self-sufficiency. *Pacific Century* newsletter recently reported that 400 high-tech "non-polluting" farms are a cornerstone of the plan to reduce the volume of imported foodstuffs (nearly all its poultry, vegetables, and seafood comes from foreign sources).

In 1988, a regional newsmagazine, *Asiaweek*, was censored in the city-state. The incident came after other publications had been reprimanded for criticisms of the ruling administration, and a global outcry was heard. Only after it was revealed that the magazine added its own text to a letter it received from a government official—a letter that appeared in *Asiaweek*'s pages—did the denunciations diminish.

The incident brings to light image problems faced by the Republic. In the past year or so, the government has been roundly criticized for impingements upon press freedom. Aspects of supposedly authoritarian tactics are attacked with equal vigor. Yet, most critics remain ignorant of the country's triumphs, and probably dismiss the delicate fabric of its ethnically based foundations too easily.

8

Malaysia: Quest for Cohesion

Malaysia holds tremendous, and often ignored, potential for an economic awakening than most Asian countries. Some of the winds of change are sweeping Malaysia, preparing it for the status of a newly industrializing country. Difficult choices lie ahead for the nation, however—choices that will determine whether Malaysia will ever realize its potential for economic might.

THE CHALLENGES FACING MALAYSIA

In the capital of Kuala Lumpur, one sees a rich mixture of ethnic groups, but the diverse population is also the greatest problem that the government must address. For centuries, this "City of Eternal Spring" has been one of Asia's most active melting pots. Moslem traders established outposts 700 years ago, followed by the Portuguese, Dutch, and British. Japan's occupation during World War II was followed by a commercial invasion of U.S. influence. The impact of Islam and its fundamentalist factions (although Malaysia is a largely Sunni nation) will also bear heavily on the direction of the nation.

Cohesion among the ethnic groups—including a Chinese bloc that represents 37 percent of the nation's 16 million inhabitants—is faltering in Malaysia in some respects. As in other countries in the region, the Chinese there ascended to commanding heights in the financial and commercial sectors. Now, regulations are in force to increase Malay participation in economic life. For example, an ambitious 1982 program created a trust agency to increase corporate control for Malays, who in 1970, ran a scant 2 percent of major businesses. The goal was to bring that figure to 33 percent in a few years, but those objectives have been partially abandoned. Some claim that this bumiputra, or "son of the soil," plan has led to boondoggles. Similar ethnic quotas apply to foreign investment projects, which has led to protests from Chinese and foreign investors alike. The Chinese—mindful of the race riots in the 1960s and 1970s—are also disturbed over policies that curtail Chinese-language studies.

Religious divisions surfaced recently, with fundamentalist Moslems demanding a larger voice in government. Regional tensions are also apparent: Two districts far from Kuala Lumpur, Sabah and Sarawak, have protested that they feel left out of the national agenda. In 1983 a plot to murder some governmental officials was uncovered, allegedly engineered by others at the highest level of government. Recent financial scandals since have also shaken the faith in national institutions.

All this comes as something of a surprise in what was supposed to be an Asian success story. After independence, over 30 years ago, the country forged ahead, scoring annual growth rates of 8 percent consecutively through the 1970s. Per capita income reached $1,865 by 1984, but fell to $1,530 in 1986. It is currently $1,800. The country is a natural resource storehouse, with 40 percent of the world's output in palm oil and tropical hardwood, a gold mine of natural rubber, a third of the world's tin, and substantial oil reserves.

Natural rubber brings in substantial foreign earnings, but rubber prices have been falling. While export earnings in tin, rubber, and timber soared 35 percent annually over the 1960s and 70s, the worldwide downturn in rubber crippled revenue. An international rubber pact in 1980 stabilized prices, but the worldwide recession hurt demand for other products, and palm oil demand has lessened because of its high cholesterol content.

Government borrowing is up sharply, bringing the national debt to new highs. Loans from abroad surpass $7 billion, and reserves fell this year. Development plans were curbed in the mid-1980s as austerity forced cutbacks in infrastructure.

The specter of a continued recession across the plantations haunts Malaysians far away in traditional rural settlements. The stock market endured a slack period through most of 1987 and 1988, and once-strong real estate tumbled in 1986–87. Genting Berhard's stock price (the casino group with large rubber holdings) was as disappointing as Sime Darby, the largest (and agricultural-based) corporation.

Dramatic events are unfolding, though, on the country's economic landscape. It is more dependent on the fate of semiconductors than ever, and much depends on a new incentives plan on electronics—anticipating, correctly, worldwide growth during 1988. To that end, investment promotion teams are touring the U.S., trying to dispel the image of Malaysia as an underdeveloped captive to commodities. Recent steps include allowing for 100 percent foreign equity participation under some conditions, permission to retain control of subsidiaries, and repatriation of profits. High technology, precision instruments, and engineering are fields given priority for tax abatements.

Dato Ahamd Sarji Bin Abdul Hamid, chairman of the Malaysian Industrial Development Authority, believes incentives "clarify" concerns over promised liberalization for foreign investors. "We have preconditions to help realize ambitious projects," especially transforming commodities into finished products, he says. "Semiconductors are well established," and the goal of more assembly manufacturing can be met by concentrating promotion campaigns on electronics sectors.

Before some multinationals retrenched, curtailing offshore electronics investments, few of them bypassed Malaysia in their offshore plans. Exports of semiconductors is a $4 billion industry there, and Malaysia has become the world's leading chip exporter and is third in the world in production.

In the high tech area, there are considerable electronics and peripheral computer-equipment manufacturers setting up shop around the capital and in Penang, the picturesque western coastal state.

Malaysia's decision in 1987 to open up its economy to foreign investment ranks as one of the most significant developments affecting the Southeast Asian region. It is one part of a two-stage effort, the second part of which consists of steps to liberalize the country's New Economic Policy (NEP). Experts like Mark van Fleet, Asia-Pacific director for the U.S. Chamber of Commerce, think a substantial rise in U.S. investment will occur as Western manufacturers explore costs and value of location.

Cutting red tape at the network of over 100 industrial estates—which include special trade zones and export processing zones—is another positive sign. Recognizing the need to develop rural sections, the Federation's incentives may succeed in luring industries to areas along the north coast, and to peninsular Malaysia. Manufacturing now makes up 20 percent of the $60 billion GNP, and more than 800,000 are employed in plants and factories, accounting for 42 percent of the $15 billion export pie.

More value-added exports are needed to revive an economy stung by negative growth in 1985 and a paltry 1 percent GNP increase in the following year. By 1988, some bright spots were visible on the economic landscape, and GNP was reaching nearly 5 percent. Citing a "narrow base" in electronics, textiles, and other industries, Primary Industries Minister Dr. Lim Keng Yaik conceded that response from multinationals has been too slow thus far. If U.S., European, and Japanese companies are lured by new incentives, perhaps technology transfer can become a reality. Despite successes in electronics, the country has not maximized the presence of foreign firms capable of introducing non-transient business.

The effort to export Proton Saga autos—priced far too high for domestic consumers—has absorbed vast amounts of capital. Protons should reach U.S. shores in 1989, and sales are anticipated to be far, far below the original forecast of 80,000 units. The U.S. holds 18 percent of Malaysia's trade, and America has a $1.2 billion balance-of-payments deficit with this country.

While uncertainties face the country, Malaysia has shown a determination to overcome obstacles in the past. It develops on its own terms, retaining indigenous culture as far as possible. The years ahead will test its inherent strengths as Malaysian society undergoes its transition.

SOCIAL GOALS AND PROGRAMS

Since independence in 1957, the nation has grappled with sharp ethnic differences. Historically, one could predict occupation based on ethnic group, with the Chinese dominating business, the Indians also primarily in trade (although a few could be found in agricultural areas), and the native Malays at the bottom of the socioeconomic ladder in the rural, poor, agricultural sector. Thus, as mentioned earlier, it was felt that the Malays needed a boost to allow them to catch up with the Chinese and Indians in terms of education, employment, and overall standard of living. Under this policy the Malays have been able to improve their standard of living to some degree.

During the 1970s, with its high-growth rates, the government was able to bring Malays into ownership of company equity without doing so at the expense of the Indians and Chinese. Today, however, with slower growth, any increase in Malay participation in the economy may occur at the expense of the other ethnic groups.

This, the government must either lengthen the schedule for Malay participation beyond 1990 (as it has already done in some instances) or risk precipitating open conflict among the various ethnic groups. Similarly, foreign investors will be needed to expand the industrial base and provide management and marketing skills, as well as the technology to manufacture various electronic and industrial equipment. Malaysia has always been fairly open to foreign investors and should continue to welcome them, but foreign investment will complicate the problem of attaining the goal of 30 percent Malay ownership of company equity by 1990. In the near term, there may be increasing pressure on the government to provide greater access to various social services, especially since most Malaysians have been experiencing a falling standard of living during the last few years, exacerbated by the removal of government subsidies on various essentials.

If ethnic peace prevails, Malaysia has a good chance to achieve a stronger role in the regional economic and political system and to improve the standard of living of its citizens. During this period, the demand for foreign technology and managerial skills will be strong, but even greater emphasis is likely to be placed on the transfer of technology and skills to Malaysians; investment in assembly industries, while welcomed for their contribution to the job pool, will probably be less favored than they have been in the past.

Infrastructural development will have to be a high priority, particularly development of communication and transportation networks. Thus, demand for imported equipment and materials as well as technical and managerial personnel will be strong. Processing industries will also be more favored during this period, and foreign investors who propose projects that allow processing and greater value added to Malaysian raw materials may be able to negotiate very favorable terms. In assessing the long-term foreign investment climate, the biggest unknown stems from the question of whether the National Front will be able to achieve a sense of national unity and purpose. Malaysian nationalism encompassing all racial groups would be desirable from the standpoint of political stability; however, if the National Front is successful in obtaining a consensus on national goals for development, there could be a tightening of controls over foreign investors. In any event, it seems unlikely that the National Front will be able to form a cohesive nationalistic government in the foreseeable future.

Access to medical care has improved greatly since independence, but access to health care is still better in urban areas than in the countryside. The Malaysian government has been successful in two major health-related efforts: elimination of the various epidemic diseases (which have devastated the population in the past) and widespread education to teach Malaysians the basics of sanitation and health care. Life expectancy has increased significantly since independence and is now at 62 years. Today, most health care is provided on an outpatient basis and is free. Hospital care is available for a small fee, usually based on income level and ability to pay. Although Malaysia still has a shortage of trained doctors, nurses, technicians, and other skilled personnel, the situation is improving; despite the limited rural facilities, overall access is improving for most Malaysians.

The Malaysian government has attached particular importance to education and thus has invested heavily to improve access to education for all Malaysians, especially for Malays, who enjoy, under the Special Rights doctrine, a preferred status for admission to institutions of higher learning. As part of the government's effort to forge a national cohesiveness, the national language, Bahasa Malay, is used in most educational institutions.

The government has set the goal of universal primary and lower secondary education; primary education is free. As in health care, rural areas lag behind the cities, but the number of schools in the countryside has increased greatly since independence. Like many other developing countries, Malaysia suffers from a lack of trained teachers and inadequate educational facilities and equipment. In recent years, a primary concern of the government, in addition to using educational institutions as a means of forming a national culture through the use of a standard curriculum and the national language, has been to encourage students to study subjects and develop skills in areas that will be needed as the economy develops further. Thus a major emphasis of government education policy has been on technical and vocational training, but the continuing public demand for general academic education has made this effort less than totally successful, as has the problem of producing adequately trained teachers. On the whole, since this is a priority area, educational levels and literacy rates should improve steadily over the next decade or so.

Finally, Malaysia has little in the way of other welfare or social security programs, but there is not much demand for such services yet. Over the next decade, as the economy grows, Malaysia should expect to face growing demands for basic services, particularly in the health and education areas.

No matter which aspect of Malaysian society is examined there always is a great disparity between the urban and rural populations (and between the Chinese and Malays). The rural populace is generally much poorer than residents in urban areas, with some 50 percent or more of the rural population living below the poverty level, while about 30 percent of the total population falls below the poverty level. Although per capita income has increased substantially during the past decade, distribution is still highly skewed in favor of urban dwellers, particularly urban Chinese who dominate business and trade.

PALM OIL

To get a glimpse of the obstacles facing this developing country, consider one of its current battles—a protracted struggle whose outcome affects exports, trade, and future growth.

Contention over palm-oil exports to the United States and the EEC is receiving wide attention around East Asia. The issue is seen by some officials as affecting future agricultural trade across both sides of the Pacific. The controversy is now having a ripple effect on America's food-processing industry as well.

Palm oil is one of several edible oils, whose number also includes safflower, coconut oil, and soybean oils. They are used in a wide range of consumer goods, especially candies, cakes, and cookies.

Malaysia has launched a publicity drive to promote palm oil, and charges protectionist interests—notably the American Soybean Association—resist imports on grounds of economic self-interest. Questions over proportions of saturated fat in the family of edible oils is emerging as the focal point of costly campaigns mounted by both sides. Evidence, from the Malaysian standpoint, is still controversial. "All vegetable oils contain amounts of saturated fat," declares Jeffrey Zeller at the Center for Science in the Public Interest in Washington, D.C. "You have to compare the percentages." Soybean, safflower, olive, and corn oil contain under 15 percent saturated fat; palm oil contains 51 percent.

Palm oil—over 95 percent of which comes from Southeast Asia—makes up just under a fifth of world edible oil production, which is 65 million tons. East Asia exported some $280 million worth of edible oils, mostly palm and coconut, to the U.S. last year. Malaysian imports of palm oil alone were $70 million of the total. While that represents a scant 3 percent of all U.S. edible oils consumption, consumption is rising rapidly in North America and in many parts of the world, and the palm oil share of edible oils is forecast by observers at the World Bank as taking half of global sales by 1999.

Palm oil's future in the United States is watched carefully, because, as one Malaysian official concedes, "the outcome of this ... could spell victory or defeat for world exports" in the 1990s. Malaysia considers America a better market than Western Europe, which will likely maintain a staunch anti-import agricultural policy for years.

Malaysia's palm oil production lagged during the 1950s and 60s, but investment in new production techniques boosted the crop by substantial amounts in the years that followed. In 1988, over 4.5 million tons were harvested, and palm oil has assumed particular importance for the country as other leading commodities such as natural rubber and tin have suffered calamitous price declines. Almost two-thirds of the 20 million acres under crop cultivation in the country is allotted for rubber and palm oil.

"Palm oil helps us integrate nearly a million farmers into modern agriculture," asserts Dr. Lim Keng Yaik, the Malaysian minister of primary industries. "This crop is keeping those small farmers and their families above the poverty line." Palm oil's fortunes rose during this decade, and the 1987 price of $800 per ton is more than enough to compensate for production costs, usually at $500 a ton.

With the country struggling to achieve the GNP growth rates enjoyed in the past, palm-oil profits are seen as a major component of plans to improve national output. For her neighbors, especially the Philippines, political stability as well as economic vitality may be at stake. Indonesian palm oil output is about 1.4 million tons, and its government has based rural development in part on the substance. For similar reasons, the Philippines is worried about fallout from any drop in its U.S. sales, according to Mark van Fleet, director of Asia-Pacific affairs at the U.S. Chamber of Commerce.

The government and farmer cooperatives are seeking foreign investment as they aim for improved techniques to raise yields above six tons per acre, but diversification of foreign investment into palm oil has been slow, largely because of uncertainty over consumer acceptance in the United States. Research on high-yielding varieties also lags.

THE OUTLOOK FOR MALAYSIA

A new generation of charismatic Moslem leaders are challenging authority in Kuala Lumpur. While the Sunni sect predominates (in contrast to the Shiites who control Iran), an Islamic resurgence—and strong fundamentalist sentiment—is on the rise. The constitution actually defines the Moslem faith as a national religion, and college campuses today abound with evidence of respect for its tenets. Dr. R. Suppiah, director of the Center for International Studies, the country's leading think tank, says, "in the past year, we have seen far greater activism than at any time in the history of the Federation." Few would challenge that assessment.

In politically sensitive Malaysia, even local political contests have a strong bearing on the outcome of national policy and on the direction of tomorrow's leaders. A blowup in the Middle East or a major economic catastrophe might polarize the nation. (In 1987, some politicians publicly alerted their people to threats of imminent invasion by Israeli forces!) Thus, the possibility for continuing tensions exists. Furthermore it seems that considerable flight capital from Chinese citizens has turned up in places like Singapore.

On the other hand, the country's history of social progress suggests that a promising future may be in store for all its citizens. Continued growth and a generally favorable world economic climate in the years ahead could enable all parties to mend fences and achieve goals of true national unity.

Because there are 22,000 Malaysians studying in the United States, and many thousands more in Canada and in the United Kingdom, some liberalization may occur once these young men and women return to positions of authority. "We believe," says Ambassador Albert S. Talalla in Washington, D.C., "that their experience in the West will introduce them to new ideas about business, about service industries, and about what role the private sector can play in national life." He is correct.

A number of key trends influence economic prospects for Malaysia in the 1990s. Privatization is a watchword of many top officials, and shipping, air transport, and services are likely candidates. Reforms must bypass political corruption as well as genuine differences of ideology, but the transition from a commodities-based economy to one with increasing levels of industrialization and technology shows that there is a natural constituency for liberalization.

Another five-year plan begins in the 1990s, and it is expected to place greater emphasis on exports. A domestic market is forecast, but not until the next century, after the government's policy of encouraging population growth has begun to show results.

Another target of reform is the banking system. The well-publicized scandals that rocked the country in the mid-1980s demonstrated domestic investment by agencies and wealthy individuals alike was necessary to prevent overconcentration of economic power. In the global debacle of October 1987, the stock exchange—closely linked to the Singapore stock market—suffered. Yet, indications in the ensuing months have demonstrated a resiliency that is characteristic of a country with real potential to diversify.

The advent of the Proton Saga, a 1300-cc passenger vehicle, may be the stumbling block in efforts to complete industrial transformation. In 1987 alone, it was generally believed that the government poured over $80 million into the project, and continuing government subsidies appear likely. The car is the prime minister's own brainchild, begun in 1982 with negotiations between the government and Mitsubishi. Proton is essentially a Japanese "kit" put together by Malaysian hands. It was conceived at a time when domestic demand had been forecast at 200,000 or so cars per year; by 1986 that estimate dropped to just over 100,000.

Yet, by that time, enough resources and prestige had been invested in the venture that it was not feasible to quit production, and foreign markets were projected to make up the shortfall. Some modest sales to New Zealand are taking place today, and the director of Florida's international commerce office indicates over 40,000 may pass through Floridian ports from October 1988 to October 1989. This is a sharp drop from earlier estimates of U.S. sales.

Will Proton be a success? It is very risky. Large numbers of Protons sitting on vacant lots would hardly add to the nation's image, and they could pose severe financial strains on the economy as a whole. The Proton comes westward just as an auto glut is appearing; total North American production capacity is over 16 million, and only 12.6 million cars were produced by all makers during 1987. If a senior General Motors vice president's prediction that "blood would be spilled" because of the overcapacity situation is accurate, Mahathir's race to produce a showcase product will result instead in creation of an embarrassing, costly white elephant.

In high technology the strong impetus by the Malaysian government to actively encourage computerization in both the public and private sectors has resulted in a fairly rapid increase in computer installations. To accommodate this changing environment, the government has formulated a new strategy, the result of which is the National Data Communication System.

The era of computer communications in the true sense of the word has recently dawned on Malaysia with the establishment of the Packet Switched Public Data Network (MAYPAC). With the availability of this data network it is now possible to achieve computer networking with greater ease.

The government plans to spend more than $60 million over the next five years on computerization to raise the effectiveness and efficiency of the public sector. Priority will be given to revenue-earning agencies; departments and agencies involved in research and development; and highly structured organizations like those involved in training.

In Selangor, the country's first mini "Silicon Valley" technology park is under way, opening its doors to foreign companies in 1988. The park consists of four basic components: laboratories and offices for research; technology sources from the higher institutions; business management facilities; and credit facilities to be provided by financial institutions, which would assist entrepreneurs in setting up businesses. Entrepreneurs wishing to use the facilities of the technology park for research must first convince the park management of the feasibility of their idea.

The government has earmarked 150 acres for the project. The site was chosen because of its proximity to several leading universities and national R&D centers. The program, which comes under the Fifth Malaysian Plan, will cost $20 million. Late in 1988, news of unionization among electronics workers sent negative ripples through much of the West and Japan, in part because of the perception, whether right or wrong, that leaders of these trade organizations were hostile to multinationals.

The timber industry has tremendous potential in Malaysia. Datuk Lim Keng Yiak, primary industries minister and a frequent visitor to the West, indicates that some value added in that sector is possible. The former physician now thinks that the output in timber, which was $1.5 billion in 1987, could reach the $2.5 billion mark by 1994. The world ecology community has been very critical of development of lumber in Sarawak, but the federal and state governments are committed to the exploitation of those resources. It has ample data to show that replanting is proceeding apace. The importance of tin has grown in the 1990s.

Malaysian industry leaders are banking on a resurgence in rubber. Malaysia is the largest producer of natural rubber, producing some 1,500 tons annually, or 35 percent of global output. (Indonesia is in second place with just over a fourth of production. Thailand, Sri Lanka, and India are also important producers.)

Two-thirds of global rubber demand is now for the synthetic form, helped by the slump in the price of the petroleum, from which synthetic rubber is made.

However, the Malaysians reason that by the 1990s, new technologies and new uses for natural rubber will reverse the industry's sagging fortunes. Increased interest in contraceptive devices in the wake of the AIDS epidemic is only one factor increasing demand for natural rubber. Radial tires, which are increasingly popular, use rubber in much higher proportions than do conventional tires. Recent breakthroughs in epoxysized natural rubber (ENR) are important to the tire market, which is the key to natural rubber's future. ENR allows for better handling on a variety of surface conditions, and improvements in vulcanization techniques enable ENR to retain its characteristics longer than was previously thought.

Natural rubber has unusual new uses as well, including its use in materials that will assist office buildings to absorb shock waves in the event of an earthquake. The global chemical industry is finding novel uses for it, too, especially in linings found in nondestructive testing processes, which are becoming increasingly important in advanced manufacturing techniques.

Competition in the rubber industry is inevitable because of relatively rapid growth in other natural rubber-producing countries, particularly Thailand, Indonesia, and China. Malaysia is projected to account for about 30 percent of the 5 million tons, and 29 percent of the 6 million tons, of the total world rubber production forecast by the Task Force of Experts for the years 1990 and 2000, or about 4 to 5 percentage points lower than Malaysia's current contribution. The land area under rubber cultivation in Malaysia is projected to decline steadily at the rate of about 1 percent a year from now until 2000 because of government policies to discourage further expansion in the smallholding subsector and of continued diversification by the estates out of rubber. Nevertheless, a growth rate of about 1.2 percent a year is projected between 1985 and 2000 on the basis of prevailing policies and organized efforts to enhance efficiency and productivity. One major thrust of these efforts is to ensure effective transfer of rubber planting and producing technologies to the smallholders who now farm more than three quarters of the rubber land.

Petrochemicals also figure to play a large role in Malaysia's future. With 63 trillion cubic feet of oil and gas in reserve, Malaysia has the potential to expand beyond the present base, which is mostly resins.

The tourist sector is only beginning to receive attention, but as new air routes traverse the Pacific and formerly off-limits regions open up, the appeal of many lush tropical regions will draw visitors and put Malaysia into direct competition with other Southeast Asian destinations.

A number of major construction projects are planned; a major four-lane highway between Johor Baru at the Singapore border and Kedha State, north of Penang, would have major consequences for the nation.

Malaysia seeks development on its own terms, and steadfastly rejects onslaughts of Western culture (as witnessed by rigid censorship of television). Westerners often fail to consider the unique outlook in this federation, a cultural and historical melange where the glimmering towers of mosques blend against Western skyscrapers and Chinese open air markets.

9

ASEAN: The Next Common Market?

Few outside Asia understand that a little-known economic confederation is quietly changing international commerce and creating vast opportunities for Western business. After 21 years, the Association of South
East Asian Nations (ASEAN) is finally coming into its own and is inching
toward a common market approach that has long-term significance for
the entire Pacific—and the rest of the world. The six member nations
(Singapore, Thailand, Malaysia, the Philippines, Indonesia, and the
newest entry to the roster of independent nations, oil-rich Brunei) have
steered a course that maximizes the vast economic potential in this
region. ASEAN is more than a ghost parliament or a debating society.
"What few Americans realize about the group," declares Dr. Sean Randolph, director of the Pacific Basic Economic Cooperation Council, "is
that they are past the point of discussing unity. They mapped out a
strategy on their own without waiting for the West, and went ahead
without getting a green light from the outside."

This event constitutes a linchpin of the Asian Century. The 7 percent
growth curve witnessed for nearly two decades among ASEAN members has been a "seven percent solution" that other developing countries
envy. At 7 percent, national wealth doubles in a decade, rises fourfold
in 20 years, and increases eightfold in 30 years. That is a simplified
version of the phenomenal success story of the ASEAN partners before
the Philippines' downfall in the early 1970s—a period of decline that
hopefully, will end early in the 1990s.

ASEAN's vitality was proved during the recent global downturns of
the '70s and '80s. Recession hardly affected the five members until

mid-1982, a full year after the slump spawned unemployment lines across the globe. The group, taken together or separately, has an array of internal strengths that enable them to withstand external economic pressures. ASEAN is far beyond the "export-or-die" stage of most other developing nations. The group has quietly built its own consumer markets. The last recession slowed this process but hardly deterred the inexorable growth that brought its members from the preindustrial phase to the threshold of the 21st century in just three decades. Combined GNP now stands at $220 billion. In a startling challenge to the advanced West and to Japan, ASEAN now appears poised to leapfrog its present technological tutors in London, Tokyo, Washington, and Paris.

DIVERSITY OF ASEAN

The Association of South East Asian Nations stretches across a swath of the world 2,000 miles from north to south and 3,000 miles from east to west. A center of trade routes for the last six centuries, the region stands today as a melange of religions, races, and cultures. Its members have a 280 million population base, one comparable to America, or Western Europe, or the U.S.S.R.

This section of the globe is a storehouse of minerals and other natural resources, strategically located along a vast and vital reach of the Pacific. With a combined GNP of $220 billion, the region is a powerhouse of mineral wealth and natural resources. Four-fifths of the world's natural rubber, 60 percent of its palm oil, and almost three-fourths of its tin are contained there. Vast amounts of oil, wood, bauxite, coal, and agricultural products (rice, sugar, fruits) are found as well. The dynamism represented by a labor force that is becoming steadily more skilled, by solid growth patterns, by sound management, and by the availability of raw materials is extremely attractive. Disparity of living standards among the members (Singapore has a per capita income about 12 times that of Indonesia) has only intensified the quest for wealth-generating development.

The basis for a common market approach in this region is found by the diversity—and hence complementation—in economic activity. For example, a banking and trade goliath, Singapore, balances well with havens of natural resources such as Malaysia and Indonesia.

Bypassing age-old animosities and many uncertainties caused by difference and distance, this loose confederacy is piecing together a fabric of regional development knitted in a unique fashion. Yet not all divisions have been eradicated. A 1981 Anglo-Dutch treaty governs the fate of territories in the Sulawesi Sea between Indonesia and Malaysia; and both contest that bit of real estate. The Philippines still quarrels with Malaysia over sections of the southernmost portion of the islands governed by Manila. Indonesia and the Philippines have their own long-standing territorial disputes. However, to its credit, the association intrepidly brought some of these issues before ministerial conferences and resolved some Thai-Malay border conflicts. Those forums may be tried again.

The various religions found in modern Southeast Asia coexist through the common threads that bind together social, cultural, and even business life. The Chinese are undisputed masters of commerce, and their Buddhist tenets allow for swift adjustment to national and global transformations. With an unshaken belief in hard work and savings, this part of the population thrives in the urban, increasingly cosmopolitan environments that are sprouting across Southeast Asia.

There are, of course, problems encountered by each member.

Islamic links in Indonesia and Malaysia are a positive harbinger. Middle Eastern banks set up shop years ago, but in the decade ahead they are certain to play an increasingly active role in providing seed money for the great natural-resource treasure hunts ahead. Moslem traditions add an international flare to Association efforts while they add leverage to its voice in world affairs.

The tiny Hindu minority is concentrated in Malaysia, where most have worked in the rural plantations and had until recently remained isolated from the benefits of the growing economy. They are now taking advantage of increased educational opportunities and social services. Hindus living in ASEAN countries may well rise to decision-making positions during the remainder of this century.

The Catholic Philippines pursue a path in keeping with its European-American orientation. However, the transplanted institutions failed to provide the citizens with the benefits that accrued from similar structures in the nations from which they were borrowed. Perhaps the republic is in limbo, trapped between a willingness to maximize democracy and a reality that reminds the Philippine leaders of a sobering fact: The nation introduced liberal democratic trappings without a historical experience that teaches people how to cope with reform.

EARLY DAYS

The organization that began with the pounding of a teak gavel at the first organizational meeting in Bangkok in 1967 was first greeted with rank skepticism. Similar experiences in World War II and increasingly bold designs by Communist powers—including major rebellions that held Manila and Kuala Lumpur at bay after the defeat of Axis forces in the region—had brought only superficial supra-nationalism. However, in the wake of the independence achieved in the postwar years, each of the countries determined to adjust its undeveloped economy and begin a headlong march toward modernization, and in August 1967 formal steps were taken to start an association whose roots were planted in different soil from that of the South East Asia Treaty Organization. Discussions among the various rulers months before were based on the assumption that another force in regional affairs was required, one nonaligned and favoring the mixed economies flourishing within the five members-to-be. The gathering in the Thai capital at that time called for an organizational structure to coordinate ASEAN aims, chiefly "regional peace and stability" and "active collaboration and mutual assistance."

A dramatic event, the 1975 U.S. evacuation from Saigon, caused old tracts about the "Domino Theory" to be dusted off. Meeting in Bali during February 1976, ASEAN heads of state used the occasion of their first conference together to launch a wide array of policies. Recognizing the need for a "move to higher levels of cooperation"—in part as a buffer to Hanoi—the members attested to a "readiness to develop fruitful relations." The weak liaisons were replaced by a permanent secretariat; preferential trade arrangements were established among the five countries; specific industrial projects were earmarked for every member.

ASEAN UNITY—AND LIMITS ON COOPERATION

The respectability earned since those early days helps the group secure diplomatic breakthroughs. "The world takes notice of ASEAN," says Mark van Fleet, international affairs director for the U.S. Chamber of Commerce. "They are seen as a block in many respects." Their cohesion is impressive to many businesspersons who see them in action. In the turbulent waters surrounding Southeast Asia, that unity—and its perception by outside powers—is a deterrent to aggression.

As ASEAN has evolved, so have modifications in the group's structure. Changes have not always kept pace with need, yet group policymakers (who use English in their parleys) try to overcome early flaws. Annual ministerial meetings serve as the key policy-making avenues for the association. A standing committee handles duties in between these gatherings and oversees the economic committees. One such economic group takes charge of food, agriculture, and forestry.

Another covers industry, minerals, and energy. Banking, transportation, and tourism are also monitored. The location of ministerial conferences is determined alphabetically, on a rotating basis, with the host country's foreign minister serving a one-year term as standing committee chief. National secretariats are given the task of coordinating Association activity within each country.

After 1976, ad-hoc groups were used to facilitate ties with the EEC, Asian non-members, and North America. The all-important ingredient of communication has been made simpler, and intraassociation contact has risen dramatically. "I can pick up the telephone now," said former Philippines Foreign Minister Carlos Romulo, "and talk directly to Adam Malik [Indonesian vice president] or Rajaratnam [then Singapore Foreign Minister]. We often find that private talks over breakfast prove more important than formal meetings."

ASEAN has witnessed economic cooperation in multiple investment projects in recent years and has shown a serious desire to carry out industrial complementation schemes. The mixed economy formula has attracted cooperation from public, private, and foreign investors. So far, the economies in this region are competitive, not complementary; until the manufacturing sector grows substantially, there is little basis for increased intraregional trade (although that trade amounts to over $20 billion, or about a sixth of the ASEAN world total). In order to build up foreign exchange, labor-intensive industries are sought in the respective national economic plans, with an eye on the early 1990s.

The group is criticized sharply for lack of economic unity, and in many cases, without justification. ASEAN was born into an era of high commodity prices and Industrial Age assumptions about continued postwar growth. Yet the six did not fall into disarray as recessions in 1973–75, and 1981–84, rent cornerstones of the global economy asunder. Only one member, the Philippines, has continuously lagged.

The group has not evolved into the true common market that some hoped for in the late 1960s. ASEAN has at times neglected innovations that would have spawned economic development. Yet critics overlook recent trends. "They proved capable of recovering from the shoals and reefs of low commodity prices," notes Mark van Fleet, director of Asia-Pacific affairs the U.S. Chamber of Commerce. "The ASEAN countries are trying privatization and are eyeing market forces."

Commerce is at the core of any cautious approach to expand ASEAN's capacity to deal with a host of other problems, including regional social development. Yet realities must be faced. Four of the venerable six are tied to petroleum. The Philippines is not the only member plagued by high external debt. Even supposedly invulnerable Singapore faced a wrenching recession in 1984–86.

Trade with the outside world consists largely of primary products exports and labor-intensive goods. Imports are mostly of capital goods and equipment. Internal practices, not just Western and Japanese restrictions, hinder best use of that trade equation, and organizational restructuring is necessary to achieve tangible gains in trade.

Barriers to trade are as various as levels of development within each of the six nations, a fact that keeps the long-proclaimed quest for intra-ASEAN trade elusive (that trade makes up only 18 percent of the members' volume of exports-imports). Despite years of negotiations, and a list of over 12,000 tariff-free items, that percentage has not grown. Most of these thousands of items are not threatening to reigning import-substitution practices. Indonesia thus keeps its own populace from benefiting from products of her more economically efficient neighbors. Thai and Philippine barriers are far more of a hinderance than those found elsewhere in the group. Meanwhile, adherence to an antiquated consensus rule in ASEAN prevents the group from making politically thorny decisions.

Yet it is possible to mesh these realities with the goal of regional economic growth. By steadily increasing the number of items on the list of preferential trade goods, the six could launch a long-term across-the-board effort to boost trade. Domestic content regulations would have to be abandoned, and nontariff barriers should likewise be reduced. Enforcement of existing rules of origin is cumbersome for exporters and importers alike.

As Japan continues to move with a vengeance to set plants on relatively low-cost ASEAN shores, the organization is taking appropriate steps. Liberalization of internal economies is desirable and should grant all foreign corporations flexibility over repatriation of capital. Other steps to streamline regulations are taking place, as is privatization.

One expert favors an end to "the ad-hoc approach" toward intra-ASEAN trade. "A great deal of harmonization is required in areas like the financial sector, and in wage-price policies, before integration takes place," notes Dr. Seiji Naya at Honolulu's East-West Center.

"ASEAN's style looks disorganized to potential foreign investors," says Dr. Naya. He favors "modest but firm goals" on intra-ASEAN commerce, advocating a regional financing mechanism, plus a revival of a 1970s idea to launch large-scale complementary industrial projects. "They will obtain the required outside investment," he admonishes, "if they create the single market which has long been awaited."

Japan's strategy in the region is shaped by a set of conclusions. The first is that the business environment in at least five of the six ASEAN members will remain favorable. The second is that new demands will be placed on Japan to transfer its technological innovations and to train native personnel. Another factor is the increased pressure seen throughout the newly-industrialized and less developed countries to have foreigners make use of more indigenous resources. Japan committed $1 billion for the initial industrial complementation projects that are the core of promised economic unity among ASEAN members.

Japan's role is substantial, and had been growing before the yen realignment. Over $8.4 billion was invested in ASEAN before 1985 through 2,400 companies with a total employment of 330,000 (3 million including subcontractors). Tokyo has been the leading foreign investor in Thailand and Indonesia (a third of the total for each country), was fourth in Singapore with 16 percent, and ranked second in the Philippines. After 1985, the trend accelerated rapidly; Japanese manufacturing investments in Singapore alone soared to $240 million in 1986, double the amount for the previous year. Increases are no less dramatic in other countries in the bloc.

The two-way ties based upon exchange of raw materials for finished products is disappearing. In its place, a true economic community is beginning, built on a strategy of complementation and competitive advantage. Shigeo Matsumoto, managing director of Ajinomoto in Malaysia, feels that advantage. His firm's Malaysian factories use locally produced tapioca starch, which is 20–30 percent more expensive than the same product in Thailand. Tariffs and quotas should drop, and local farmers should move to other crops (sugar cane was supported by government funds, but is equally unprofitable). Matsumoto and others believe that an end to trade barriers would boost intra-ASEAN trade and plant the seed of another EEC. That issue is something the six must negotiate, at their own pace, as the regional agenda is harmonized.

THE OUTLOOK FOR ASEAN

From Tokyo comes the sense that a greater Pacific Community is possible, if not inevitable. Encouraging this approach, Japan promotes serious international dialogues among professionals in all fields of finance and business. Increased contact continues as the six nations, lying at both ends of the world's most dynamic economic region, harness their full potential. Over $1.5 billion in credits and grants was extended through 1981 by Tokyo's official aid program, but development aid since then totals over $9 billion—more than the total of U.S. official assistance.

Over half of Tokyo's development monies reach ASEAN (the Philippines alone receives a fourth of the total outlay, while Malaysia was given under $200 million last year).

As investment policies are codified, corporations must research the rules of the game in six separate entities—while preparing for joint marketing approaches. Complementation has a profound impact on future business strategies, and reflects on the evolving common market. It makes little sense to establish a presence in Indonesia, for example, without planning on at least some future marketing in Malaysia. Association members are willing to accommodate joint ventures that affect all six—and appreciate the style of internationalism found in the region. A common external tariff zone and a free trade zone are likely events in this decade. Both will help promote U.S. goods and services in a flow across borders.

Restructuring of the six economies can be accomplished with increased Western participation. In high tech, consulting, agriculture, and telecommunications there are vast opportunities, and many U.S. industries still maintain a competitive edge. "The Japanese are admiring grudgingly," says Laurence Krause, director of the University of California, San Diego's new international business program. "They still come out as somewhat menacing. All ASEAN countries explicitly or implicitly look to the U.S."

Progress in complementation schemes—enabling specialization in product lines—have ushered in an era of high growth rates. Trade barriers have fallen dramatically, leading to an EEC-styled, regional commerce. Industrial projects, once slow to fruition, proceed apace. Plans for the mid-1980s include construction of a regional grains terminal, a fish cannery, and a meat processing facility—all with impressive quantities of finished products set on the drawing boards. Marketing of sugar-based products, spices, and copra is seriously discussed. A shipping corporation to serve the six members is likely. Common policy for attracting investment capital to the region and a multinational solution to the woes of double taxation are also sought. Joint marketing programs are possible.

Cooperation continues to grow. A regional bank and the ASEAN Finance Corporation provide equity and capital and should stimulate joint ventures. With her neighbors in Manila and Bangkok hard-pressed for costly fossil fuel, Indonesia has offered bargain deals on the crude, and joint processing of crude with Singapore is expected. Some insiders expect a commodities cartel to emerge with Kuala Lumpur in the lead. The aim of this confederation would be to secure processing rights for exports. (A regional police force, patterned on the INTERPOL model, and an Association arms factory are being discussed. Already, joint military maneuvers—limited to patrols on land and sea—are carried out for defensive purposes.) The range of other economic projects being considered is broad, encompassing telecommunications equipment, petrochemicals, agricultural machinery, rubber industries, and electronic appliances. Each country has pledged $20 million for a stand-by credit arrangement to provide temporary aid through multi-currency swaps. Some 50,000 metric tons of rice have been reserved for another sharing plan, and members will be given preference for supplies in the event of oil shortages.

"Certain objectives cannot be achieved as quickly as some of us would have wished them to be," observes Singapore Prime Minister Lee Kuan Yew. "There are difficulties which, for a variety of reasons, cannot be overcome as simply as we would wish. As a result, we have to accept a pace ... which is more congenial to all of us, even though it may be less than what is achievable if we all set our sights higher."

"I have trouble with people in my own ministry," an economic boss in one of the six confides, "because there is usually the sense that different interests are competing against each other for attention and implementation of stated national objectives. It's perfectly true, energy comes into conflict with, say, food, and so on. When requests come from the ASEAN secretariat, though, there is a form of priority given to them; suddenly, the narrower interests lose meaning in the face of the reminder that the future of six countries is at stake."

In 1989, the U.S. government gave strong consideration to a plan that would create a special "free trade zone" between the U.S. and ASEAN. As the world witnesses distinct economic blocs emerging (the EEC and North America, through the special American-Canadian pact to end tariffs), creation of such a new relationship will propel growth within the region. That growth, says Dr. Kernial Sandhu, director of the Sin-gapore-based Center on Southeast Asian Studies, may build a new bloc whose potential rivals that of the EEC.

INDEX

A

ADB—*See Asian Development Bank*
Africa 14, 16
Agriculture 13, 29, 77, 79, 82, 110, 141-143, 191, 202, 210, 217, 224—*See also specific countries*
Ahn Seung-Chul 115
Alic, John 10
American Telephone & Telegraph Co. (AT&T) 61, 197
Amoco Corp. 24
ARCO—*See Atlantic Richfield Co.*
Armaments 17
Armentrout, Fred 166
Artificial Intelligence 58, 65
ASEAN—*See Association of Southeast Asian Nations*
Asian Development Bank (ADB) 14, 26-27, 35, 38, 78, 116
Assembly Line 2
Association of Southeast Asian Nations (ASEAN) xi, 18, 76, 143, 216-224
Atlantic Richfield Co. (ARCO) 105
Atomic Energy 23, 141, 163—*See also specific countries*
AT&T—*See American Telephone & Telegraph Co.*
Audio Equipment 8
Australia, Commonwealth of x, 5, 10, 25, 46, 200
Automation 12, 38, 70, 146, 187-191
Automobile Industry x-1, 8-10, 12, 25, 34-35, 39, 57, 96, 103, 107, 120, 128, 150, 153, 207, 212—*See also specific countries*
Aviation Industry 17, 30, 79, 129, 149, 168, 184, 196, 201, 212—*See also specific countries*

B

Bader, Jeffrey 77
Balance of Payments 8, 13
Banking & Finance 8, 24-25, 49-50, 78, 93, 99, 102, 126, 130, 133, 135, 140, 149, 160, 164-167, 177, 200, 212, 217, 220, 223—*See also specific countries*
Barnett, Stephen 33
Barry, John 148
Bennett, John 116, 121, 125, 127
Bergsten, C. Fred 17
Berkeley Roundtable on the World Economy 13
Biotechnology Industry 6-7, 37, 67-70, 125-126, 129-130, 159, 172, 190, 196—*See also specific countries*
Birth Control & Family Planning 28, 100
Black Monday 25
Bloom, Justin 39, 48, 57, 60, 68
Boeing Co., The 129
Boo Kheng Hua 147, 194
Borrus, Michael 13
Brazil, Federative Republic of 34
Brookings Institution 17
Brunei xi, 18, 76, 143, 200, 216-224
Buddhism 53, 83
Bush, George Herbert Walker 161
Business & Industry—*See specific industry*

C

Canada, Dominion of x-xi, 2, 5-6, 8, 40
Carroll, Steven 146
Cathay Pacific Airways 163
Cetron, Marvin 46, 59, 65
Chaitt, Ed 69
Chamber of Commerce, U.S. 48

Chan, S. K. 170, 174
Chang, Parris 28, 78, 83, 97, 105, 156
Chase Econometrics 13
Chemical Industry 33, 40, 73, 117, 123, 141, 154, 171, 190, 214—*See also specific countries*
Cheng, Richard T. 90
Cheng, Vincent 96, 170, 174
Chiang Ching-kuo 139, 156
Chiang Kai-shek 139, 156
Chien, Frederick 156
China, People's Republic of x
  Automobile Industry 96, 103, 107
  Banking & Finance 78, 93, 99, 102
  Commodities Industries 24, 105, 215
  Construction Industry 82
  Demographics & Social Issues 27, 79, 82, 100-101, 103
  Economy & Labor x-xi, 12, 15, 76-112
  Electronics Industry 6, 87, 94, 97, 103, 105-106
  Energy Industry 12, 22, 80, 83, 86, 103-104, 199
  Environment 21, 107-108, 110
  Foreign Exchange & Investment 83-84, 95, 102, 110
  Government & Politics 103-104
  Hong Kong Relations 89, 102, 158-176
  Ship Building & Shipping 30, 81
  Space Industry 81, 111
  Steel & Iron Industry 34, 86
  Taiwan Relations 89, 102, 153-157
  Textile Industry 87, 97, 108-109, 111
  Tourism 86-87, 109
China, Republic of (Taiwan) x
  Automobile Industry 34, 150, 153
  Banking & Finance 25, 140, 149, 200
  Biotechnology Industry 7
  Chemical Industry 141, 154
  Chinese Relations 89, 102, 153-157
  Demographics & Social Issues 27-28, 140
  Economy & Labor x-xi, 8, 11-13, 16, 28, 138-157
  Electronics Industry 6, 10, 14, 139, 143, 150-153
  Energy Industry 12, 139, 141, 143-145, 154
  Environment 21, 28, 142, 155
  Foreign Exchange & Investment 11, 20, 144-146
  Ship Building & Shipping 29-30, 149, 153
  Steel & Iron Industry 34, 39, 149, 153
  Textile Industry 140, 144
Cho, Lee-Jay 100, 136
Chongsoo, Kim 121

Choy, John 44
Chrysler Corp. 96
Chu, Godwin 185
Chu, Paul 72
Chung Se Yung 128
Chun Hwa Lee 122
Chun Hwan Doo 126
Clare, Tod 96
Coal Industry 22
Cobalt 23-24
Commerce, U.S. Department of 18, 131, 150
Commodities & Commodity Trading 1, 9-10, 12, 30, 44, 133, 178, 210—*See also specific countries*
Computer and Business Equipment Manufacturers Association 5, 66
Computer Industry 4-6, 11, 55-66, 116, 128, 150-151, 184—*See also specific countries*
Confucianism 4, 26, 140, 153, 157, 179
Construction Industry 11, 40, 82, 115, 131, 181-185, 199, 215—*See also specific countries*
Cooney, Stephen 35, 167
Corn 17
Cotton 17
Countertrade 15
Couteaux, Pierre 108
Crane, Alan 77-78, 110
Culture—*See specific countries*
Currency 19-20, 25—*See also Foreign Exchange*
Current Accounts Deficit 19
Cyert, Richard 72

D

Danielian, Ronald 9, 127
Darby, Larry T. 66
Dataquest 6
Dato Ahamd Sarji Bin Abdul Hamid 206
Debt 16, 47, 49, 116, 120, 126, 130, 133, 205, 221
Deficits—*See Debt*
Demographics 1, 7, 27, 52-54, 101, 103—*See also specific countries*
Deng Xiaoping 77, 84, 91, 96, 98, 109-110, 155, 161
Developing Countries—*See specific countries*
Dickson, John 64
Dore, Ronald 42
Dorward, William 158

Drug Industry—*See Pharmaceutical Industry*
Dui Tui Leong 192
Dunning, John 14
Du Pont de Nemours & Co. Inc., E. I. 69, 190

E

Eastern Computers Inc. 90-91
EC—*See European Community*
Economy—*See specific countries*
Education 4, 11, 26-29, 41, 55-56, 100, 117, 123, 131-132, 198, 209—*See also specific countries*
EEC—*See European Community*
Electronics Industry 1, 5-6, 8, 10-12, 14, 16, 37, 94, 97, 103, 105-106, 115-116, 122-125, 130, 139, 143, 150, 153, 160, 163-164, 169-171, 173, 182, 186, 188, 190, 194, 205-207, 214, 224—*See also specific countries*
Energy Industry 1, 20-22, 116—*See also specific countries*
Environment & Pollution 1, 20-21, 27, 107-108, 110, 134, 136, 141, 155, 176—*See also specific countries*
Erdman, Paul 30
Estes, Richard 26
Europe—*See specific countries*
European Community (EC) x-xi, 12, 40, 63
European Space Agency (ESA) 72
Exports—*See Trade*
Exxon Corp. 199

F

Facsimile Machines 5, 59, 122, 168
Fairbanks, Richard 18
Family Planning—*See Birth Control*
Fang, Samuel 169-170
Fertilizers 15
Ford Motor Co. 128
Foreign Exchange & Investment 1, 11, 13-15, 19-20, 25, 83-84, 95, 102, 110, 114, 117, 121-126, 144-146, 164-167, 174, 186, 193-203, 206, 211, 222—*See also specific countries*
Foreign Trade—*See Trade*
France 2-3, 17, 111
Frisbie, John 80, 98
Fujitsu Ltd. 58, 60-61, 67-68, 168

G

Galbraith, John Kenneth 186
Gao Yin 109

Gas, Natural 22
GATT—*See General Agreement on Tariffs and Trade*
General Agreement on Tariffs and Trade (GATT) 78
General Electric Co. (GE) 129
General Motors Corp. (GMC) 128, 197
Germany, Federal Republic of (West) 2-3, 5, 17, 111
Gibbons, John 66
Godown, Richard 68
Great Britain & Northern Ireland, United Kingdom of (UK) 2-3, 17
Gross National Product (GNP) xi, 25

H

Hammer, Armand 105
Handicapped 27, 29
Han Xu 109
Harding, Harry 77, 79, 82, 91, 98, 101
Harding, Peter 36
Harris, Martha 56
Haruo, Maekawa 48
Hayakawa, S. I. 140, 155
Hayashi, Iomonao 71
Hewlett-Packard Co. 147, 149, 197
High-Definition TV (HDTV) 65-67
Higuchi, Yoshio 42
Hirohito, Emperor (Japan) 53
Hitachi Ltd. 5, 55, 58, 60, 67-68, 201
Hitomi, Katsundo 38
Ho, Irving 149
Ho, Walter 172
Hong Kong (British colony) x
  Banking & Finance 24-25, 160, 164-167
  Biotechnology Industry 7, 159, 172
  Chemical Industry 171
  Chinese Relations 89, 102, 158-176
  Demographics & Social Issues 27-29, 168-169
  Economy & Labor x-xi, 8, 11-13, 15, 158-176
  Electronics Industry 6, 14, 160, 163-164, 169-171, 173
  Energy Industry 163
  Environment 29, 176
  Foreign Exchange & Investment 20, 164-167, 174
  Government & Politics 18
  Ship Building & Shipping 30, 32, 168, 199
  Textile Industry 36, 164, 175
  Toy Industry 9, 164, 169-171

Housing 26-29, 46, 49, 53, 101, 131, 136,
179-180—*See also specific countries*
Hu, Richard 200
Huang Xiang 94
Humphrey, Arthur 68-69
Hurd, Jane 103
Hyundai Group 10, 35, 117, 128, 184

I

IBM—*See International Business Machines*
Illiteracy 26
Imports—*See Trade*
India, Republic of 3
Indonesia, Republic of
ASEAN xi, 18, 76, 143, 216-224
Commodities Industries 24, 215
Economy & Labor 8, 211
Energy Industry 10, 22, 199
Foreign Exchange & Investment 222
Ship Building & Shipping 200
Infant Mortality 28
Insurance 11, 130, 135
Intel Corp. 63
International Bank for Reconstruction and
Development—*See World Bank*
International Business Machines Corp.
(IBM) 19, 55, 59, 61, 63, 105, 175
International Economic Policy Associa-
tion 9
International Energy Agency (IEA) 21
International Savings Bank Institute 20
International Telephone & Telegraph
Corp.—*See ITT Corp.*
Investment—*See Foreign Exchange*
Ishak, Rikki 89
Islam 18, 204-205, 211, 213
ITT Corp. 4, 104

J

James, William 116, 128
Japan
Automobile Industry 39, 57, 107
Banking & Finance 24, 49-50
Biotechnology Industry 67-70
Commodities Industries 22
Demographics & Social Issues 27, 41,
43-46, 49, 51-56
Economy & Labor ix, xi, 7, 10, 15, 37-75
Electronics Industry 5-6, 9, 55-67
Energy Industry 12, 23, 46
Environment 21
Foreign Exchange & Investment 14, 19-
20, 38, 165, 222
Research & Development 2
Ship Building & Shipping 29-30, 32

Space Industry 70-72
Steel & Iron Industry 33, 39, 73
Textile Industry 36, 73
Jeffrey, Brian 63
Jenkins, Ray 23
Jia-Ming Shyu 148
Johnson, Charles 23-24
Jones, Lionel (Skip) 34
Joun Yung Sun 129

K

Kang Ki-chae 36
Kato, Hitoshi 53
Kennecott Corp. (of Sohio) 24
Kent, Reginald 31, 166, 168
Kishi, Sakae 74
Korea, Republic of (South Korea)
Automobile Industry 10, 35, 120, 128
Banking & Finance 25, 126, 130, 133,
135, 200
Biotechnology Industry 6-7, 125-126,
129-130
Chemical Industry 117, 123
Commodities Industries 114
Demographics & Social Issues 28, 117,
123, 131-132, 134, 136
Economy & Labor x-xi, 8, 11-13, 15-16,
113-137
Electronics Industry 5-6, 16, 115-116,
122-125, 128, 130
Energy Industry 23, 116
Environment 21, 28, 134, 136
Foreign Exchange & Investment 20,
117, 121-126
Government & Politics 18, 113-117, 126-
128
Ship Building & Shipping 10, 29-30, 32,
120, 131-132
Steel & Iron Industry 10, 16, 33-34, 39,
120, 131
Textile Industry 16, 36, 115, 122, 131,
135
Krause, Lawrence 114, 223
Kwang Shih-chan 151
Kyle, Joe 141

L

Labor—*See specific countries*
Labor, U.S. Department of 17, 43
Lai, Alice 164, 169, 171-172
Language & Linguistics 59, 65, 90, 151,
179, 184-185, 205, 209
Latin America 14, 16
Lawrence, Robert 18
Leather Industry 10

Lee, Chung 9
Lee, Irene 174
Lee, Kim M. 125
Lee, Martin 162
Lee Kuan Yew 178-179, 199, 201-202, 224
Lee Yee 163
Leisure Industry 51-52
Levenson, Rachel 69
Levine, Rep. Mel (D, Calif.) 66
Li, Victor 4
Liang Xiang 89
Li Hao 96
Lim Keng Yaik 206, 211
Lin, W. S. 147
Ling, James 187, 190
Liquified Natural Gas (LNG)—*See Gas*
Li Yi-ning 110
Loh See Hong 183
Lord, Winston 92
Lumber Industry 10, 46, 205, 214, 217
Lyles, Jimmy 144

M

Major, John 92
Malaysia
 ASEAN xi, 18, 76, 143, 216-224
 Automobile Industry 34, 207, 212
 Banking & Finance 25, 205, 212
 Chemical Industry 214-215
 Commodities Industries 9-11, 22, 29, 205, 210, 214
 Demographics & Social Issues 27, 204-215
 Economy & Labor 8, 11-13, 15, 29, 204-215
 Electronics Industry 6, 11, 14, 205-207, 214
 Energy Industry 11-12, 205
 Environment 21
 Foreign Exchange & Investment 206, 211
 Government & Politics 18
 Oil & Fat Industry 205, 210-211
 Ship Building & Shipping 212
 Textile Industry 206
Malik, Adam 220
Management Consulting 11
Manufacturing—*See specific industry*
Masayoshi, Okhita 38
Medicine & Health 26-29, 131, 196, 208—
 See also specific countries
Mental Health 27
Microprocessors 6
Middle East 14

Minerals & Mining 22-24, 105, 114—*See also specific mineral*
Mining—*See Minerals*
Mitsubishi Ltd. 32, 60, 212
Mooney, James L. 49
Morrisson, Charles 47, 49
Mowery, David 16
Mulally, Jim 25
Multinational Corporations (MNCs) 14—
 See also specific corporation
Munasinghe, Mohan 21, 105

N

Nakasone, Yasuhiro 45, 47
Narendram, N. 198
NASA—*See National Aeronautics & Space Administration*
National Aeronautics & Space Administration (NASA) 71, 111
Naya, Seiji 9-11, 15, 35, 100, 164, 221
NEC Corp. 5, 55, 57-58, 60
Neptune Orient Lines 31
Netherlands, Kingdom of the 3
New Technology Society 2
New York Stock Exchange (NYSE) 24
Nga Been Hen 191
Nomura Research 4
Northern Telecom Ltd. 5
Nuclear Power—*See Atomic Energy*

O

Occidental Petroleum Corp. 105
Office Equipment—*See specific industry*
Oil & Fat Industry 11, 205, 210-211, 217
Oksenberg, Michael 79, 161-162
Ooi Inn Bok 187, 189
OPEC—*See Organization of Petroleum Exporting Countries*
Open Door Policy 76, 79, 84, 94, 96, 99, 109
Organization of Petroleum Exporting Countries (OPEC) 22, 199
Oshima, Yoshiso 74

P

Palm Oil—*See Oil*
Panyarachun, Anand 18
Pao, Y. K. 30
Park Chung Hee 114
Park Pil-Soo 129
Parks & Recreation Areas 29
Pascale, Richard 42

Patents & Copyrights 55, 60, 130, 145, 151, 153
Pei, I. M. 163
Petrochemicals—*See Chemical Industry*
Petroleum Industry ix, 10-12, 16, 21-22, 40, 46, 80, 83, 86, 103, 116, 120, 139, 141, 143-145, 154, 177, 182, 199, 205, 214, 217, 220, 223-224—*See also specific countries*
Pharmaceutical Industry 7, 69, 73, 97, 125, 129, 143, 171—*See also specific countries*
Philippines, Republic of the
ASEAN xi, 18, 76, 143, 216-224
Economy & Labor 8, 10, 16, 211
Foreign Exchange & Investment 222
Government & Politics 211
Philips Gloeilampenfabrieken N.V. 62, 147, 188
Pickett, John 5, 66
Pintz, Sam 24
Politics—*See specific countries*
Poverty—*See Welfare*
Protectionism—*See Trade*

R

Raffles, Sir Stamford 177-178
Railroads 33, 44, 168
Rand Corp. 57
Randolph, Sean 216
Research and Development (R&D) 2, 4-5, 7
Rha Woong Bae 130
Rhee, Synghman 114
Roh Tae Woo 120
Romulo, Carlos 220
Rubber Industry 9-11, 29, 182, 205, 210, 214-215, 217, 224—*See also specific countries*
Ruthvin, Phil 2

S

Sakamura, Ken 59
Salmon, Kurt 36
Samsung Electronics Co. Ltd. 122-124, 126, 129
Sandhu, Kernial 224
Satellites—*See Space*
Saudi Arabia 22
Saxonhouse, Gary 56
Semiconductors 6, 11, 14, 17, 60-61, 106, 120, 122, 149, 186, 205
Serlin, Omri 56
Service Industries 10-11, 13, 114, 135, 143, 167, 194, 199, 212—*See also specific industry*

Seung Bum Oh 130
Sewage & Water Treatment 26, 28
Shapre, Sir Eric 168
Sharp Electronics Corp. 67
Shell Oil Co. (of Royal Dutch Shell) 199
Shilling, A. Gary 12, 14, 25, 35, 50
Shimbun, Yomiuri xi
Ship Building & Shipping 10, 29-33, 39, 79-80, 120, 131-132, 153, 168, 177, 182, 200, 212—*See also specific countries*
Shultz, George 161
Siemens AG 5, 62
Singapore
ASEAN xi, 18, 76, 143, 216-224
Banking & Finance 24-25, 177, 200
Biotechnology Industry 6-7, 190, 196
Chemical Industry 190
Commodities Industries 182
Demographics & Social Issues 27-28, 179-180, 196
Economy & Labor x-xi, 8, 11-13, 15, 177-203
Electronics Industry 6, 182, 184, 186, 188, 190, 194
Energy Industry ix, 12, 177, 182, 199
Foreign Exchange & Investment 20, 186, 193-203, 222
Government & Politics 18, 202-203
Ship Building & Shipping 32, 177, 182, 200
Textile Industry 14, 190, 194
Tourism 181-182, 185, 192-193
Toy Industry 194
Singapore Airlines 201
Smith, Kirk 21, 27
Soga Shosha 43-44, 73
Solarz, Rep. Stephen (D, N.Y.) 77
Sony Corp. 38, 67
South Africa, Republic of 23
South America—*See Latin America*
South Korea—*See Korea, Republic of*
Soybeans 17
Space Industry 70-72, 81, 111—*See also specific countries*
Sri Lanka, Democratic Socialist Republic of 14
St. Laurent, Yves 109
Steel & Iron Industry 8, 10, 16, 33-34, 39, 73, 86, 120, 131, 149, 153—*See also specific countries*
Sternlieb, George 11
Stocks, Bonds & Securities 24-25—*See also Banking*
Sugar Industry 10
Superconductivity 37, 72-73, 81, 111
Sweeney, Kirk 25

T

Taiwan—*See China, Republic of*
Talalla, Albert S. 212
Tanaka, Shoji 73
Tank Kok Kheng 191
Tan Puay Chuan 192
Technology 1-7, 13—*See also specific industry*
Technology Assessment, U.S. Office of 10, 34
Telecommunications Industry 4-6, 17, 45, 58, 87, 122, 129, 152, 164, 168, 184, 186, 194, 200, 224—*See also specific countries*
Telephones—*See Telecommunications*
Textile Industry x-1, 8-11, 14, 16, 35-36, 73, 87, 97, 108-109, 111, 115, 122, 131, 135, 140, 144, 164, 175, 190, 194, 206—*See also specific countries*
Thailand, Kingdom of xi, 8-9, 18, 21, 76, 143, 215-224
Thatcher, Margaret 160
Timber Industry—*See Lumber*
Tin Industry 11, 178, 205, 210, 214, 217—*See also specific countries*
Toshiba Corp. 60-61, 67-68, 196
Toshida, Seiji 53
Tourism Industry 52, 86-87, 109, 181-182, 185, 192-193, 215, 220
Toy Industry 9, 164, 169-171, 194—*See also specific countries*
Toyota Motor Corp Ltd. 38
Trade, Foreign 1, 5, 7-13, 217, 221—*See also specific countries*
Transportation Industry 208, 215—*See also specific industry*

U

UK—*See Great Britain*
Unger, A. J. Marshall 65
Union of Soviet Socialist Republics (USSR) 2
United States of America (USA) x, 2, 8, 12, 16-17, 19-20, 67-70
United Technologies Corp. 129
Urbanization 21, 26
U.S. Steel Corp. 24, 131

USSR—*See Union of Soviet Socialist Republics*

V

Van Fleet, Mark 48, 87, 93, 145, 166, 206, 211, 220
Vatt, Bill 43
VCRs—*See Video Cassette Recorders*
Veel, Stewart 146-148
Video Cassette Recorders (VCRs) 5, 9, 66

W

Wada, Toshiko 41
Welfare & Poverty 26-29
Westphal, Larry 28-29, 113, 132, 136
Wheat 17
Williamson, John 19, 127
Wolf, Charles 57
Women 1, 27, 43, 53, 155
Wong Kok Seng 186
World Bank (International Bank for Reconstruction and Development) 16, 21, 33, 35, 78, 82, 86, 91, 103, 105, 121, 200

X

Xin Dingou 22
Xu Jiatun 162

Y

Ye Jian 79, 91, 96
Yeo, Philip 32, 188, 197
Yeung, K. Y. 169
Yip, Vincent 185, 188
Yong-Sea Teoh 186
Yoshida, Toyoaki 55
Yuan, Robert 7
Yue-kong Pao 163
Yue Loong 142
Yung, T. C. 185

Z

Zeller, Jeffrey 210
Zhao Ziyang 160